HARDBALL RELIGION

Smyth & Helwys Publishing, Inc.
6316 Peake Road
Macon, Georgia 31210-3960
1-800-747-3016
©2009 by Smyth & Helwys Publishing

The paper used in this publication meets the minimum requirements of
American National Standard for Information Sciences—
Permanence of Paper for Printed Library Materials.
ANSI Z39.48–1984. (alk. paper)

Library of Congress Cataloging-in-Publication Data

Burleson, Wade.
Hardball Religion: Feeling the Fury of Fundamentalism / by Wade Burleson.
p. cm.
Includes bibliographical references and index.
ISBN 978-1-57312-527-7 (pbk. : alk. paper)
1. Burleson, Wade.
2. Southern Baptist Convention. International Mission Board—History—21st century.
3. Church controversies—Southern Baptist Convention—History—21st century.
4. Southern Baptist Convention—Doctrines—History—21st century.
5. Fundamentalism—History—21st century. I. Title.
BV2520.A5S682 2009 266'.6132—dc22
2009000760

HARDBALL

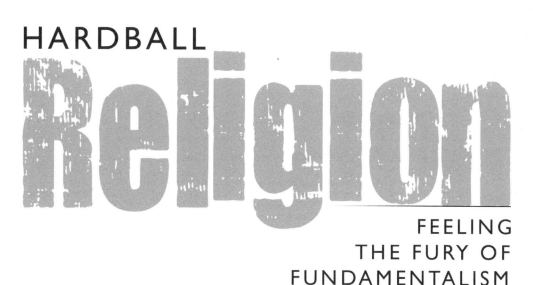

Religion

FEELING
THE FURY OF
FUNDAMENTALISM

WADE BURLESON

DEDICATION

To our missionaries; they understand.

ACKNOWLEDGMENTS

There are several people I wish to thank for their assistance in working on this book.

First, I would like to thank the finest church any pastor could ever dream of serving, the Emmanuel Baptist Church of Enid, Oklahoma. To the deacons and staff who have consistently, courageously, and publicly expressed their support, you can never fully appreciate what you have meant to the Burleson family. To all Emmanuel members, I express my love to you for your love and support, which can never be repaid, but will never be forgotten.

I would also like to express my gratitude to several current International Mission Board trustees for their friendship and support, many of whom desire to remain unnamed for obvious reasons. But to trustees Rick Thompson and John Click, I would like to thank you for your very public and courageous expressions of love and support for me personally.

My appreciation for my family runs deep. My father, Paul Burleson, has given me immeasurable wisdom at times it was sorely needed. My mother, Mary Burleson, a professional editor, ensured that I was always precise and accurate in what I wrote. Without their support, I would not have been able to finish the course. My four children, Charis, Kade, Boe, and Logan have all given joy to me in terms of their walk with Christ. I am grateful that their understanding of grace and true Christianity has not been tainted by the ugly politics of denominationalism. My wife, Rachelle, has lived every minute of this narrative with me, displaying true Christian grace as she has assisted me in thinking through many issues we faced together.

Finally, I would like to thank Southern Baptists who have stayed the course in terms of ministry and missions. I write not to discourage Southern Baptists from participating, but to encourage Southern Baptists to speak up and speak out. The kingdom needs us all, not just a few.

In His Grace,
Wade

CONTENTS

FOREWORD

In the preface to John Warburton's autobiographical classic *Mercies of a Covenant God*, the famous nineteenth-century Baptist J. C. Philpot makes a classic statement about the miserable and painful experiences of Pastor Warburton's life: "When dark clouds rested upon him in providence, when poverty and want knocked hard at his door, when little work and scanty wages, hard times and an increasing family plunged him into a sea of embarrassment and distress, *he was still learning deep and blessed lessons.* . . ."[1]

I first read Warburton in 1982 when I was a Baylor University student, and my appreciation for the goodness of divine providence, greatly deepened by reading his autobiography, hasn't wavered since. God's goodness, even in the midst of hard times, has sustained me when nothing else could. Though I have found it difficult to explain the circumstances in which I found myself during the years of 2005 through 2008, I have continued to learn *deep and blessed lessons* through the recounting of those events.

Since the inception of the Southern Baptist Convention (SBC) in 1845, a trustee serving on one of the dozen SBC agency boards had never been recommended for removal from service; that is, until January 2006, when a majority of the trustees of the SBC International Mission Board (IMB) voted for my removal. In addition, the recorded minutes of all Southern Baptist agency proceedings, including the minutes of the Southern Baptist mission boards, seminary boards, literature board, and executive board, reflect that no sitting trustee had ever been censured—until a majority of the trustees of the IMB voted officially to censure me in November 2007.

Southern Baptist trustees have been found guilty of criminal conduct by federal courts and sent to prison, arrested for soliciting homosexual prostitutes, ended their marriages by having adulterous affairs, and even, in one case, charged with murder, but never has a Southern Baptist trustee been recommended for removal or officially censured until I experienced both between 2005 and 2008. The aforementioned extraordinary steps were taken to discredit me in order to silence my public opposition to two new doctrinal policies that a majority of IMB trustees had voted to adopt in November 2005. I believed these policies exceeded the 2000 *Baptist Faith & Message* (2000 *BFM*) and disqualified hundreds of Southern Baptists who could not agree with them from serving on the mission field. It was initially difficult to overcome the shock of such strong-arm tactics by trustee leaders. I responded as any normal pastor would respond; I defended myself and looked to others, including some of my fellow trustees, to offer a vigorous defense on my behalf. Many, as you will read, took up that challenge with vigor.

My greatest personal tool of defense, however, became my blog (short for *Web log*), which I began in fall 2005 to voice my public opposition to the two new doctrinal policies. A blog is a form of communication, via the Internet, where one can instantly make known what is happening in his or her life. It is like an instantly published autobiography. What served as my defense also happened to be the greatest irritant for those who wished to silence me. What you will read in the pages that follow is supported by the blog posts I wrote months and even years ago. One of the advantages of writing a blog is that I have a record of what happened when it happened, and I am not required to rely solely upon fading memory. Thanks to the written record, this book will portray as accurately as possible the events that transpired during the years 2005 through 2008 in the International Mission Board and the Southern Baptist Convention.

The blog served to hone my writing skills and allowed me to see with greater clarity my own frailties. I've reviewed most of the things I wrote in the beginning of the IMB controversy, and I see my concern for preserving my personal reputation. This may have been due to the initial shock of the unique circumstances in which I found myself in the SBC. It is not pleasant to be on the receiving end of tactics designed to destroy your ministry. When a pastor's reputation is in danger, he faces the possibility of losing everything associated with his calling. For this reason, I sought to keep the record straight through an accurate accounting of events at the IMB on my blog.

Time and experience, however, have seasoned my understanding of what is important. I did not fully understand at the beginning of the controversy the extraordinary benefit of being pastor of the same church for fifteen years. The people of Emmanuel Baptist Church knew me. Nothing changed in terms of my ministry to them, though their pastor was now in the national news. I continued to pastor this great church. My family was both encouraging to me personally and supportive of my ongoing involvement in the SBC. For these reasons, my writings, both on my blog and in this book, have taken on new directions.

First, I now write for the sake of others, not myself. I have conversed with Southern Baptists over the past three years who have lost their denominational jobs for opposing the ideological philosophies and idiosyncrasies of the Fundamentalists. I have witnessed people in our convention literally cry in fear of losing their jobs because they have questioned authority. I have observed a pastor, whose wife was dying of cancer, become the victim of a false rumor that he was having an affair, simply because this pastor opposed a certain viewpoint held by those who controlled the board on which he served. I have heard the pain expressed by another Southern Baptist leader over an intentional rumor that he had experienced a mental breakdown—a rumor spread in a concerted attempt to minimize his influence.

I have seen a female employee of one of our Southern Baptist agencies lose the job of her dreams, sell her blood to meet expenses, and face the humiliation of being called a tool of Satan, all because, according to a handful of Fundamentalists in control of the agency where she worked, she was a "woman in a position reserved for men." I have met missionaries who lost their jobs overseas because they refused to bow to the political pressure of their superiors and submit to demands for conformity, and then sacrificed their children's college education funds in an attempt to fulfill their divine call and stay on the mission field. I have met a number of Southern Baptists who have been abused, lied about, discriminated against, mistreated, and even terminated from jobs for being, quite simply, Baptists with a conscience. They are now fighting to right the ship of their lives. I wish to help them all, but if I help just one, I will have accomplished more by writing this book than by sitting idly by, as I have done in years past, and saying nothing. There is no valid reason to remain silent when fellow Southern Baptists are being destroyed by a political machine hiding behind a mask of spirituality.

I began to realize in 2005, to my horror, that the issue causing such pain in the Southern Baptist Convention was not a battle for a belief in the inspired, inerrant word of God. I discovered as a trustee of the IMB that we are battling a much worse problem in the SBC. That battle is against Fundamentalism, or legalism, that threatens to destroy the fabric of our cooperation. Frankly, because of the way I have seen some Southern Baptists who hold to inerrancy treated by other Southern Baptists who also profess to hold to inerrancy, I now wonder if some actually believe and practice the Bible we call inerrant. I am now writing to help other Southern Baptists who have been burned by the fires of Fundamentalism and to keep others from becoming its victims.

Second, I now write with the desire to change the Southern Baptist Convention by quenching the fires of Fundamentalism. We need a "gospel resurgence." Southern Baptist churches should focus on the primacy of the gospel. Our convention should awake to the damage done when we boycott Disney, rail against the sexually immoral, look down in disdain at other denominations, and boast of our own numbers, power, and cultural influence. We should only boast of Christ and show sinners his transforming power to change lives. When we Southern Baptists are more concerned with being identified with Christ and his people than we are with our "Baptist identity," we will withstand the pressure to conform to autocratic decrees of denominational bureaucracies, particularly when those decrees violate both Scripture and conscience.

The Southern Baptist Convention, born in 1845, came of age during the Civil War. The eighteenth anniversary of the Southern Baptist Convention occurred during the summer of 1863, the same season in which the Battle of Gettysburg stemmed the high tide of Confederate aggression. Prior to Gettysburg, the South looked virtually invincible, but Gettysburg changed both the course of the war and the ultimate destiny of our country. By the end of the Civil War, federal authority had expanded to the point that citizens changed the way they referred to the United States of America. Prior to the war it was appropriate to say "The United States of America *are*," but after 1865 the vast majority of people would refer to our country by saying "The United States of America *is*."[2] The states that made up the United States of America had become a singular noun; the plurality of identity and purpose that characterized individual states prior to the Civil War had been lost.

Such solidarity and unity are a benefit to a country, but the same process in the Southern Baptist Convention does not yield the same result. It has taken nearly one hundred and fifty years, but the churches of the Southern Baptist Convention are now undergoing a similar transformation. Southern Baptist Convention agencies like the IMB are now exerting a kind of federal authority, demanding that individual, autonomous churches comply with their authoritative, denominational decrees. An internal civil war is being waged within our convention. Some Southern Baptist churches and pastors are continuing to hold fiercely to local church autonomy, congregational authority, and a *cooperative* ministry among a plurality of churches with differing identities, while Fundamentalists in the SBC are emphasizing absolute conformity to denominational confessions, ecclesiastical hierarchies of authority, and a Baptist identity that goes far beyond our historic Baptist heritage. In other words, some are trying to turn the SBC into one big church, with a pope as her head and all members conforming to the bulls issued by our anointed leader.

Though it would cause old-time Southern Baptists to cringe if someone were ever to say "The churches of the Southern Baptist Convention *is*," events of the past few years in my life have convinced me that some Southern Baptist leaders have desired, and have worked tirelessly toward, an absolute conformity within Southern Baptist churches on all things *nonessential* to genuine Christian faith. The idea of a *cooperating* convention of autonomous Baptist churches has been superseded by an authoritative denominational control that demands conformity to a specific ideology called Fundamentalism. Those who hold to Fundamental ideology seem willing to stop at nothing to see that their goal of a *uniform* Baptist identity arises. Of course, that identity is defined by them and their peculiar interpretations of the sacred text. Ironically, it is the demand for conformity on all things nonessential to the Christian faith, and a quiet submission to this demand, that is causing the historic *nonconformist* identity of Baptist people to be in jeopardy. Baptists have traditionally enjoyed the freedom that comes from defending liberty of conscience, soul competency, the priestly authority of every believer, and local church autonomy. I now write, joining the chorus of others who have written before me, to seek to restore those cherished Baptist ideals to the Southern Baptist Convention. Some Southern Baptist leaders who resist my call for greater cooperation will call me a "liberal," but by the time you finish reading this book, you will know that I am as conservative as Spurgeon, Gill, Boyce, Dagg, and other Baptist forefathers when it comes to the essential doctrines of the faith. Those at war against cooperation commonly call those who view nonessentials differently than they "liberals." It is a tactic that may have worked in the 1980s, but it won't anymore. Likewise, I do not care for the tag "Fundamentalists," but as of yet I have found no better word to describe the ideology you will read about in this book. I have no problem with Fundamentalists being a part of our convention; but I have a huge problem with Fundamentalists demanding that everyone else share their interpretations of Scripture or be removed from convention leadership or cooperative missions ministry.

There may not be many Southern Baptists under the age of forty-five who understand the significance of Southern Baptist churches maintaining separate, autonomous identities. Sometimes Southern Baptists must be *made* to understand the importance of local church autonomy. It's similar to pre-kindergarten students not caring much for reading, or third grade students for algebra, but at the end of their education, they would regret it if someone didn't force them to care. The goal of this book is to help Southern Baptist Christians understand and cherish church autonomy, soul competency, and church liberty and thus resist the demands for doctrinal conformity on the nonessentials of the faith. Further, it is a call for Southern Baptists to see the importance of having multiple voices speak out, representing different positions on various issues, when some Southern Baptists are vigorously pushing to silence all dissent within our convention. The chorus of forced uniformity and unity that is being sung by some SBC leaders must be interrupted by the individual voices of reason that cannot be silenced.

Were I to write a tome on the above subject matter alone, it would be both unsold and unread. So I have decided to write a narrative that will help illuminate the problem. Preachers will tell you that the two things most people remember about a message are the stories and the illustrations. I remember hearing an elderly pastor calling illustrations "windows that give light to the soul." I will illustrate for you the significance of the fight that Southern Baptists now face through the telling of stories that are designed to make you interested in the outcome of this ideological war.

The narrative of the events at the International Mission Board of the Southern Baptist Convention will read like fiction to most. Some of the stories are so bizarre that some will say, "There's no way those things happened." To be confronted in a threatening manner with a knife by a fellow sitting trustee, to overhear trustees collaborating on how to get rid of an IMB vice president because she is simply *female*, and to endure the illogical rants of a tobacco-tasting trustee as he turns purple with rage over my attempt to reconcile a relationship with him might prove more than the reader can comprehend. But be assured that everything I write is the truth from my perspective. I would never intentionally say something that I know or think to be untrue. Is it possible that my perspective may be skewed? Of course it is. That is one of the reasons I am grateful for my blog. It allows me to read what I wrote months ago, with added time removing the emotion of the moment, and to write with even more reflective objectivity. Hindsight, as they say, is 20/20.

Not everyone will like what I write. I will seek to illustrate how narrow Fundamentalism, Baptist identity radicalism, and ecclesiological dogmatism are destroying the fabric of our cooperative convention and harming people in the process. I will issue a caution to anyone who loses sight of the nature of true Christianity because the shadow of our denomination overtakes the centrality of Jesus Christ and his commandment to love one another. I initially thought I would not write this book, but a federal judge changed my mind in March 2008 when he granted the summary judgment of Southwestern Baptist Theological Seminary and dismissed the suit of Dr. Sheri Klouda. Dr. Klouda, a tenure track Hebrew professor at Southwestern who was denied the tenure process after Paige Patterson became the institution's president, had sued her former employer for breach of contract due to gender discrimination. Leadership at Southwestern, under the direction of Paige Patterson, had informed Dr. Klouda that she "was a woman in a position reserved for men." After her removal, Dr. Klouda moved her family to Indiana, taking a lower paying job at an evangelical college, and resorted to selling her own blood to pay for the medical expenses of her husband who had suffered a heart attack after her dismissal. In granting the summary judgment, United States district judge John McBryde ruled that the courts had no jurisdiction if a seminary professor were to be removed for gender reasons since a "church" was protected by the First Amendment. The judge then wrote the following:

> The court is satisfied from the summary judgment record that the decision of Patterson and other members of Seminary's Board of Trustees to terminate plaintiff was religiously motivated. . . . [M]ere inquiry into those areas [by the court] would be an unconstitutional intrusion into the affairs of Seminary as a religious organization . . . . In the Baptist denomination, the Convention is formed to serve all participating local congregations . . . . [The] Seminary is principally supported and *wholly controlled* by the Convention . . . .[3]

The judge convinced me to write this book. The federal courts, by constitution, should have nothing to do with regulating, supervising, or determining the just behavior of seminaries, agencies, or ministries of the Southern Baptist Convention. That is our job as Southern Baptists. It is up to the congregations of local churches and Southern Baptist pastors to change things. If we don't like what we see happening within our convention, then we need to change it. This book is my small attempt to change the direction of the Southern Baptist Convention. Twenty-five years ago I joined the effort to stem what I had been told was a growing tide of liberalism within our convention. That tide, which may have been only a small current, has been stemmed. It's now time to correct the current that is moving our convention too far to the right into Fundamentalism. It is time to restore us to our heritage of individual and church freedom and focus on the sharing of the gospel of Jesus Christ.

The Southern Baptist Convention has gone far enough. Those who believe it is time for a "gospel resurgence" need to speak up, speak out, and be prepared. I've discovered that sometimes the attempts to keep our convention focused on the gospel and evangelical cooperation is not as easy as it seems. There are many who want to play a rough-and-tumble game of hardball religion.

Notes

1. J. C. Philpot, "Preface," in John Warburton, *The Mercies of a Covenant God,* (Swengel PA: Reiner Publications, 1964), xv–xvi. My emphasis.

2. "One Must Say the United States Are," *New York Times,* 24 June 1895.

3. *Klouda v. Southwestern Baptist Theological Seminary,* no. 4:07-cv-0061, doc. 78-2, U.S. District Court, Northern District of Texas, Judge John McBryde. My emphasis.

Chapter 1

BLINDSIDED!

The International Mission Board Headquarters
Richmond, Virginia
January 2006

"I move that the trustees request the Southern Baptist Convention remove Wade Burleson from the International Mission Board as soon as possible."

I was stunned. As I realized what IMB trustee Jerry Corbaley was saying, the universe began to move in slow motion around me. My mind raced as I tried to fathom the words, but my emotions acted as molasses to my mind, slowing my comprehension of the environment around me to the point that I did not recall until later his next words.

". . . that the trustees reprimand him for gossip and slander that hurts the work of the board; that the chairman make public the nature of the reprimand in the manner of the chairman's choosing; and that Mr. Burleson be removed from all trustee committees until such time as the Southern Baptist Convention rules otherwise."

I was seated next to my good friend Rick Thompson, pastor of Council Road Baptist Church in Bethany, Oklahoma, a suburb of Oklahoma City. Rick's church is one of the largest Southern Baptist churches in Oklahoma in both attendance and contributions to the Cooperative Program. Rick leaned over to me and whispered, "Can you believe this?"

I could not believe it. Precisely a month earlier, on December 10, 2005, I had gone public with my opposition to two new doctrinal policies that a majority of the International Mission Board trustees had passed at our November 2005 trustee meeting. I had attended my first IMB trustee meeting the previous summer, in July 2005, and it was there that I first learned about the proposed new doctrinal policies. My opposition to them had been according to protocol, consistent, and respectful at the three previous trustee meetings. I now found myself enduring heavy-handed tactics from trustee leadership in an effort to silence my opposition to their proposed policies. They had refused to give me any anecdotal evidence of a problem on the mission field that would be solved by adopting the new doctrinal policies. They had refused my repeated requests that the IMB's professional administrative staff, including the candidate consultants, be allowed to give to the trustees their professional opinion regarding these new doctrinal policies. Worse, written attempts by the president of the International Mission Board to inform the trustees that these policies, in his view, were harmful to the cooperative mission efforts of the Southern Baptist Convention had been completely stifled by trustee leadership. When the new doctrinal policies were passed by a majority of trustees in November 2005, under a disputed vote count, I had no choice but to make my opposition to them known to the entire Southern Baptist Convention. I felt it my duty as a trustee to express my dissent to the people who had put their *trust* (i.e., "the root word of trustee") in me to represent them on the board.

The first new doctrinal policy required that a missionary desiring to be appointed by the IMB be baptized in a Southern Baptist church, or at least in a church that taught "eternal security." This new doctrinal policy violated the Bible's teaching that baptism is identification with Christ, not a swearing of allegiance to a "system of local church beliefs." Baptists nearly 400 years ago confessed belief that "the persons designed by Christ, to dispense this ordinance [baptism], the Scriptures hold forth to be a preaching disciple, *it being nowhere tied to a particular church.*"[1] Landmark and Campbellite (Church of Christ) doctrines have placed emphasis on the qualifications of the baptizer; but Baptists, particularly Southern Baptists, have resisted such doctrinal demands, as evidenced by the silence on this subject by our only consensus confession, the 2000 *Baptist Faith & Message* (2000 *BFM*).

The second of the two new doctrinal policies required IMB trustees to ask prospective Southern Baptist missionaries if they prayed in tongues in the privacy of their prayer closets. If they answered "yes," then those missionaries would be immediately disqualified. The International Mission Board *already* had a policy that prohibited the *public* expression of tongues on the mission field, but now trustee leadership sought to enter the prayer closets of missionary candidates, forcing them to confess to something that was supposed to be private, and then disqualify them based on an honest answer. In doing so, trustees were doing the opposite of what the Apostle Paul clearly stated in 1 Corinthians 14:39: "Do not forbid the speaking in tongues . . . ."

Again, this new doctrinal policy exceeded the 2000 *BFM*, and in the opinion of many, it contradicted the expressed command of the Apostle Paul.

Back in the 1970s, trustees had wrangled with then Foreign Mission Board president Baker James Cauthen over spiritual gifts. Dr. Cauthen had been a missionary in northern China, and he was familiar with the famous Shantung Revival. He knew that the so-called "sign gifts"—miracles, healings, tongues, and interpretations of tongues—had been a part of the Shantung Revival. He told the trustees that if they did not recognize the gifts as being valid today, he would have to tender his resignation as president of the Foreign Mission Board. The trustees were stunned; they could not afford to lose him. He was an effective leader with an anointing for his task. Dr. Cauthen put his reputation and his pension on the line for what he knew to be true, and the trustees backed down. In a manner similar to Dr. Cauthen,[2] I had gone public with my opposition to the International Mission Board trustees narrowing the doctrinal parameters of missionary cooperation and doing what I believed only the Southern Baptist Convention as a whole had the prerogative to do—establishing the doctrinal boundaries of our convention's missions cooperation.

Some IMB trustees seemed to me to be driven by ideological, theological, and philosophical Fundamentalism and "Baptist identity" separatism that demands everybody else agree with them on every single doctrine. This uniformity and demand for conformity is one of the hallmarks of religious Fundamentalism. I had reminded my fellow trustees that our convention was built on cooperation, and cooperation necessitated differences among those who came together for greater, common causes—such as missions and evangelism. I don't mind Landmarkers who happen to be Southern Baptists cooperating with us in missions; we just can't have Landmark IMB trustees demanding that all Southern Baptists agree with them on baptism. Likewise, I do not speak in tongues, nor have I ever sought that particular gift, and I know how to fellowship and cooperate with people who believe that particular spiritual gifts have ceased (cessationists). But, in my understanding of what it means to be a Southern Baptist, it is totally inappropriate for IMB trustee leaders, who happen to believe in the cessation of certain spiritual gifts, to set aside otherwise qualified Southern Baptists for being honest about what they do in the privacy of their prayer closets. That's a demand for conformity, not the delight of cooperation. Worse, this private prayer language policy would have disqualified even the International Mission Board president, Dr. Jerry Rankin, if it were in place at the time of his commissioning. It would also have disqualified the great missionary Miss Bertha Smith and others who confessed to "praying in the Spirit."[3] I also knew that these two new doctrinal policies at the IMB, in place for only a couple of months, had already disqualified dozens upon dozens of otherwise qualified Southern Baptists who felt called by God to the mission field.

Though I had voiced my concerns privately to my fellow trustees, once the doctrinal policies passed, I felt it my duty as a trustee to inform the people of the Southern Baptist Convention about the dangers these two new doctrinal policies represented to our cooperation. I had begun posting articles on my blog website a month earlier, only speaking to the issues and not the personalities involved. Now, I was facing the wrath of IMB trustee leadership for speaking out. It was a cool, cloudy Tuesday afternoon, January 10, 2006, and I was attending only my *fourth* trustee meeting of the International Mission Board. We were gathered in the main meeting room of the IMB headquarters in Richmond, Virginia, and the cloudy sky outside seemed to fall supernaturally through the roof into the room. Just a couple of minutes earlier the IMB chairman of the board, Arkansan Tom Hatley, had ordered all reporters, staff, and guests out of the room. We were behind closed doors—a place trustee leadership craved as ducks crave the water.

Jerry Corbaley, the trustee who made the motion to remove me, was at the time the director of missions for the North Coast Baptist Association in California. He served with me and eighty-seven other Southern Baptists who formed the International Mission Board, overseeing the work of the largest missions-sending agency in the world. I did not know Jerry Corbaley prior to being appointed as a trustee in June 2005, and my only personal contact with him had been through two or three brief conversations in the hallways or hotel lobby. I had been told by former IMB trustees that Jerry loved to talk, and during my previous three IMB meetings the observations of those former trustees seemed to me to be dead on. This "bloviator" with a penchant for dressing in khaki caught me completely off guard with his recommendation; a recommendation that had already been approved for presentation to the board by trustee leadership.

The yearly January meetings of the IMB board of trustees are held in Richmond, Virginia, and it is historically the lowest attended trustee meeting of the year. This meeting was no exception. Being in the former capital of the Confederacy in the dead of winter is not on the wish list of many, including a large number of trustees who took the opportunity to skip this particular meeting. Attendance was deemed so poor that the next January board meeting (2007) was moved from Richmond to California and to even warmer climates for the January board meetings in years to come.

The trustees who were present at this January 2006 IMB meeting were as surprised as I was when they heard Corbaley's recommendation for my removal. As is the case with most agencies in the SBC, quiet, godly men and women follow the wishes of trustee leadership unless they become aware that there is a problem. Trustee leaders hold the power on SBC boards, and trustee leaders kept me and everyone else in the dark regarding their attempts to remove me. In addition, most trustees were unaware of problems between IMB trustee leadership and our IMB administrative leadership and professional staff. The only evidence they had of a problem between trustee leaders and IMB staff, though they may not have been able to place their finger on the source, was the hostile attitudes displayed toward Jerry Rankin behind closed doors by certain trustees. For example, IMB trustees in the 1990s and early 2000s included men such as Paul Pressler, Paige Patterson, and a who's-who list of leaders of the conservative resurgence. IMB board leadership had been stacked with their family and close friends in the intervening years. They had a history of giving Dr. Rankin grief.

The executive committee of the International Mission Board composed the IMB trustee leadership, and they absolutely controlled the board through their appointments. The chairman of the board of trustees, who also chairs the executive committee, is elected by a simple majority vote of his fellow trustees during the May trustee meeting. Once he becomes chairman, he has the sole power to appoint whomever he desires as chairmen of the trustee standing committees, all of whom come together to form the executive committee of the IMB. Nothing comes before the full board in the form of an agenda item unless it is preordained and preapproved by the trustee leaders who form the executive committee of the IMB. From 2004 to 2006, pastor Tom Hatley from Arkansas, graduate of Criswell College and close friend of Paige Patterson, served as chairman of the IMB trustees; from 2006 to 2008, John Floyd from Tennessee, a former IMB executive with a grudge against Rankin and currently an administrator at Mid-America Seminary in Memphis, served as chairman of the board. John's fellow administrator at Mid-America, Van McClain, concurrently served as chairman of the board of trustees at Southwestern Baptist Theological Seminary. The appointment of chairmen is more controlled than SBC presidential elections—for good reason.

It has been said that the president of the Southern Baptist Convention has tremendous influence, but it is the chairmen of the boards of the respective Southern Baptist agencies who possess the real power. At this January 2006 meeting in Richmond, Tom Hatley was nearing the end of his second year as the IMB chairman of the board. In 2004, the night before Hatley was elected to his first term as chairman, a female trustee overheard through the thin walls of the hotel room conversations among a group of trustees who were meeting with Hatley, vowing to get him elected as chairman the next day if he would promise to appoint certain people as chairmen of the standing committees.[4] In many ways the International Mission Board is a microcosm of the Southern Baptist Convention in terms of government, with one exception—the IMB chairman, or for that matter any chairman of a SBC board, has far less accountability than the president of the Southern Baptist Convention. Few Southern Baptists know what takes place at agency board meetings, yet that is where Southern Baptist business is conducted.

The president of the Southern Baptist Convention appoints the committee on committees. This committee recommends to the Southern Baptist Convention men and women to serve on the SBC nominating committee. The nominating committee in turn presents to the convention the men and women they are nominating to serve as trustees at our various Southern Baptist agencies (i.e., LifeWay, the seminaries, the Annuity Board, etc.). The president of the Southern Baptist Convention only has indirect influence on the convention, but each chairman of the respective boards of our Southern Baptist agencies has much more power than the president of the SBC. The various chairmen *directly* appoint the chairmen of the major committees on that board, with no approval necessary. And in the case of the IMB, as I will show you, the chairman can keep anyone he dislikes from even serving on a committee. Once trustees with certain ideologies or theological idiosyncrasies gain control of a board and oppose the professional paid staff of our convention, it is impossible for an agency president, such as Jerry Rankin, to do anything without constantly having to fight trustee leadership who oppose him or what he believes. Therefore, the ultimate control of the entire SBC is in the hands of trustee leaders of our SBC agencies.

The trustees who formed the executive committee of the International Mission Board in 2006 ruled with an iron fist. These men included John Floyd from Tennessee, Tom Hatley from Arkansas, Chuck McAlister from Arkansas, Lonnie Wascom from Louisiana, and about ten others that I will introduce later. They set the board's agenda and its direction. The members of the executive committee had approved in advance Corbaley's recommendation for my removal, and sought direction from legal counsel on how to get it passed. Yet, no one on the executive committee came to me to tell me the motion was coming. No one showed common Christian courtesy or civil decency to explain to me what they intended to do. Their actions would have brought severe consequences to the typical Southern Baptist pastor at his home church, but not one trustee in leadership seemed to care about the repercussions of their rash actions, or asked if they had a moral obligation to share their charges privately with me before making them public.

And I knew why. They had an agenda. I stood in the way. I asked too many questions, and I was too persistent, particularly for a "rookie" trustee. I had discovered their attempts to remove Jerry Rankin for what they declared to be poor theology and poor leadership. I had overhead their plans to fire Wendy Norvelle, vice president of the IMB, simply because she was a woman in too powerful of a position. Even before my first IMB meeting, I was invited by the trustees who thought they were in charge to join their select group and meet secretly at a hotel or restaurant during the trustee meeting, skipping the missionary appointment service, to plan their next attack against Jerry Rankin's leadership. Some of them told me Jerry had misappropriated funds, which I later learned was a blatant lie. Others told me that the trustees were three votes short of removing Rankin, and they were counting on me, a new trustee, to be one of those three. They had recently discovered that not only was I not sympathetic to their cause, but I had informed them they were wrong in the *manner* by which they were trying to undermine the administrative leadership of the IMB and undermine the principles of trustee conduct as laid out in our manual called the "Blue Book" (because of its blue cover). One such unpleasant confrontation occurred between the caucus group of trustees and me the night before the recommendation for my removal. Now they were getting their revenge.

Once Jerry Corbaley made his recommendation, he was allowed to speak in support of it. He held in his hand a copy of an article I had written on my blog, titled "Crusading Conservatives vs. Cooperating Conservatives: The Battle for the Future of the Southern Baptist Convention." Corbaley said the article was "slanderous" and full of "gossip." It seems he didn't think about making enough copies for the board to read it for themselves, and he also happened to neglect to point out any specifics to support his charges. He assumed the full board would take his and the IMB executive committee's recommendation at face value. They felt the trustees should vote to remove me because they—trustee leadership—simply *said* I was a problem, and that problem was spreading gossip and slander. When Michigan trustee Rochelle Davis interrupted and asked for specifics of the gossip and slander, Hatley responded that the trustees needed to *trust* their leaders and that the specifics would be given to them later. It was important this matter be dealt with promptly. Of course, later never came.

When the Baptist Press reported on the motion for my removal, they quoted an official statement given to them by Chairman Tom Hatley after the meeting: "This difficult measure was not taken without due deliberation and exploration of other ways to handle an impasse between Wade Burleson and the Board. In taking this action, trustees addressed issues involving broken trust and resistance to accountability, not Burleson's opposition to policies recently enacted by the board."[5] I laughed when I read that statement. If my total and complete lack of awareness of trustee leadership's recommendation for my removal prior to it being presented to the full board is considered "due deliberation," and if the refusal to provide specifics to support their allegations of gossip and slander is considered "due diligence," then Tom either lied or exhibited a poor understanding of the English language. I would later be told that Hatley and the executive committee had researched the bylaws of the Southern Baptist Convention and knew that it was necessary for this recommendation for my removal to be presented to the executive committee of the Southern Baptist Convention a set number of days before the June meeting. That deadline was at hand, so due diligence was out the window. On with the show. It seemed never to occur to IMB trustee leadership at the time that the Southern Baptist Convention might not take too kindly to a group of trustees seeking to remove one who disagreed with them, or that I would be given an opportunity to defend myself. They totally miscalculated the enormous backlash about to come their way. Baptists are independent by nature, and anything that smacks of heavy-handed conformity doesn't sit well with the average person in the pew.

After Corbaley spoke to his recommendation, I was given an opportunity to speak behind closed doors. I was totally unprepared. I honestly didn't know what to say. I stumbled through several sentences and then asked the trustees if they had even personally read what I had written about the new doctrinal policies on my blog. It was then that I was interrupted by Hatley and told that this was not an appropriate question. I happened to think it was since on the previous day one of the trustees had explained in the trustee forum (again, behind closed doors) that "blogging" was akin to "internet pornography." I was unsure that the trustees, many of whom didn't even know what a blog was, knew what was causing trustee leadership so much consternation. I didn't argue with the chairman about the relevancy of the question, took a moment to compose myself, and went on to explain that everything I wrote on my blog was truth, not slander, and it couldn't be gossip because *everything* I had written on my blog I had already said personally to all the trustees. I was simply repeating the arguments against the policies that they had already heard me give. Gossip is talking *about* people and not *to* people. Further, I explained that I was always positive on my blog about our work on the IMB; I had never named any individual trustee when criticizing the new doctrinal policies, and only spoke about the issues at hand, not personalities. I said that if any trustee would present any evidence that what I had written was incorrect, I would immediately apologize to all involved and correct it. However, until I knew the specifics of what trustee leadership considered "gossip and slander" on my blog, it was impossible for me to apologize.

After I spoke, one of the members of the executive committee called for the question, which is a parliamentary procedure to end debate. Rick Thompson told me later he found it humorous that someone felt it necessary to call for the end of debate when there never was one. The vote for my removal was taken and the motion passed, though the vote total was not announced. Several trustees voted against the motion, and even more later told me they voted against it, but everyone was sworn to secrecy by Hatley, so those trustees who did vote against my removal and were irate over the heavy-handed tactics they witnessed, were forbidden from saying anything regarding their feelings—at least publicly.

Before this closed door meeting was dismissed, Chairman Hatley, after informing the trustees that they were not to speak about this recommendation, told me before the entire board that he was going to give me the opportunity to resign. The carrot he held out to me as an incentive to resign was clear. He said if I did resign, then this motion that had been introduced by Corbaley and trustee leaders behind closed doors would never be reported to the media or the Southern Baptist Convention. I would simply leave the IMB and there would be no personal embarrassment. To me, this is a prime example of why nothing should be done behind closed doors in the Southern Baptist Convention. If a Southern Baptist leader doesn't have the courage to say what needs to be said for the good of the convention publicly, he ought never to say it in secret. The scrutiny brought to bear by the eyes of the public would ensure that fiascos such as the one IMB trustees were about to enter, one of their own making, would never happen.

Some have suggested that I was right in opposing the doctrinal policies in principle, but the manner by which I informed the Southern Baptist Convention of my opposition to the policies was wrong. These "peace at all costs" Southern Baptists believe that a unified front is essential, and once something is done by a board, we should be quiet about it. However, it is a good thing that kind of thinking wasn't in vogue during the conservative resurgence, or changing the boards by publicly opposing "liberal" practices would never have seen the light of day. It's amazing to me how those in control are the ones who always wish to silence dissent. Further, wise men in leadership understand that the freedom to dissent only strengthens those who are in control. Those who blew the whole IMB issue out of the water were trustee leaders who were too insecure to allow one little trustee to publicly voice his disapproval to the new doctrinal policies. Their unprecedented action of removing me—an action similar to taking a hammer to smash a gnat—ignited this latest controversy in the SBC. The best way to deal with dissent is to allow it to occur—fully and freely. If dissent is without merit, it goes away. If it has merit, those in leadership are in trouble.

During the next several hours, many trustee leaders sought me out personally and urged me to resign. They again promised me that the embarrassing motion for my removal would be kept confidential if I would simply step down. I was reminded how painful it would be for me to go through the public ridicule that was about to come my way. Some suggested that my ministry would be in jeopardy if the actions of the board against me were to be made public. I steadfastly resisted any and all pressure to resign. The next morning, with all the trustees present and the doors still closed, I was asked one final time by Chairman Hatley, for the good of the SBC, to step down. I told the chairman that not only would I not resign, but I also stood by every word, sentence, and paragraph I had ever written on my blog. I added that though I found the circumstances we were now in very unfortunate, trustee leadership could look forward to a vigorous defense from me in Greensboro, North Carolina, at the 2006 Southern Baptist Convention when the convention would vote on the trustees' recommendation that I be removed. Frustrated, Chairman Hatley ordered the doors opened to the public and media, and the motion for my removal was read into the record.

Since this was the first time the public, including missionaries and IMB staff, were hearing the motion, I went to the microphone and requested that

I be allowed to read a statement into the record in response to the motion. I had learned the day before to anticipate board leaders' actions against me, and I had prepared a statement to read that expressed my love for my fellow trustees, but my belief that the Southern Baptist Convention needed to grant trustees the freedom to dissent on issues of conscience. Chairman Hatley refused me the privilege of reading my statement. I knew then that this motion for my removal did not stand a proverbial snowball's chance in hell of passing before the convention. Trustee leadership was scared of my ability to convince people that they were wrong. They had believed that I would simply resign under the *threat* of removal, but they had miscalculated my resolve.

I left the meeting a little early to catch a plane home, and as I walked down the hall toward the building's exit, IMB trustee Bill Sutton, Paige Patterson's close friend and confidante, came running up behind me. "Wade, Wade, stop! Listen to me. Please. What do I have to do to get you to resign? I'll wash your feet; I'll kiss your butt. Please, just tell me, what can I do to get you to step down for the good of everyone involved?" Someone told me later that I should have dropped my drawers right there. Regardless, I like Bill and said to him, "Bill, you still don't understand. This is a matter of principle for me. I can't resign. I'll see you in Greensboro."

When the official recommendation for my removal was presented to the media later that Wednesday morning, the wording of the motion had been changed. No longer was I being ousted for "gossip and slander"; now the "official" trustee reasons were "broken trust and resistance to accountability." The dishonesty involved with trustee leadership presenting "gossip and slander" as the reasons for my removal behind closed doors, and then later publicly presenting the reasons for my removal as "broken trust and resistance to accountability," is unconscionable behavior in my opinion. This kind of dishonesty began a pattern of conduct that characterized many actions of IMB trustee leadership until my eventual resignation in 2008.

Before I caught my plane home to Oklahoma from Richmond, I wrote and published an article on my blog. I think it gives the reader a sense of what I was feeling on the day the motion for my removal became public.

The Chairman has just read a statement into the record that the Southern Baptist Convention is being requested by the trustees of the International Mission Board that I be removed as a trustee of the IMB. I hope reporters were present since the doors had been opened and the public was invited in. I had several questions about the basis for the motion to remove me, but after the Chairman read his statement, my request to read a statement into the record was denied.

Because I am returning to a family, a church, and a state I love, I believe it is essential that I issue this statement . . .

Dear Southern Baptist Family,

I am deeply grieved by the action of the trustees of the International Mission Board in recommending to the Southern Baptist Convention that I be removed as a trustee of the IMB. This is a very difficult day for me, but I wish to express my love to the missionaries, staff, and particularly President Jerry Rankin for their outstanding service in taking the gospel to the ends of the earth. This recommendation is not from staff, but rather it is trustee initiated.

Before you make a judgment regarding the basis for their recommendation to the convention, I invite you to thoroughly read the articles that I have posted on my website at www.kerussocharis.blogspot.com or www.wadeburleson.com. I have consistently maintained that a growing problem within our convention is the removal from leadership and service those who do not conform to specific interpretations of the Bible. We Southern Baptists have already fought the battle for the Bible, but I sense that the new battle that must be waged is for the freedom of Baptists to disagree on interpretations of difficult texts in the Bible, and to always remain in fellowship and cooperation with each other in our mission.

My desire has always been to capture the interest and commitment of what I believe is a critical mass of conservative SBC members in general, and a younger generation of SBC pastors and leaders in particular, who are increasingly feeling disenfranchised because of attempts to demand conformity to interpretations of the Bible with which even reasonable, conservative inerrantists may disagree.

I am very uncomfortable with the knowledge that for the next few months of my life, my wife and children will probably have to endure an attempt by a few to discredit my character or to disparage my integrity. I place my concern in God's hands, knowing my own heart in this matter. I have sought to be gracious with others, and even though it may not be reciprocated, I am committed to always speak the truth in love.

As you probably know, a trustee is elected by a vote of the entire Southern Baptist Convention and a trustee can only be removed by a vote of the entire Southern Baptist Convention. The vote to remove me as a trustee of the International Mission Board will be June 13-14, in Greensboro, North Carolina.

> I simply ask that you vote your conscience. As for me, here I stand. I can do no other. [6]

Some have asked me, in hindsight, if I should have resigned in order to avoid all the public humiliation and embarrassment that ensued over the next several months. There have been huge consequences for my family and me but the issues at stake were much more important to me than anything personal. I would much rather have fewer speaking opportunities than a convention that stifles dissent. I would much rather have people spread false rumors about me than other Southern Baptists not appointed to the mission field for an unwillingness to conform to Fundamentalist interpretations of the Bible. In other words, sometimes causes are much bigger than any one person or family.

Once the International Mission Board made it official in fall 2005 to adopt the new doctrinal policies, one prohibiting the appointment of missionaries who confessed to having a private prayer language, and the other demanding that baptism of a missionary be performed at the hands of an IMB "authorized" baptizer, I believed it was time for the entire convention to weigh in on this matter. Again, some are under the impression that dissent should cease when a measure or policy is passed by a majority of SBC trustees. "Majority rules!" they adamantly cry. I agree that the trustees on the losing side of a vote should acquiesce to the majority, except in an instance where the dissent is a principled dissent (based upon a violation of conscience or Scripture), or when the majority of trustees have violated the will of the convention, or when a policy is passed surreptitiously in order to achieve something other than the stated purpose for which the policy is allegedly needed. All three reasons above drove me not to resign from the IMB. In light of this, I have no regrets for not resigning—even though the next two years would be wilder than a roller coaster ride without rails.

Notes

1. *The First London Confession of Faith,* article 41, London, England, 1644 (http://www.reformedreader.org/ccc/h.htm). Emphasis mine.

2. Diane Deevers, former IMB missionary, to Wade Burleson, 8 March 2006, in author's personal files.

3. "Cheers for Miss Bertha Smith," http://kerussocharis.blogspot.com/2006/01/tears-for-miss-bertha-smith-then.html, 6 January 2006.

4. Pam Blume, former IMB trustee, e-mail to Wade Burleson, 30 January 2006.

    5. Baptist Press, "Mission Board Trustees Seek Removal of Trustee Burleson," http://www.bpnews.net/bpnews.asp?id=22424, 11 January 2006.

    6. "Grace and Truth to You, To My Friends, Family, Church, and the Southern Baptist Convention," http://kerussocharis.blogspot.com/2006/01/to-my-friends-family-church-and.html, 11 January 2006.

Chapter 2

AT HOME ON THE RANGE

Though I am not, as Merle Haggard would say in his country and western hit, "an Okie from Muskogee," I am definitely an Oklahoman by birth and at heart. I arrived home in Enid, Oklahoma, from Richmond in January 2006 to a warm reception by my church and family. The motion for my removal from the IMB had been picked up by the Associated Press and was now making national headlines. An Associated Press photographer and reporter flew in from New York to be in the worship service on Sunday, January 15, 2006, as I explained to my church why I was the first Southern Baptist ever to be recommended for removal from a board. By and large, Oklahoma Southern Baptists are a fiercely independent group of Christian people, composed of rugged individualists who never hesitate to stand for what they believe to be right. The people of Emmanuel Baptist Church are no different. They respected the stand their pastor had taken in order to attempt to foster greater cooperation among Southern Baptists with differing opinions on tertiary issues. They also understood completely why it was necessary to seek to prevent the exclusionary practices by those who sought to narrow the doctrinal parameters of cooperation *beyond* the 2000 *BFM*. It has been said that Oklahoma was built on "soil, oil, and toil," but it can equally be said that Southern Baptists in Oklahoma, with just a few exceptions, sustain personal relationships through "amazing grace and a smiling face." I have met many a transplanted northerner who has remarked to me how odd it is to see Oklahoma people wave and smile at complete strangers as if they were long-lost friends. That is Oklahoma culture, including Southern Baptist Oklahoma culture, and I love it.

I was born two days after Christmas, December 27, 1961, in the newly opened Oklahoma City Baptist Hospital, a hospital that was built and operated by the Baptist General Convention of Oklahoma until the early 1980s. At the time of my birth, my father and mother, Paul and Mary Burleson, were already serving on staff at their second Southern Baptist church in

Oklahoma, and my mother had already given birth a year earlier to my older sister. My dad was only twenty-one years of age and my mother was barely twenty. My father was commuting from Oklahoma City to Shawnee, Oklahoma, to finish his major in Bible and minor in history from Oklahoma Baptist University.

The Oklahoma City Burlesons in 1961 were hardly as famous as our Texas Baptist forefather of a hundred years earlier. Ancestor Rufus Burleson had served as president of the Baptist General Convention of Texas in the mid-1800s and had also been president of Baylor University. I grew up hearing stories of Texas Baptists, the Alamo, Baylor University, etc. The Burleson name is still prevalent in Texas, as seen in the city of Burleson, Texas, a fast-growing southern suburb of Fort Worth, named in honor of Rufus. A clan of the Burleson family also settled around Cleburne, Texas, but my branch of the Burleson family eventually looked for their prosperity in Oklahoma, and crossed the northern border of Texas in the early 1900s.

The Baptist gene in the Oklahoma Burlesons mutated during the twentieth century, leaving no appetite for religion in my immediate ancestry. Legend has it that Reed Burleson, my alcoholic grandfather, was in the poker game where the owner of the famous Oklahoma City Cattlemen's Restaurant threw the deed of his restaurant onto the table to cover his bet—and lost the hand. My great-grandfather William "Arthur" owned and operated an Oklahoma City grocery store, called Burleson's Grocery. It was located just south of the downtown railroad tracks, not far from the cattle stockyards, on May Avenue. My great-grandfather sold liquor out the back door during the days of prohibition and would tell stories of serving the rich and famous that came to Burleson's Grocery in disguise. The Burleson legacy in Oklahoma in the early 1900s is not one for the history books, but fortunately, God remains interested in the lost sheep as much as he is the ninety and nine in the fold.

Through the influence of a small Southern Baptist church in Oklahoma City and my praying grandmother, Margaret Burleson, my father and his siblings eventually came to faith in Christ. My dad and his only brother, Jim, became Southern Baptist ministers, and Dad had sons and sons-in-law who were gospel ministers. My aunt Betty Burleson married a Southern Baptist International Mission Board missionary, Frank Coy, who would later become president of the Santiago Theological Seminary in Chile. The Coys' boys, Terry and Jerry, would follow in their father's steps and become ministers of the gospel as well, with Jerry serving with the IMB as a missionary in

Chile and Terry on the church-planting staff at the Southern Baptist Convention of Texas. My only other aunt, Fern Burleson, faithfully took her children to the local Southern Baptist church in her poor Oklahoma City neighborhood until her death. Her grandchildren are now faithfully serving Christ in Southern Baptist churches, including Alicia Pharaoh, whose husband serves as youth pastor at a fast-growing Southern Baptist church in Idaho. We have always appreciated the ministry of small Southern Baptist churches and a praying grandmother because of the influence they both had on the OKC Burleson family in the late last half of the twentieth century.

In addition to growing up in a Southern Baptist culture, I developed at an early age an appreciation for ethnic, social, and economic diversity. My great-great-grandfather Burleson had married what was then unfortunately called a "half-breed" (half American Indian, half Caucasion), and there was also "Indian blood" on my mother's side of the family. I believe that my Indian heritage, however small a percentage of Indian blood that courses through my veins, as well as my understanding of the unique history and culture of Oklahoma, have helped shape my desire to champion anyone I perceive to be the underdog. Abuses of power, manipulative tactics, broken promises, and coercion of the weak have been characteristics of the United States government's actions toward the Indian tribes of Oklahoma. Anyone familiar with Oklahoma's history will always cast a wary eye against those who use positions of power to abuse.

"Oklahoma" is a Choctaw word that means "red people." From 1817 to 1842, the United States actively sought to remove the Indians (or "red people") from eastern colonial states by giving them land where they could settle and practice their ancient rituals without interference from the white man. Ironically, Baptist missionary Isaac McCoy and his son John C. McCoy (founder of Kansas City), recommended to President John Quincy Adams that the land most suitable for Indian relocation was a portion of the territory called the Louisiana Purchase, obtained from Napoleon's France in 1803 for pennies an acre. This land, suitable for the Indians, would eventually be labeled "Indian Territory" by the United States. Indian Territory in the 1800s encompassed all of present-day Oklahoma. Baptist missionary Isaac McCoy wrote in the 1820s, during his trips throughout the region, that the country was "far better than I had expected"[1]—no small statement from the man who devoted his life to the cause of the Indians and had first recommended this territory for the Indians because of its natural beauty and resources.

The five "civilized" Indian tribes (Choctaw, Cherokee, Chickasaw, Creek, and Seminole) from Alabama, Mississippi, Tennessee, North Carolina, Georgia, and Florida were relocated to Indian Territory in the 1820s, '30s, and '40s by means of journeys that killed thousands of them because of the harsh winter weather, poor provisions, and shoddy government planning. Though the Cherokees call their relocation to Tahlequah, Oklahoma, "The Trail of Tears," each of these five tribes have their share of horror stories and their own trails of tears as they made their way to their new home. The United States government established forts in Indian Territory and staffed them with soldiers to keep the native "Plainsmen" Indians (Comanche, Osage, Kiowa, Apache, etc.) of Indian Territory from attacking the unwelcome and newly relocated "civilized" Indians. By 1842, most forced relocations of the five civilized tribes of the east were finished, but Indian Territory was eventually home to sixty-seven different tribes that often warred with each other more than they did the neighboring white man in Kansas and Texas or the white men who used government trails through Indian Territory on their way to California.

The town in which I have served as pastor for the past seventeen years is called Enid, Oklahoma. The high school mascot is the Plainsman Indian, a fierce-looking chief that represents the "uncivilized" natives who lived in Indian Territory prior to the forced relocation of the "civilized" tribes from the eastern United States. For about fourteen years, from 1847 to 1861, the United States government soldiers stationed in Indian Territory did fairly well at keeping the various Indian tribes at bay from each other, but when the Civil War broke out, all the Indian tribes in Indian Territory banded together to side with the Confederacy, and the United States government found itself at the receiving end of Indian uprisings. The attacks by organized Indian Confederate horsemen and infantrymen led to the withdrawal of Federal troops and the abandonment of Federal forts during the Civil War. A little known fact about the Civil War is that the last Confederate general to surrender was General Stand Watie, a Cherokee Indian who led a Confederate company of Cherokee, Creek, and Seminole Indian soldiers into battles against union loyalists. General Watie signed a ceasefire agreement with Union representatives on June 23, 1865, at Fort Towson (Oklahoma Territory), more than two months after Robert E. Lee's surrender at Appomattox.

After the close of the Civil War, animosity over the Indian tribes siding with the Confederacy, as well as envy over the natural resources located on the beautiful "Indian" lands, caused the United States government to decide to open Indian Territory to white settlement in a series of "land runs"— including the 1889 Land Run that turned the Oklahoma Depot (railroad stop) at the center of the state into "Oklahoma City" overnight. Another infamous 1893 land run, made famous by the 1993 Tom Cruise and Nicole Kidman movie *Far and Away,* resulted in the founding of Enid, Oklahoma. Within the short span of ten years, "Indian Territory" became a region populated by hundreds of thousands of white people looking for a new start. The Indians quickly became a minority race in the land the United States government had given them in exchange for relocating from the east coast states. More than a quarter million whites raced into Oklahoma to claim the free quarter section of land (160 acres) promised them by the United States government if they would simply build a dwelling, plant a crop, and occupy it for five consecutive years. Some enterprising whites decided to risk their lives by jumping the shotgun starts of the five major land races in order to stake out the best quarter section of land before anyone else could beat them to it. These illegal "Sooners" knew full well they would be shot dead by federal marshals if caught. In addition, if they were fortunate enough not to be caught, but were later discovered to have cheated when they went to file a land claim, they would endure the derision of the Oklahoma "Boomers" who had waited for the proper start and staked their land according to the law. If you ever have the good fortune to attend an Oklahoma Sooners football game in the 90,000-seat arena in Norman, Oklahoma, you will hear half the crowd shout "Boomer" and the other half "Sooner" before the kickoff. I'm not sure if the modern Indians who participate in this football chant prior to the game would yell quite so loudly if they fully comprehended that the "Boomer Sooner" land runs took from them what the United States government had promised would be the possession of the Indians "as long as the grass grows and the rivers run."[2]

Promises by those in authority can be broken unless there is enough grassroots willingness to hold leaders accountable. Sadly, many times the majority simply doesn't care about the integrity of its leaders. Without moral fortitude and integrity characterizing those in power, there can be no inherent basis to believe the promises of those leaders. The more centralized power becomes, the greater the need for character among leaders—or strict accountability brought to bear against those leaders by those being led. One should not assume, even among Christians, that there is integrity in the hearts of those in power. Every individual struggles with the primacy of self-interest, and unless checked by intentional structures of accountability, power corrupts even the best of characters. I was to learn this lesson well while serving as a trustee of the International Mission Board of the Southern Baptist Convention. Although there cannot, nor should there be, any comparison between the suffering of Native Americans and conflict between those in power and those not, the lessons of history should teach all Americans that power corrupts and absolute power corrupts absolutely.

While I was still a child, my father moved the family south of the Red River to take the pastorate at a small church in St. Joe, Texas. Then, following five-year stints, respectively, as pastor of Fairway Baptist Church in Wichita Falls, Texas, and First Baptist Church, Borger, Texas, my father became pastor of the large Southcliff Baptist Church in Fort Worth, Texas. It was in Fort Worth, Texas, that I would spend my high school years, graduating as one of four valedictorian students at Southwest High School, located in the shadow of the neighborhood of Southwestern Baptist Theological Seminary. Upon high school graduation in 1980, I attended Baylor University.

My wife, Rachelle, and I met on a blind date at Baylor University in fall 1981. Some look at me and accuse her of still being blind, but I can assure you my eyesight is perfect, and I fell in love with a beautiful woman. She, too, is a native Oklahoman and made her home in Hong Kong during her college years. Her father worked at the time for the Asian office of Phillips 66 Petroleum, an Oklahoma-based oil company that takes its name from Frank Phillips, the founder, and the historic interstate highway called Route 66 that runs from Los Angeles to Chicago and literally dissects the state of Oklahoma from southwest to northeast. Rachelle's parents, Don and Nancy, now work for Southern Baptist cooperative missions in a secure region overseas.

Rachelle and I dated for more than a year while attending Baylor, and then I was called in early 1982 to serve as the youth director for First Baptist Church, Holdenville, Oklahoma. I transferred my full-time college education from Baylor to a part-time effort at East Central University, Ada, Oklahoma, where I pursued a Bachelor of Science degree in finance while working full-time at FBC Holdenville. I was able to save just enough money to purchase an engagement ring on my $200 a week salary, and Rachelle and I were married in August 1983 in Bartlesville, Oklahoma, her original hometown.

I owe a great deal to the people of First Baptist Church, Holdenville. The church asked me to be their interim pastor in 1984 when their pastor, James Robinson, left. Within a few weeks, the pulpit committee asked me if I would consider becoming their permanent pastor. The pulpit committee was not unanimous in this recommendation, with two of the five members telling church people I was too young, too inexperienced, and lacked a formal theological education. I publicly agreed with the minority on the committee and declined the majority's invitation to become the church's pastor. Six months later the majority of the pulpit committee insisted again that they were going to recommend to the church that I be their pastor. This time they told me they felt so strongly that it was God's will for me to be their pastor that they would resign if either the church or I refused. After seeking counsel from my father and family friend Jack Taylor, I agreed to let the church decide.

The two pulpit committee members against me began making phone calls encouraging people to show up to vote against the prospective pastor. The three pulpit committee members who were for me came to me and explained what the other two were doing. They asked if they should begin making phone calls on my behalf. I asked them what the two men were saying. They said that the two pulpit committee members were telling church members that I was young, I had no formal theological degree, and I had no experience as a senior pastor. I told the three members that what the two were saying about me was true, and there was no need for them to call anyone on my behalf. I felt that the people of First Baptist, who had been under my interim pastoral leadership for seven months, could determine for themselves whether or not I would make a good pastor for them. My under-standing of allowing committee members to voice their dissent on a majority decision has been shaped by my personal experiences.

On September 13, 1985, the auditorium of First Baptist Church, Holdenville, was standing room only as the church decided on whether or not to call a twenty-three-year-old college kid to be the pastor of their his-toric one-hundred-year-old church. I was called with a 97 percent vote of the church. Only the two men on the pulpit committee, their wives, and their voting-age children voted against me. I learned a great deal during this time about how God ultimately brings about his purposes, and it does not require either our manipulations or our conniving for his will to occur. Those two men remained my friends, though one eventually left the church, and the other moved away a short time later because of work.

I spent a total of five years at First Baptist Church, Holdenville, before I was called to be the pastor of Sheridan Road Baptist Church in Tulsa, Oklahoma. In Tulsa, Rachelle and I spent an additional five years working among some wonderful Southern Baptists. We often heard stories from the old-timers of how Johnny Bisagnio, who used to be a member of the church in his teens, would play the trumpet during the Sunday school hour. Sheridan Road was in what could be called a tough, transitional neighborhood of Tulsa, but as in Holdenville, God was gracious in giving to the church solid, steady growth during those five years. Attendance doubled and our experience at Sheridan Road Baptist Church was both fulfilling and enjoyable.

In 1992, Emmanuel Baptist Church called me to be their pastor. I was twenty-nine years old at the time, and this church already possessed a great history of well-known pastors. Dr. Gary Smith left Emmanuel to become pastor of Fielder Road Baptist Church in Arlington, Texas, in 1991. Before Gary, Dr. Hayes Wicker was pastor, and he left Emmanuel eventually to become pastor of First Baptist Church, Lubbock, Texas. Hayes is currently pastor at First Baptist Church, Naples, Florida, the home church of Christian apologist extraordinaire and former Watergate co-conspirator Chuck Colson. Dr. C. Mack Roark, for many years the professor of Greek at Oklahoma Baptist University, was the founding pastor of Emmanuel. Dr. Roark was serving for the third time as the interim pastor of Emmanuel when I was called to be their full-time senior pastor.

I went in view of a call to Emmanuel on February 2, 1992, just two days after hosting at Sheridan Road Baptist Church a celebration service commemorating the life of Charles Spurgeon. The prince of preachers had died on January 31, 1882, and on Friday night, January 31, 1992, 100 years to the day of his death, our church hosted a unique event celebrating Spurgeon's ministry. Dr. Lewis Drummond, president of Southeastern Seminary and author of the newly released biographical account of Spurgeon's life, was the featured speaker. Dr. Tom Nettles, professor of Church History at Southern Seminary, also spoke. I wrote a script on the life of Charles Haddon Spurgeon, narrated it with background music and slides, and played it as a eulogy for the two hundred or so pastors who came for the event. During my research on Spurgeon's life I discovered that when he left his small country church to become pastor of the historic London church that would eventually be known as Metropolitan Tabernacle, he received five "no" votes from the members of Metropolitan. At the time I read that account, I remember setting down the book and asking God, "Lord, if I could only receive five 'no' votes when I go in view of a call to Emmanuel, I would be so grateful." I felt that receiving enough votes to become pastor of Emmanuel, a required 90 percent of all votes cast, would be a difficult feat since members would be voting on such a young pastor. If I were called, I would be by several years the youngest pastor on Emmanuel's staff, though I would carry the title "senior pastor." Figure that one out. Frankly, I didn't want my wife or me, or the church, to be embarrassed with a numerous amount of "no" votes.

I received five "no" votes out of several hundred cast on that February Sunday at Emmanuel, and I took that as confirmation from the Lord that I was to move my wife and by now three young kids (Charis, Kade, and Boe) to Enid, Oklahoma, and become pastor of Emmanuel Baptist Church. We began our ministry at Emmanuel Baptist Church, Enid, on Sunday, March 2, 1992, and for the last seventeen years we have experienced a piece of heaven. The people are gracious and kind. The leaders are servants. The church has her priorities straight. She is missions minded and grace filled. Though we are located in a rural city, we have experienced steady growth, and I thank the Lord regularly for being so kind to give me a place like Emmanuel to pastor. During my tenure at Emmanuel, I have served two terms as president of the Baptist General Convention of Oklahoma, two terms as its vice president, and in the early 1990s I also chaired the denominational calendar committee for the Southern Baptist Convention and served a term on the nominating committee of the SBC. My church has been both understanding and supportive of my involvement in state and national Southern Baptist Convention matters.

However, for ten years, from 1995 to 2005, I concentrated on pastoring the church, providing leadership for our state convention, and being a dad to my four kids (our youngest son, Logan, was born the second year we lived in Enid). Though I had supported the conservative resurgence in the Southern Baptist Convention during the 1980s, even traveling with Paul Pressler as he toured Oklahoma raising support for pastors to attend the Southern Baptist Convention and vote "conservative," I had lost track of the developments within the convention for nearly a decade. I assumed there was a sweet spirit among the people, a high degree of trust in convention leaders, and a focus on cooperative efforts to share the gospel with the world at large—similar to the spirit of the Southern Baptist churches I'd had the privilege to pastor.

It took only one phone call in early spring 2005 to change my perceptions of what was going on in the Southern Baptist Convention.

Notes

1. Randolph O. Yeager, *Indian Enterprises of Isaac McCoy,* 1817–1846, unpublished Ph.D. diss., University of Oklahoma, 1955.

2. *Indian Affairs: Laws and Treaties,* ed. Charles Kappler, vol. 2 (Washington DC: Government Printing Office, 1904), 284.

Chapter 3

THE PHONE CALL

The Beginning: Pastor's Office
Emmanuel Baptist Church
March 2005

I was sitting at my desk one day in March 2005 when my secretary used the intercom to tell me Winston Curtis wanted to speak with me.[1] I knew Winston fairly well, though it would not be accurate to call him a close friend. He was the pastor of a small church in Duncan, Oklahoma, and we had shared a few conversations regarding state matters while I served as president of the Baptist General Convention of Oklahoma. Winston felt comfortable enough with me that he had requested a few months earlier that I recommend him to First Baptist Church, Blackwell, Oklahoma, or any other church in Oklahoma that I felt would be a good fit for him, and he also asked if I would serve as one of the references on his résumé. I was happy to do so, not because I could vouch for his ministry abilities (and would tell the pulpit committee so), but because I liked him personally and believed him to have a pastoral heart.

Winston greeted me with his warm, cheery "How ya doin' Wade?" and we spent a few minutes talking about family and church. Then Winston explained why he had called. He told me he was serving as a trustee of the International Mission Board. The reminder was unnecessary since I remembered clearly that when Winston had asked me to recommend him to various churches, he had stipulated that churches be in Oklahoma because he did not want to lose his position as a trustee on the IMB—which he would if he were to move out of state. Winston proceeded to relay to me that the IMB was in trouble and he believed I could help.

Winston asked me if I knew Jerry Rankin. I told him I had met him on a couple of occasions, and had heard him preach at our state convention in 2004 when we held a missionary appointment service on Tuesday night in conjunction with the convention. I was moderating the Tuesday night business meeting and had welcomed Dr. Rankin to Oklahoma, which was the only personal conversation I had ever had with him. Winston asked if I met Tom Hatley that night as well. I told him I had been reintroduced to Tom, who was then the IMB's chairman of the board, and that I remembered Tom from his difficult days as pastor of Frink Baptist Church, near McAlester, Oklahoma, about twenty years earlier.

Winston then proceeded to tell me that he liked Jerry Rankin personally, but there were problems with his administration at the IMB. He then said something that is as clear to me today as it was the day he said it. He said Jerry had taken "Southern Baptist money and buried it at Monument Avenue." I'll never forget that statement because it conjured up an image in my mind. One of my favorite movies of all time, *Pirates of the Caribbean: The Curse of the Black Pearl*, had been released the year before, and I could imagine Jerry Rankin putting money in a chest, taking it home, and burying it in his back yard. So I asked Winston, "You mean Dr. Rankin has stolen money and buried it in his backyard?"

Winston laughed and said no. He explained to me that Monument Avenue is the name trustees give for International Mission Board headquarters in Richmond, Virginia. Jerry had misappropriated, according to Winston, millions of dollars for remodeling without trustee approval. Winston then asked if I knew Judge Paul Pressler. I told him I did. He suggested I call Judge Pressler and he would explain to me how and where all the money had been buried. It seems that Paul Pressler and Paige Patterson both had been trustees during Jerry Rankin's tenure, and they would have nothing good to say of his administration, nor would a host of other trustees who felt that the tenure of Jerry Rankin should come to an end. Some of the other problems with Jerry Rankin were his lack of theological acumen, his unwillingness to move headquarters from liberal Richmond to a place in the southwest, and his inability to distance himself from money and people affiliated with the Southern Baptist churches aligned with the Cooperative Baptist Fellowship (CBF).

I was curious as to why Winston was calling me, and reminded him that if Jerry Rankin had actually misappropriated funds, it was the fiduciary duty of trustees to terminate him. I also said I wasn't sure it was appropriate to tell people that misappropriation had taken place unless you were willing to back it up by holding accountable the people who were responsible. Winston explained that Jerry was a popular person, even among some trustees, and they did not have enough votes to deal with the matter appropriately. They needed more trustees who were strong, independent people who would not back down from doing the right thing. He said he had observed me lead our state as president and he knew I would do the right thing, no matter how unpopular the action might be.

I thanked Winston for his compliment, but having myself served on the Southern Baptist nominating committee in 1995, I knew that the decision regarding the appointment of trustees was in the hands of that committee, not sitting trustees of the IMB. Winston said a group of IMB trustees met on a regular basis to "help" the IMB correct her course, and at the last meeting, trustees had been assigned the responsibility of getting good people from their home states nominated to serve on the IMB. Winston said he was looking forward to the opportunity of serving with me on the IMB, and he would be in touch once I had been approved by the nominating committee. Winston then asked how much our church gave to the Cooperative Program, Lottie Moon, and missions in general. He was vetting me to ensure I had the credentials that would get me nominated by the committee, and eventually elected by the Southern Baptist Convention. We hung up after about a thirty-minute phone conversation, and other than being curious about the alleged misappropriation of funds, I did not think more about the conversation—until the Southern Baptist nominating committee contacted me three weeks later.

The nominating committee of the Southern Baptist Convention meets in March to nominate Southern Baptists to serve as trustees of our Southern Baptist entities. The president of the Southern Baptist Convention appoints the committee on committees, which then recommends two members from each state to serve on the nominating committee. The convention votes on the nominating committee in June, and the following March, the nominating committee meets in Nashville to carry out their work recommending various Southern Baptists to serve as trustees of our various Southern Baptist agencies such as the International Mission Board, the North American Mission Board, LifeWay, Guidestone, the executive committee, our six Southern Baptist seminaries, and the various standing committees of the convention. The process is supposed to be independent, without any tampering from either agency heads or sitting trustees to stack their respective boards with like-minded people.

The member of the nominating committee from Oklahoma who called me was a layman, but a man I knew well because he had dated one of the single women in our church. Our conversation over the phone was cordial, and he informed me that I had been recommended to him as a person who would represent Southern Baptists well on the International Mission Board. I did not ask him who recommended me, but from my earlier phone conversation with Winston, I had no doubt who it was. He asked me questions about our church's Cooperative Program giving and other missions emphases and told me that he and his fellow nominating committee member would be nominating me for a trustee position on the IMB.

It was only later that I would learn the specifics of how a group of trustees on the IMB, led by a contingent from Texas, Arkansas, and a hodge-podge of other states, were intentionally attempting to control the direction of the IMB by manipulating the process through which trustees were elected. There are 89 trustees on the IMB, but only about two dozen (who gather in an informal caucus, in violation of trustee bylaws) control the direction of the entire board. This caucus wanted trustees to bring about a change of administration at the IMB by removing Rankin. In his book *Witness to the Truth*, IMB trustee Louis Moore explained how the chairman of the SBC nominating committee had been influenced by sitting IMB trustee Bob Pearle, who also happened to be Paige Patterson's pastor, to select Louis as the new IMB trustee from Texas.[2] It is not, according to the Southern Baptist Convention's own constitution, the role of sitting IMB trustees to find replacements for vacancies on the IMB. That is the role of the SBC nominating committee. But the IMB caucus group was active in ensuring that only those who agreed with them were nominated—an act that violated the bylaws.

In February 2006, the aforementioned IMB trustee Bob Pearle, who served as pastor of Birchman Avenue Baptist Church in Fort Worth, Texas, and was the close friend and pastor of Dr. Paige Patterson, spoke with a couple of people in a coffee shop and told them that the IMB was three votes short of either forcing Jerry Rankin to retire or to get him terminated, and Wade Burleson had been counted on as being one of those votes.[3] I received an e-mail from someone to whom it was said that trustee leadership could count on my vote. These people only confirmed what I had personally experienced in conversations with other trustees during the months following my initial contact with Winston Curtis.

When Winston Curtis made that original phone call to me in spring 2005, I know there was nothing malicious or malevolent in his intentions. Winston is a man who loves the Lord and serves him faithfully, but as with everyone else, there is a tendency to lose perspective when you get in a position of influence or are surrounded by people you have long admired. I do not for a minute believe that Winston Curtis would have initiated any plan to orchestrate the removal of Jerry Rankin, but he had surrounded himself on the IMB with men (and at least one woman trustee) who were all highly influenced by Paige Patterson and his animosity toward Jerry Rankin. I discovered later that an outside auditing firm had cleared Dr. Rankin and all IMB administration of any wrongdoing in the remodeling of IMB headquarters in Richmond. The approach that the trustees were now taking to get rid of Rankin, as I would soon learn, was to pass a policy forbidding any missionary from being appointed to the mission field who confessed to having a "private prayer language." The ridiculousness of asking someone about something that should be private is almost as bizarre as passing a policy that would disqualify the president of the International Mission Board from serving as a missionary in the very organization over which he presides.

Winston Curtis is not an opposition leader to Jerry Rankin. It's not that he agrees with Rankin, but he is not a leader. He is a nice Oklahoma pastor who got involved with people who play a game of hardball religion and are not used to anyone questioning their intentions or their actions. Some of these men and women who served on the International Mission Board in 2005 and 2006 include the following:

(1) Bob Pearle (Texas). The aforementioned pastor is a pleasant man with whom to converse, and he knows how to tell a good joke. He is Paige Patterson's pastor and I have seen him take direct aim at Dr. Rankin while serving as chairman of one of the major standing committees. He was involved in the informal caucus of trustees who sought to orchestrate Rankin's removal. The Texas contingent of IMB trustees, under the influence of Paige Patterson, sought to control the direction of the IMB through critical letters from Paige Patterson sent to IMB trustees regarding Jerry Rankin's vision and leadership, letters sent while Paige Patterson was serving as president of Southeastern Baptist Theological Seminary in North Carolina.[4] When Paige became president of Southwestern Baptist Theological Seminary in Fort Worth, Texas, he joined the church of IMB trustee and friend Bob Pearle.

(2) Louis Moore (Texas). This man is a self-described independent journalist from the *Houston Chronicle* who was "given" sole access to the suite in which Paige Patterson and Paul Pressler oversaw the 1979 Southern Baptist

Convention. His recent book, *Witness to the Truth*, is a diatribe against Rankin's leadership, probably tainted by Moore's poor opinion of Rankin while working at the International Mission Board. Louis, a disgruntled former IMB employee, pulls no punches in alleging "misappropriation of funds" and that Carl Johnson, the IMB treasurer, resigned in order "to get Jerry off the hook" with the board.[5] This is exactly the kind of allegation trustee Winston used in an attempt to get me on the board as a trustee to remove Rankin. I would later learn these allegations were demonstrably proven false by an external audit. Louis Moore alleges in his book that I stated to him that he was the only trustee who treated me with kindness,[6] a statement as preposterous as it is hollow. It makes me question the veracity of other things he's written in his book, particularly when there are at least two dozen other IMB trustees whom I count as close friends.

(3) Skeet Workman (Texas). Mrs. Workman is an elderly Texan with a fierce temper. She buttonholed me during my second trustee meeting, after she discovered I had questioned the new policy forbidding the appointment of missionaries who confessed to having a private prayer language, shook her finger in my face, and said, "Young man, do you realize if we don't pass this policy we will have charismatics on the mission field?" I thought about asking her who did her nails, but simply responded, "No, ma'am, I did not realize that." Skeet is a close personal friend of Judge Paul Pressler. She was also in the habit, as were other members of the caucus, of blind carbon-copying e-mails to her friends that she had written to me. This tactic would come back to bite her in January 2006.

(4) Albert Green (Texas). Albert is a good old boy who wears University of Texas clothing and likes to give the "aw shucks" kind of attitude. He was involved in the informal trustee caucus meeting in the lobby of the hotel in January 2006 where I confronted them about their desires to fire Wendy Norvelle, acting vice president of communications for the IMB. I never will forget his part in this formal introduction to hardball religion, described in more detail in chapter 11.

(5) Tom Hatley (Arkansas). Tom is a graduate of Criswell College and was the chairman of the IMB from 2002 to 2004. Tom's temper is legendary. Anecdotes of his anger at both the churches he served as pastor and in a handful of meetings he chaired at the IMB when he got upset are often told. I was the recipient of his anger from the beginning of my service on the board, and I saw his temper flash publicly toward Dr. Rankin more than

once. Though I never personally saw Tom in a caucus setting, other former IMB trustees did.[7]

(6) Mary Nichols (Alaska). Mary Nichols is a quiet, home-schooling mom. She's married to a law enforcement official who was promoted to head of security for Southwestern Baptist Theological Seminary under Paige Patterson. Dean Nichols, Mary's husband, is Paige Patterson's close hunting buddy, and though Mary would be averse to identifying herself with a group of men, she was definitely counted on to vote with the party line and be supportive of the agenda of the caucus.

(7) Bill Sutton (Texas). Bill Sutton is the granddaddy of the caucus group. He served on the International Mission Board an astonishing sixteen years, and is also the hunting buddy of Paige Patterson, along with Dean Nichols. I like Bill because you never have to wonder where he stands, and he is not plagued with the super-spiritual lingo with which so many trustees seem to be infected. He tells it like it is, and by golly, the enemies of the SBC are liberals and charismatics! Some of my funniest memories of serving as a trustee involve Bill Sutton.

(8) Steve Swofford (Texas). Steve served as president of the Southern Baptist Conservatives of Texas. Ideologically, he is right in line with the Landmark, Fundamentalist movement that typifies the direction Paige Patterson wishes to take the Southern Baptist Convention. As everyone else in the caucus, Steve was given various leadership positions within the IMB. Also, as everyone in the caucus, Steve regularly violated the trustee guidelines by speaking ill of me to anyone who would listen. At the retirement for Dr. Bell at Dallas Baptist University in summer 2006, a pastor friend of mine overheard Steve tell a group of four or five men that Wade Burleson was "crazy." Steve was confronted by both the pastor and me personally about his comments.[8]

(9) Chuck McAlister (Arkansas). Chuck is known for a syndicated television hunting show in his home state of Arkansas. Chuck set his sights on me during my tenure on the board, and of all the off-the-wall, hardball tactics perpetrated by trustees against me, Chuck McAlister's antics rank right up there with Jerry Corbaley's, Tom Hatley's, and John Floyd's. He is the trustee who recommended in the March 2006 trustee meeting that I pay my own way to board meetings, never be recognized at a microphone, and not be able to vote. His motion died for lack of a second.

(10) Bill Sanderson (North Carolina). Bill Sanderson, another good friend of Paige Patterson and former Southeastern and Southwestern seminaries missions strategist Keith Eitel, was always publicly cordial to my wife and me. I

enjoyed his company and appreciated his cordiality. However, it is Bill Sanderson, along with Bill Sutton, whom Dr. Rankin pointed out to me privately in his office as the men who caused him the most concern and formed the unofficial leaders of the opposition to IMB administration under Rankin. Bill Sanderson played a key role in undermining Rankin's leadership in 2002–2003. He did this by partnering with Southeastern Baptist Theological Seminary (SEBTS) president Paige Patterson and SEBTS missions professor Keith Eitel to encourage IMB journeymen to "spy" on the IMB and report to them regarding any theological aberrations, including weak ecclesiology (planting churches on the mission field with women in leadership, or partnering with non-Southern Baptist groups, etc.), imbalanced Pheumatology (any teaching on the gifts that was non-cessationist in nature), and other "problems" they might see on the mission field under Rankin's leadership. This subversive, intrusive activity at the IMB by Paige Patterson resulted in every IMB trustee receiving critical letters from Patterson and Eitel regarding the direction of the IMB.[9]

The ten trustees above never formed an official organization, had no "Skulls and Bones"-style initiation and would deny their involvement in organized opposition to Dr. Rankin, but it was clear to me and others that whatever their motives, they deemed that Dr. Rankin needed to be gone for the good of the convention. Ultimately, the man orchestrating the removal of Dr. Rankin was Paige Patterson himself,[10] who, after the IMB trustees passed the new "private prayer language" policy in November 2005, wrote Dr. Rankin a personal letter asking him if it was now time to step aside as president of the IMB since his own trustees had turned against him. Patterson's friendship, influence, and guidance are obvious in the ten IMB trustees named above. Other trustees were also involved in undermining Rankin's leadership, but they used the "doctrinal purity" rationale for passing two doctrinal policies in November 2005 that Rankin opposed. Some of these "doctrinally pure" men (another way of saying "Baptist identity" men) included former IMB employee and openly Landmark trustee John Floyd, trustee Jerry Corbaley, trustee Paul Chitwood (who told me he would boot his own grandmother out of the SBC if she were Southern Baptist because she speaks in tongues), and trustee Winston Curtis. They pushed the IMB to pass doctrinal policies that exceeded the 2000 *BFM*, and then excluded otherwise qualified Southern Baptists from serving in cooperative missions and ministries based upon those two doctrinal policies because they believed they were *right*. They never stopped to consider that the Southern Baptist Convention was built on cooperation, and cooperation necessitates diversity of opinions on nonessentials of the faith. The 2000 *BFM* is the doctrinal basis of cooperation, not a collection of the mere whims of individual trustees. The two new IMB doctrinal policies, a prohibition for missionaries to confess having a private prayer language and the demand that a missionary be baptized by an IMB-approved administrator of Christian baptism, were either intended to embarrass or ultimately remove President Rankin (as was the intention of Sanderson, Pearle, Workman, etc.), or were pushed because of the peculiar Landmark, fundamental, cessational, and ecclesiological ideologies of the trustees who wrote them (as in the case of Floyd, Corbaley, Chitwood, etc.). Some of the trustees might argue that they had no idea Dr. Jerry Rankin was targeted by the new policies, and that may be true, but any trustee who voted for policies that would disqualify the president of the IMB from serving as a missionary in the very agency over which he allegedly presides should have his or her head examined.

I'm not sure Winston Curtis ever understood that he was being played like a fiddle by people who had an agenda for the IMB, but his phone call to me began a long, tough journey for my family and me.

Notes

1. Details of this phone conversation are found in an affidavit dated February 2006 by Wade Burleson and Randy Long, Attorney at Law.

2. Louis Moore, *Witness to the Truth* (Garland: Hannibal Books, 2008), 316.

3. Ben Cole, personal letter to the author, 20 April 2008.

4. Paige Patterson to IMB trustees, March 2003.

5. Moore, *Witness to the Truth*, 284.

6. Ibid., 316.

7. Pam Blume, letter to the author, 8 January 2006.

8. Wade Burleson to Steve Swofford, 15 January 2007.

9. See chapter 8, "Grace and Truth," for references to these attempts at undermining Dr. Jerry Rankin.

10. According to Dr. Jerry Rankin, in a conversation held during a meeting of various denomination officials gathered to discuss the IMB trustee motion for my removal, St. Louis MO, February 2006.

Chapter 4

THE IMB POLICIES
THAT BECAME A FUSE

IMB New Trustee Orientation
Richmond, Virginia
July 2005

The Southern Baptist Convention approved my appointment as a trustee for the International Mission Board at the 2005 convention in Nashville, Tennessee. I was not present at that particular convention, but I received a large packet of material from the International Mission Board in late June with instructions regarding the IMB orientation and trustee meeting scheduled for Richmond, Virginia, in the middle of July 2005. The orientation for new trustees takes place at the International Learning Center (ILC) about thirty minutes west of IMB headquarters in Richmond. I arrived late Sunday night, July 10, 2005, ready for four solid days of instruction and orientation.

For several years prior to my two-year stint as president of the Baptist General Convention of Oklahoma (2002–2004), I served as its parliamentarian. The importance of governing documents is not a fact that others need to impress upon me, and before I arrived at the ILC I had read through all the governing documents of the IMB, including the bylaws, the "Blue Book" (trustee conduct manual), and the thick policy book that governs administrative actions of the largest missions-sending agency in the world.

The orientation for new trustees began early Monday morning and did not end until Thursday. Interspersed between orientation meetings was a regularly scheduled trustee meeting. New trustees were already assigned to committees, with my position being on the personnel committee of the IMB, chaired by former IMB missionary and soon to be trustee chairman, John Floyd. When I attended my first personnel committee meeting early

Tuesday morning, July 12, 2005, I met John Floyd for the first time. It was to be a memorable meeting.

John had been an employee of the International Mission Board for many years, having eventually been promoted to regional leadership by the time Jerry Rankin was hired as president of the IMB. Interestingly, both Rankin and Floyd were equals in terms of positions on the IMB—until Rankin was promoted by trustees to the presidency. When structural changes were made at the IMB under Rankin, John Floyd resigned and took a position as vice president at Mid-America Theological Seminary in Memphis, Tennessee. John did not keep it to himself that he had problems with Jerry Rankin's theology, administrative style, and vision for the International Mission Board. Similar to other disgruntled former employees of the IMB, including Vice President David Button and communications specialist Louis Moore, Floyd was strategically placed on the IMB board of trustees by the Patterson coalition in an attempt to end Rankin's tenure as president.

At this first trustee meeting of my tenure as an IMB trustee, my ears were alert to the attempts to undermine Rankin. I had already turned down an invitation by Winston Curtis and a group of caucus trustees to meet with them at a restaurant offsite in order to discuss IMB business. In fact, I informed them that their meeting was a violation of the "Blue Book" rules that set the boundaries for trustee conduct. This did not sit well with the caucus trustees, and I'm sure my refusal to meet with them played a part in launching the harsh treatment I would receive over the next few months. I told the caucus trustees that I would be willing to perform my fiduciary duty as a trustee and, if there were problems with Rankin, I would not be afraid to confront him. However, my stomach was already being turned by the gossip, innuendo, and in some cases outright slander by caucus trustees as they spoke of Rankin to me.

The personnel committee of the IMB approves every single appointment of Southern Baptist missionaries to the mission field. In 2005, the committee broke up into three subgroups, called subgroups A, B, and C, and every missionary candidate applying for appointment with the IMB appeared before one of those subgroups for interviews, questions, and ultimately approval. Then, the personnel committee subgroups brought their separate missionary appointment recommendations into one unified recommendation that was voted on by the entire board. Once the IMB trustees gave their consent to a missionary being appointed, that missionary would then be set aside at a special "Missionary Appointment Service" that would be held in a local Southern Baptist church on either Tuesday or Wednesday night of the IMB trustee meeting.

At this first personnel committee meeting I attended, we interviewed a delightful young man whom we unanimously voted to appoint. After the vote, committee chairman John Floyd said, "Well, it's a good thing this man came to us at this meeting, because had he come before us at our next meeting in September we would have had to reject him because of the new doctrinal policies." I then innocently asked the one question that lit the fuse that ultimately became a full-fledged blowup at the IMB.

"Mr. Chairman, what new doctrinal policies?"

I was given a brief synopsis of the two new policies that the personnel committee had adopted and would enforce at the September 2005 board meeting. The two new doctrinal policies were as follows:

1. A missionary candidate's baptism must take place in a church that practices believer's baptism by immersion alone, does not view baptism as sacramental or regenerative, and in a church that embraces the doctrine of the security of the believer. A candidate who has not been baptized in a Southern Baptist church or in a church which meets the standards listed above is expected to request baptism in his/her Southern Baptist church as a testimony of identification with the system of belief held by Southern Baptist churches.
2. In terms of general practice, the majority of Southern Baptists do not accept what is referred to as "private prayer language." Therefore, if "private prayer language" is an ongoing part of his or her conviction and practice, the candidate has eliminated himself or herself from being a representative of the IMB of the SBC.

I was absolutely shocked when the two new policies were explained to me. Seriously, you could have knocked me over with a feather. I tried to gather my thoughts during the rest of the personnel committee meeting as we continued to interview missionary candidates, but my mind was racing. Several thoughts immediately came to mind.

First, besides the fact that the policies were horribly written, I was stunned that the IMB was taking the heirachial position of telling *individual Southern Baptist churches that the baptism of their members was not legitimate.* That turned every Southern Baptist principle of the autonomy of the local church on its ear. In essence, if a man or woman joined my church, and we examined their individual faith and baptism and concluded each had been scripturally baptized (by immersion, after having come to faith in Christ), the IMB was taking a Landmark position that the baptism was legitimate only if the *baptizer* had legitimate Baptist credentials, and was rejecting that missionary candidate because of his "improper" baptism. Thus, even if our church accepted the prospective member's baptism as biblical, if that member were to eventually apply to be a missionary with the IMB, he or she would have to be "rebaptized"—according to this new doctrinal policy. To me, that was absurd. It was Campbellite (Church of Christ—"our baptism is the only legitimate baptism"), Landmark ("our church is the only legitimate church"), and totally anti-scriptural. When I later privately questioned John Floyd about this new Landmark doctrinal policy, he responded, "I'm a Landmarker and proud of it."

Second, the private prayer language prohibition seemed to me to be a direct strike against Dr. Jerry Rankin. I knew that when Jerry had been hired in 1993, it had been publicly revealed that he was not a cessationist, and had personally experienced the gift of tongues. However, the presidential search committee made it clear he was not a Pentecostal, but was simply a Southern Baptist with a continuation view of the gifts—and his speaking in tongues would be in private and never be public. Thus, this new doctrinal policy prohibiting missionaries from possessing a "private prayer language," in effect, would disqualify the president of the IMB from serving as a missionary in the very organization over which he presumably presided. When it was later explained to me that this policy was an attempt to address "charismatic problems" on the field, I repeatedly requested that I be given anecdotal evidence that proved there was a problem. As a trustee, I needed to know about the problems. I was never given one piece of paper, one verbal anecdote, one scrap of evidence that there was a "charismatic" problem on the Southern Baptist mission field that was not properly handled by the policies and processes already in place. Nobody could substantiate why this new policy was needed. Eventually John Floyd admitted to me that there was no evidence of a charismatic problem among Southern Baptist missionaries, and these new policies were "doctrinal" in nature—the board didn't need evidence of a problem, and the policies were put in place to ensure doctrinal purity at the IMB.

Third, I was deeply bothered by new doctrinal policies on two different fronts. I felt that if these policies were kept in place, the fabric of cooperation among Southern Baptist churches would be ripped from top to bottom. The idea that a board would establish doctrinal policies that exceeded the 2000 *BFM*, and then disqualify otherwise qualified Southern Baptist missionaries from serving because they disagreed with those policies, was a jolt to my Baptist soul. In addition, I was offended that trustee leadership, many of whom were personally involved in manipulating the process to get like-minded trustees on the board, including me (or at least so they thought), were now using a backdoor policy to either embarrass or remove Jerry Rankin from his leadership position at the IMB.

All these thoughts led me to ask a series of questions of John Floyd after we interviewed our last missionary candidate that Tuesday. Other trustees on the personnel committee, subgroup A, and several candidate consultants (IMB employees) were in the meeting and listening as I asked the questions.

"Dr. Floyd," I began, "are you aware that the bylaws of the IMB do not allow the personnel committee to establish policy—and that the full board must approve them? Has the full board voted on these doctrinal policies?" John responded that I was incorrect in my understanding of the bylaws, and that the full board had not voted on the policies and did not need to. John would eventually be proven wrong on this point by the IMB attorney, Matt Bristol, and the full board would vote on the new doctrinal policies four months later.

I continued, "Dr. Floyd, how does IMB administration feel about these new policies?" John informed me that trustees had the responsibility to establish policy and it was unnecessary to find out the feelings of administration. I then asked, "Dr. Floyd, would *you* give me the rationale for why these policies are needed?" It was at this point, after my third question in a row, that Dr. Floyd showed his agitation. He informed me that the personnel committee had been working on this new policy since 2003 (a fact that caused me to make a mental note of that year), and that as a "new" trustee I should be quiet and let those who understood the process lead. I am able to recognize a putdown when I hear one, and chose to not ask the additional questions I had written on the paper in front of me. The questions included these: "Is not the Baptist Faith & Message the only consensus doctrinal statement approved by the full convenetion, and is it wise to exclude Southern Baptists from cooperative missionary service based upon disagreement with doctrinal policies that exceed the 2000 *BFM*? Dr. Floyd, I've read the policy manual twice, and the previous missionary candidates' policies on baptism and tongues were excellent: who wrote the new policies and what led those authors to believe the old policies were inadequate? Dr. Floyd, will the passing of these new policies embarrass our president?"

After the meeting I was stopped by at least five employees of the IMB who listened to the dialogue between John Floyd and myself, with some pulling me aside in separate rooms, encouraging me to keep asking questions. I was told that there was a climate of fear at the IMB, and that no IMB staff member could question trustee leadership without fearing their job would be in jeopardy. Those staff members reminded me that I was appointed by the Southern Baptist Convention and I should not stop asking questions until I received answers, no matter how difficult trustee leadership would make it for me.

They need not have been concerned that I would cease asking questions. The issue was important to me personally because I believed the cooperative nature of Southern Baptist missions and the future health of our convention depended upon these questions being asked. The International Mission Board unifies the 45,000 churches of the Southern Baptist Convention by facilitating a cooperative mission effort among all Southern Baptist churches. The IMB thrives when churches feel that the missionaries they (the churches) send to the mission field are given help and support by the IMB. Churches need to know the board acts as servants to the churches—not bishops over the churches.

IMB trustees are constantly reminded by IMB administration that the highest authority on the board is the local church, but it seemed to me that among trustees, that counsel was falling on deaf ears. My initial experiences as a trustee led me to believe that trustee leadership had a sense that they possessed higher authority than even the local church, since John Floyd was suggesting that the trustee board knew better as to what qualified as a scriptural baptism than the local church or even the 2000 *BFM*.

I guess word spread among trustee leadership at that first meeting in July 2005 that the new trustee from Oklahoma they were counting on to help them was asking some embarrassing questions. Some have alleged that I came on the board to "protect" Dr. Rankin, but there could be nothing further from the truth. The issue to me was never about Dr. Rankin—it was about being true to the cooperative nature of our convention and refusing to narrow the doctrinal parameters of cooperation within our Southern Baptist missions ministry.

A few weeks before I went to that first trustee meeting, a former IMB missionary from Central Asia, a man I will call "Steve" for the sake of his own security (he is still in that country preaching the gospel with another organization), traveled to Enid, Oklahoma, to visit with me about some embezzlement that had occurred among a couple of IMB administrative missionaries in his region. The embezzlement was huge (several hundred thousand dollars), and "Steve" did not believe IMB administration in Richmond had investigated enough, disciplined enough, and implemented enough controls to prevent a future fraud of similar magnitude. This particular "embezzlement" has been the subject of at least two Southern Baptist Convention motions,[1] and it caused me to spend three hours in intense meetings with administration and trustees trying to get to the bottom of the situation. In the end, I believe the IMB administration in Richmond did all they could possibly do to correct the situation, and if there is any fault with administration, it is in the false belief that if something bad happens in an agency of the SBC, it should be kept quiet. I believe the SBC has a right to know about everything that goes on in our agencies—both the good and the bad. My point, however, in relating this particular anecdote, is to show that I did not come onto the board to protect Rankin. I came to do my job as a trustee for the SBC.

And it was about to get harder.

Note

1. 2006 SBC meeting in Greensboro; 2007 SBC meeting in San Antonio.

Chapter 5

THE CHAIRMAN'S OUTBURST AT PENSACOLA BEACH

There are a couple of reasons that lead people to believe serving as a trustee for the International Mission Board is the plum assignment of all potential service for Southern Baptists. First, the frequency of meetings and the exotic locations chosen to host these meetings are sometimes the only trips small church pastors make in the course of the year. There are not too many assignments where SBC pastors have their travel, food, and lodging paid for as they traverse the United States. Second, the opportunities to travel for the IMB trustee are frequent. Including overseas trips, IMB trustees meet between six to eight times a year, all expenses paid. Other than the traditional July meeting in Richmond, the other trustee meetings are now held in various locations around the United States and, in some instances, overseas.

IMB Trustee Meeting
Pensacola Beach, Florida
September 2005

My second trustee meeting with the International Mission Board was in Pensacola, Florida, at a swanky hotel on Pensacola Beach. I had planned to fly to Florida, but on the way to Will Rogers Airport in Oklahoma City, my car hydroplaned off the road and I ended up in a ditch with a demolished front end. I missed my flight, rented a car in Oklahoma City, and drove all night in order to reach Pensacola Beach for the trustee forum on Monday afternoon. Without catching up on my sleep, I attended the afternoon forum.

Trustee forums are closed-door sessions where only trustees and select administrators of the IMB are allowed to attend, and they are usually held on Monday afternoon of every board meeting—the first time the full board gets together. There is something strange about Baptist trustees meeting behind closed doors before they do anything else. The manual of conduct for trustees specifically states that no trustee business can be conducted during these "forums," and they are simply designed to be an informal gathering of trustees to air different opinions about upcoming business. But I am totally, 100 percent against forums because they become a place where people say things they ought not say with impunity. Further, those in control of trustee boards can influence the direction of an entire board outside the watchful eye of the Southern Baptist Convention.

It was in one of these trustee forums in 2000 that IMB trustee Paul Pressler excoriated Jerry Rankin for his leadership with language and temper rarely seen in Baptist circles. The hostile display by Pressler caused the mild-mannered IMB trustee from Nevada, Johnny Nantz, to chastise Pressler publicly for his outburst. Nantz's display of courage in taking on the judge effectively ended any possibility of Pastor Nantz ever holding a leadership position within the board of trustees.[1] It was common for IMB trustee forums, from 2000 and beyond, to become loud referendums on the inadequacy of Rankin's leadership. Whether or not the animosity of trustee leadership toward Rankin had any merit is irrelevant to my point here. I advocate open doors because it causes all trustees to consider seriously the appropriateness of their words *before* they say them.

The IMB trustee forum in Pensacola Beach in September 2005 was an intense discussion over whether or not the personnel committee, the committee assigned to interview prospective missionaries from Southern Baptist churches, had the authority to establish doctrinal policies without full approval of the board. It had been my contention at the July meeting that the bylaws of the IMB did not give to the personnel committee, chaired by trustee John Floyd, the authority to establish board policy in terms of new doctrinal standards. The attorney for the IMB, Matt Bristol, eventually gave his legal opinion to the full board that the personnel committee, just as I had stated, did not have such authority. The fact that a rookie trustee had been right, and that the chairman of the board, Tom Hatley, and the chairman of the personnel committee, John Floyd, had been wrong, did not sit well with the rest of trustee leadership. Now the full board, not just the personnel committee, would have to debate the new doctrinal policies. Questions that would be asked would include these: "What precipitated and instigated the drafting of the new policies?" "What is the rationale for the new doctrinal policies?" "Why were the old policies deemed insufficient by trustee leadership?" "Does administration believe the new doctrinal policies are needed?"

When it was announced at that September 2005 IMB trustee meeting that a board vote on the proposed policies would take place at the November 2005 trustee meeting in Huntsville, Alabama, trustee leadership began to direct their anger toward me personally. In the Wednesday morning plenary session at the hotel in Pensacola Beach, Tom Hatley directed strong, stinging remarks my way. I had never had any personal or private conversations about the IMB with Tom prior to that Wednesday morning, but two things became obvious to me as I listened to him speak. First, John Floyd had communicated with Tom that I had derailed the personnel committee's plans to implement the new doctrinal standards on baptism and private prayer language, and, second, Tom Hatley did not like the fact that a "rookie" trustee had forced the board to vote on the doctrinal policies that, in his opinion, should have already been implemented by the board. He called me a "rookie" trustee and suggested that "rookies" should keep their mouths shut and learn from those who have been involved in "the system" for many years. He further added that it was impossible for new trustees to know what was best for the board. In essence, Hatley's diatribe against me was intended to put me in my place.

As Hatley railed against me publicly, I leaned over to Wendy Norvelle, vice president of the IMB, who was sitting next to me, and said, "Why is he doing this?" She responded that she did not know, but thought it wise if I said nothing publicly to Hatley. I took her advice and waited until after the meeting and went up to Hatley at the podium, shook his soft, fleshy hand, and said, "Tom, I just want you to know that I am not intimidated by your bullying tactics. I will continue to do my job as a trustee, regardless of your attempts to silence me." According to Dr. Rankin, who witnessed my conversation with Hatley, I walked away from the podium and Hatley muttered under his breath, "I am going to get that man off this board."

By my second meeting, I had become the target of trustees who were used to playing a game of hardball religion. Whereas I felt that some trustees wanted Rankin off the board, the larger problem to me was the trivial manner in which trustees played fast and loose with the *Baptist Faith & Message*. On the one hand, IMB trustee leadership wanted everyone fired who would not affirm the 2000 *BFM*, yet on the other hand, they wanted to write new doctrinal policies that far exceeded the 2000 *BFM* and disqualify any Southern Baptist from missionary service who wouldn't affirm their

Landmark and cessationist beliefs. A convergence of desires to rid the IMB of Rankin's leadership with the desire of doctrinally "purifying" the IMB led trustee leadership to push policies detrimental to our cooperative nature as the Southern Baptist Convention. I immediately sensed a line in the sand had to be drawn regarding these two policies.

The issue to me was not a private prayer language or the qualifications of the baptizer; the issue to me was the demand by trustee leadership that everyone agree with them in their interpretation of these tertiary doctrines. The new policies were never about condoning "tongues" and were never about preventing "infant" baptism. The new policies were about excluding people who privately prayed in tongues and people who were not baptized in a Baptist church. I had spoken maybe a couple of times to the personnel committee about my opposition to the new policies by the time the September meeting rolled around, and I can only assume it was my opposition to trustee leadership that caused me to enter the game of hardball religion.

During the September (and, later, November) opportunity to debate the proposed new policies, I shared with the board my convictions about them. I was not alone in my opposition to the policies, and several other trustees voiced their concerns, including Alan McHam of South Carolina, Rick Thompson of Oklahoma, John Click of Kansas, and a host of others. It would be appropriate at this point to articulate my opposition to the policies, similar to the manner in which I did before the board.

First, I objected to the baptism policy, which required a missionary candidate to be baptized in a "Baptist" church, because the policy was both Landmark and hierarchical in nature. Trustee chairman John Floyd once told me "Landmarkism is nothing with which we ought to be ashamed." Bill Sutton echoed, "I'm Landmarkist and proud of it." The Landmarkers left the SBC in the 1850s because they couldn't get the mission boards to agree with their ecclesiology; the cooperating Baptists stayed in the Southern Baptist Convention and the Landmarkers left. Landmarkism almost destroyed the Southern Baptist Convention in the 1850s, and it is rearing its ugly head at the dawn of the new millennium within our Convention.

Several years ago a man named Bob Ross took it upon himself to republish the messages of Charles Haddon Spurgeon by reprinting *The Metropolitan Tabernacle Series*, a multi-volume set of every message preached by Spurgeon during his pastoral ministry. Many Southern Baptist pastors, myself included, have this Metropolitan series in their libraries. In 2005, Bob

Ross sent me a letter explaining his background in Landmarkism, his eventual repudiation of this belief system, and where the writings of Charles Spurgeon helped him see the error of Landmarkism.

Dear Brother Burleson:

I surely hate to see that it is apparently rising again to some significance among Southern Baptists.

I spent the first several years of my Christian life in Landmarkism, after having been baptized at Parkview Baptist (SBC), Jackson, Tennessee, in 1953 by a godly and beloved Pastor (now deceased) who first introduced me to the writings of J. R. Graves.

I left the SBC over Neo-orthodoxy in the schools (particularly at Union University) in 1954, and spent the next eleven years of my life advocating Landmarkism among the "strong as a bear's breath" type of independent Baptists. In the Providence of God, I was enabled by His grace to study my way out of it and abandoned it in 1964.

Since I knew Landmarkism very well from the "inside" of independent Baptists and saw its divisive and sectarian character, I wrote a book, *Old Landmarkism and the Baptists*, briefly discussing the history and teachings of Graves and other Landmark Baptists, including myself. If you have not seen the book, I will be happy to send you a free copy. It is a 188-page paperback, fully documented.

Over the past 41 years, I have received many testimonies from readers—especially preachers—who have been helped by my various writings on the erroneous theories and practices of Landmarkism.

Here in Texas, as recently as this week I read the SBTC [Southern Baptists of Texas Convention] *Texan* magazine article by Jim Richards, which advocated some of the principles involved in Landmarkism (Feb. 6, 2006, page 5). I hate to see the SBTC leadership get on this dead-end trail which leads to the type of Landmark sectarianism which I have witnessed among independent Baptists, the American Baptist Association (Texarkana headquarters), and the Baptist Missionary Association (Little Rock headquarters).

I have tried my best to maintain fellowship with Christian brethren who hold to Landmarkism, but they usually have held me at arm's length and regard me as a heretic!

Bob L. Ross
Pilgrim Publications
Pasadena, Texas

Bob then sent to me an excerpt from the foreword of his excellent work on the subject. Someone has suggested that the best way to understand the future is to learn history, and Ross does an admirable job of warning modern Baptists of the errors of Landmarkism—a warning IMB trustees intentionally ignore.

While the tenets of Landmarkism may be strange to many readers, I believe understanding it is key to comprehending what has taken place in the SBC over the past two decades. Many of our SBC's influential trustee and administrative leaders (e.g., Paige Patterson, John Floyd, Keith Eitel, Bill Sutton, Malcolm Yarnell) over the past few years have had strong Landmark tendencies. Bob Ross gives an excellent overview:

> According to Landmarkers, there is no authority in either the Word or from the Spirit for doing the work of the Great Commission; this authority comes solely from the local Baptist church. . . . It is asserted that a church is unscriptural, baptism is invalid, and ministers are not duly ordained unless there is proper Church Authority for them. This is Landmarkism's "chief cornerstone."
>
> Some writers of the past referred to this position as "high churchism." Consequently, the Landmark view is that Baptist Churches ALONE have the authority of Christ to evangelize, baptize and carry out all aspects of the commission. . . . Generally therefore, they believe that (1) the true and scriptural organization of a church, (2) the valid administration of baptism, and (3) the proper ordination of a gospel minister, all MUST all be enacted upon the authority of a sound and true, scriptural church, namely, a church that was born through the authority of a "mother" church continuing in like manner back to the original apostolic church of Matthew 28 where "church authority" first "began."
>
> In refuting these errors, Baptists and other Christians today can believe in the continuity of Christianity since Christ and may devote themselves to regulating their faith and practice by the Scriptures (in an orderly manner) without adhering to the Landmark teachings of church authority and succession. The authority which validates baptism, or any other scriptural action of our time, does not reside in the church institution any more than does the authority which validates salvation itself; authority resides in Jesus Christ and is expressed in His Word. The church itself is dependent upon this authority, but this authority is not dependent upon the church. . . .
>
> —Bob L. Ross[2]

It's important to understand that Paige Patterson serves on the board of a large Landmark college in Texas. The Southern Baptist Convention of Texas makes donations to Landmark colleges. Kentucky, Arkansas, and Texas are filled with Landmark Baptists who have made their way back into the Southern Baptist Convention, many of whom are now serving as trustees at the IMB, Southwestern and Southern seminaries, and other SBC agencies.

I can cooperate with a Landmark believer any day of the year in the area of missions, but the essence of Landmarkism is to separate from everyone who does not view the administrator of baptism with the same level of importance as Landmarks do. Through the new Baptist identity movement within our convention, we are in danger of being overrun again by Landmarkism and facing another fracture within the SBC unless we remind people of the need for cooperation in the midst of disagreement over ecclesiology and the ordinances.

Charles Spurgeon himself wrote on the subject of Baptist popery and the belief that the only valid baptism is that performed at the hand of a Baptist minister or in connection with a Baptist church:

Fragments of Popery among Nonconformists

It is very natural that our friends should desire their minister to baptize them, and yet there is no reason why he should do so on account of his office. It does not appear from the Scriptures to have been an act peculiar to preachers; in fact, at least one of them, and he by no means the least, was not sent to baptize, but to preach the gospel. A vigorous Christian member of the church is far more in his place in the baptismal waters than his ailing, consumptive, or rheumatic pastor. Any objection urged against this assertion is another unconscious leaning to tradition, if not a relic of superstition.

The usefulness of the ordinance does not depend upon the baptizer, but upon the gracious meditation and earnest prayer of the person baptized: the good which he will receive will depend upon how far his whole soul is receptive of the divine influence, and in no sense, manner, or degree upon the agent of the baptism.

We do not know what Paedobaptists think upon their ceremony, but we fear that the most of them must have the minister to do it, and would hardly like their infants to be left to the operation of an unordained man. If it be so, we do not so very much wonder at their belief, for as it is clear that no good arises to an infant from its own prayers or meditations during the ceremony, there is a natural tendency to look for some official importance in the performer of the rite; but yet we do not and cannot believe that our Paedobaptist friends have fallen so low as that; we make no charge, and hope we shall never have cause to do so.

For Baptists to attach the smallest importance to the ordinance of baptism being administered either by a minister or a private member would be to the last degree inconsistent, and yet we are not sure that the inconsistency is not to be found in many quarters. It behooves ministers to break down in time every tendency to make us into necessary adjuncts of the ordinances, for this is one step towards making us priests.[3]

Regarding the second policy, I have never spoken in tongues and I have no desire for a private prayer language. I fully affirmed the previous policy of the IMB that forbade any missionary from publicly speaking in tongues. We are paying our missionaries to share the gospel intelligently with those to whom they minister. Yet, if a missionary prays in tongues in private, and does not do so in public, then the prohibition of the Apostle Paul, "Forbid not the speaking in tongues" (1 Cor 14:39), seems to be an inspired, biblical command from the sacred, infallible text that we ought not lightly dismiss. Further, the 2000 *BFM* is silent on this issue.

It was also during this September meeting that a trustee named Randy Davis from Tennessee asked me to speak with him in the lobby of our hotel. He expressed his appreciation for the position of cooperation I had articulated to the board as I stated my opposition to the proposed policies, and informed me that the narrowing of the doctrinal parameters for missionary participation had been orchestrated by Paige Patterson. Randy was not the first person to tell me about Dr. Patterson's attempt to control the direction of the International Mission Board. During this September meeting, I repeatedly had asked that trustee leadership provide me with examples of charismatic abuses on the field. They could not, because there were none. I could only suspect, as stated previously, that the desire for "doctrinal" purity at the IMB was being led by Landmark, fundamental, separatist, cessationist Baptist trustees, influenced by their mentor Paige Patterson. These trustees demanded that everyone else believe as they did, arguing that they possessed true "Baptist identity."

What was absolutely mind-boggling to me is that trustee leadership sought to stifle anyone who sought articulately to oppose the new doctrinal policies, including President Jerry Rankin. In the end, though, the bylaws of the International Mission Board had to be followed, and a vote on these doctrinal policies would have to be taken by the full board, not just the personnel committee. That vote was scheduled for a trustee meeting scheduled for November 15, 2005, in Huntsville, Alabama. Debate on the policies was to occur in the trustee forum, trustee luncheon, and other committee meetings prior to the vote in plenary (public) session. Of course, all the opportunities to debate the policies as trustees were behind closed doors. Then we were supposed to act unified before the public eye. The debate should have happened in public, because then Southern Baptists would have seen that there was, in reality, no debate at all. One side was totally shut out even from speaking, and of course, that side was the one in opposition to trustee leadership.

Notes

1. Pam Blume, e-mail to author, 9 February 2006.

2. Bob L. Ross, *Old Landmarkism and the Baptists* (Pasadena TX: Pilgrim Publications 1979). For a longer excerpt, see the Appendix.

3. C. H. Spurgeon, *The Sword and Trowel* (Pasadena TX: Pilgrim, 1974), 267, 268.

Chapter 6

THE DAY ADRIAN ROGERS DIED

IMB Trustee Meeting
Huntsville, Alabama
November 2005

November 15, 2005, is a day that will go down in Southern Baptist Convention infamy. It is the day trustees of the International Mission Board adopted two new doctrinal policies that exceeded the SBC's 2000 *Baptist Faith & Message*. Sadly, it also happens to be the day legendary SBC pastor Adrian Rogers died. Adrian's own son, IMB missionary son David Rogers (Spain), eventually spoke out against these new policies. Adrian's childhood friend and wife of five decades, Joyce, joined her son and criticized the "narrowing of doctrinal parameters of missionary cooperation" at the 2006 Southern Baptist Convention. It is ironic to me that on the day the pastor who is attributed with bringing about the conservative resurgence died, the resurgence itself died to the ideals for which it began. Southern Baptists were told that the conservative resurgence was a battle for the Bible, but on November 15, 2005, trustees of the IMB, many of whom were strong proponents and participants in the resurgence, passed two doctrinal policies that exceeded both the Bible and the 2000 *BFM*. They then ruled that nobody could participate in Southern Baptist missions ministry unless they agreed with the new doctrinal policies.

In the debate leading up to the vote on whether or not to adopt the new policies, several trustees opposed to them, including Rick Thompson, Alan McWhite, John Click, Thurman Marshall, myself, and others, tried to ask questions during the closed-door meetings, including the forum, trustee working luncheons, and personnel committee meetings. Specifically, in one personnel committee meeting where I was serving as a member, the IMB candidate consultants were forbidden to speak. The consultants are men paid by the IMB to interview, coach, and ultimately recommend prospective

Southern Baptist missionaries for approval by IMB trustees. I had asked personnel committee chairman John Floyd to allow the candidate consultants to tell trustees on the committee what they thought about the policies. Chairman Floyd refused to let them speak. In addition, top-paid management for the IMB, men who serve as regional leaders, were not allowed to speak publicly to the trustees about their feelings regarding the policies. One such leader, Rodney Hammer, later resigned over the mistreatment he received at the hands of trustee leadership as he sought to voice his opposition to the policies. All of the regional leaders were opposed to the policies, but they too were forbidden to speak to trustees by personnel committee chairman John Floyd and board chairman Tom Hatley.

But the coup de grâce was what happened to IMB president Jerry Rankin as he sought to express his opposition to the new doctrinal policies. In April 2005, just two months before the Southern Baptist Convention elected me to serve as a trustee of the IMB, Dr. Rankin wrote a letter to chairman Tom Hatley and personnel committee chairman John Floyd expressing his respectful but heartfelt opposition to the proposed new doctrinal policies that the personnel committee sought to implement. Rankin verbally requested that his letter, as well as a compromise proposal from his administration, be forwarded to every trustee. This request was denied. Rankin's letter is a clear refutation of the logic behind the new doctrinal policies. The ability of Tom Hatley and John Floyd to stifle the distribution of this letter illustrates the problem of how just a few strategically placed leaders in the SBC can control the direction of the entire missions ministry of our Convention.

April 28, 2005

Dear Tom and John:

I appreciate your leadership and efforts to deal with the very controversial and potentially divisive issues of baptism and private prayer language. The process review committee has been working on proposed guidelines for two years; the difficulty in coming to a consensus recommendation should indicate the need for caution and whether or not there are compelling reasons for installing these guidelines.

As I have discussed with you, there is concern on the part of staff about the process as well as the proposed guidelines themselves. I'm sure you share our conviction that every effort should be made to consider every viewpoint objectively and also take into consideration the implications of imposing these guidelines.

I have discussed my perspective on these issues with the two of you personally and attempted to communicate this appropriately in discussions within the process review committee and the full personnel committee. It is my understanding, John, that you are planning to bring both these proposals before the personnel committee in May. And Tom, you have indicated that you might allow these issues to be introduced and discussed in the forum. I would hope that you would let us know what to expect, but also that you would use your leadership to keep something from being adopted that would be detrimental to the unity and focus the board has had this year as well as creating difficulties for the staff to implement.

I am attaching a draft of my assessment of the two proposals. I would like assurance that this perspective will be given appropriate consideration or advise me as to how my position and these concerns should be communicated constructively.

Tom, you may not be aware of a scenario that occurred last week in one of the personnel committee meetings which is likely to become commonplace if the proposed baptism guideline is adopted.

In the meeting on April 19 in Richmond, it was reported that one of the candidates, a member of a large, conservative Southern Baptist church, had been baptized in a Free Will Baptist Church. It was reported that these churches generally do not believe in the security of the believer, which is inconsistent with Southern Baptist faith and practice. Someone on the committee also perceived that these churches practice baptismal regeneration (which is contrary to my understanding, and subsequent research has failed to affirm this perception). It was not confirmed that this was true in the committee, or if that particular church believed this as perceived—and it would have taken an undue effort on the part of the candidate consultant to determine this. The candidate himself affirmed he did not believe in baptismal regeneration and did not understand his baptism in that regard, nevertheless approval of appointment was denied until he was rebaptized.

The church of which this candidate is a member is Second Baptist of Springfield, Missouri, one of the most passionate supporters of the IMB, functioning as a hub church in Middle America and sending scores of volunteers and missionaries to the field. The pastor, John Marshall, affirmed they had examined thoroughly this person's baptism and considered it valid. Many churches and pastors would be offended and angry at such a legalistic judgment on their authority to administer the ordinances by an outside entity.

However, John indicated he would be willing to take the candidate up to the church and baptize him if that were necessary for him to be appointed by the IMB, but all it would be is a "dunking"—meaning nothing to the individual or to the church because he had already been baptized. Is this kind of Pharisaical legalism necessary to maintain doctrinal integrity? Is this the reputation we want to reflect, and does it enhance our ability to relate to churches in a way that will enhance mobilization, serving churches to fulfill our ministry assignments?

I appreciate so much the way you, John, and Bill Curp and the personnel committee responded to handle and resolve this sensitively and appropriately by reversing the decision, and I am confident we are all committed to doing what is right. However, this experience has left our consultants even more confused. Are they to require a candidate to be rebaptized if they were baptized in a non-Southern Baptist church that does not adhere to our faith and practice, except when it is a large church with a prominent pastor, or if the pastor affirms the baptism as being valid? I have suggested alternative guidelines which I feel to be appropriate and satisfactory to deal with the issues in question in the attached drafts.

I hope to discuss this with you prior to our board meeting and look forward to your advice. I trust we can work together to come out with a win-win solution for the diverse elements on the board, but especially for the kingdom of God.

Sincerely yours,
Jerry Rankin

The other trustees and I did not find out about the president's letter until the November trustee meeting, six months after it had been written, and it took a motion from this "rookie" trustee (as Dr. Tom Hatley called me publicly), to get the letter before the board prior to the vote on the proposed doctrinal policies. My recommendation for the trustees to see the letter, a recommendation opposed by trustee leadership, barely passed during a lunch meeting of the full board, and when it did, we were told that we would be given the letter several hours later, after trustee leadership had an opportunity to prepare it for distribution. We did get the letter several hours later, with handwritten notes from Dr. John Floyd scribbled all over it.[1]

The notes Dr. Floyd wrote speak for themselves, illustrating what I have said has been taking place for the past few years in the IMB and the Southern Baptist Convention as a whole. Ideological, like-minded Southern Baptists are attempting to marginalize, and in some instances remove, those who disagree. To call the arguments and conclusions of the president of the IMB "ridiculous," "unscriptural," "illogical," and the like is unconscionable conduct, particularly considering the timing of the release of the letter (right before a vote by the board on the policies).

What is the difference between a blog that sways SBC opinion after the adoption of a policy, and Dr. Floyd who used his position to keep from the board of trustees valuable information in a letter from the president, only to release it when forced to do so, and then with handwritten criticisms covering the letter? The old way of keeping control by limiting the flow of information, stifling dissent, and ridiculing those who disagree is over. The Southern Baptist Convention needs and demands transparency, the free flow of information, the ability to dissent, and cooperation in the midst of differences on tertiary issues.

Our convention of cooperating churches is harmed over demands for a uniform, homogenous Baptist identity that some seek. In addition, agencies are harmed when there is never any true debate allowed among the trustees. To act as if God is only on one side of an issue, and assert that it is "our side," is the height of spiritual arrogance. Unhindered and transparent debate keeps all Southern Baptists humble and honest. Southern Baptists must realize that the power of the gospel cannot be replaced by the power politics of a Baptist identity religion.

Finally, I believe Dr. Rankin's letter quoted above proves that the reason some don't like blogs is because they lose control of both the amount and kind of information they wish released. The IMB president desired his letter to be communicated widely. Southern Baptists operate *Christian* ministries, and Rankin's request for open communication is the mark of genuine, Christ-like leadership. The ability to debate issues among Southern Baptists with civility, cooperate with brothers and sisters holding to divergent views, and keep our focus on the gospel is essential. Hopefully, the IMB will cease pressing for narrower and narrower doctrinal parameters that shrink the participation pool of Southern Baptist churches.

John 12:42 said that of the many who believed in Christ, some "did not confess him, lest they should be put out of the synagogue." It is time Southern Baptists become more concerned about cooperative missions than we are about our fear of being branded or removed from denominational service by leaders who wish to define Baptist identity according to their own narrow beliefs. In time, the SBC will be better because the pastors and churches that support her Cooperative Program speak up and speak out for cooperation.

When the trustees of the International Mission Board voted during the plenary session on the proposed new doctrinal policies at this meeting, the vote count was in immediate dispute. Wendy Norvelle, the acting vice president in charge of media relations, reported that there were a number of no votes (which there were), but the number she reported infuriated trustee leadership. Though there was no roll call, no electronic vote tabulation, and no official vote tally, Chairman Hatley said he scribbled the vote total down on a piece of paper (he allegedly counted the raising of hands), and he felt that Wendy's report of the number of "no" votes was inaccurate. Regardless of the number of votes for (or against) the new doctrinal policies that limited Southern Baptist cooperation, policies that were not approved by the Southern Baptist Convention at large, on November 15, 2008, by the efforts of a small group of strategically placed trustees at the IMB, new doctrinal policies were instituted that would have prohibited Jerry Rankin, Bertha Smith, Yacouba Seydou, and a host of other incredibly gifted missionaries from ever serving for the International Mission Board.

It is appropriate to end this chapter on the adoption of the new IMB doctrinal policies with a letter from IMB missionary David Rogers to all the trustees of the International Mission Board. Remember, these doctrinal policies were adopted on the day David's father, Dr. Adrian Rogers, died. Were the following letter to have been written by a missionary other than David Rogers, that missionary would have been fired. The IMB has changed to the point that no dissent, no disagreement, no questioning of "authority" is tolerated by trustees. Eventually, more missionary leaders such as David Rogers will speak out, and the direction of our convention will be reversed. Until they do, allow David Rogers's letter to IMB trustees to encourage you with the knowledge that some people do understand what Southern Baptist cooperation is all about. David's letter was written in January 2006, three months after the adoption of the new policies and shortly after the recommendation for my removal was made public.

> Dear IMB Trustee,
>
> After much prayer and thought, I have decided to write and express my concerns to each of you regarding the developments at the IMB which have been in the news recently. . . .
>
> I must say now that I am concerned with what seems to me to be a general direction on the part of the Board of Trustees, much of which I have only recently been made aware. It would seem to me that much of the ground gained for the glory of God and the advance of His kingdom through the "conservative resurgence" in the SBC, in which my father played such an integral role, is in danger of being commandeered in a new, more extreme direction. . . .

Specifically, I do not think the recent policy change approved in the November Trustee meeting disqualifying missionary candidates who acknowledge having a "private prayer language" or those who were baptized by immersion as believers outside of a church deemed to be doctrinally compatible with Southern Baptists is a move in the right direction.

I myself do not practice a "private prayer language." However, in the course of my Christian ministry, I have known many fellow servants of Christ who have professed to have had this experience and for whom I have the utmost respect, due to their evident love for Christ, His Word, and His work, as well as sterling Christian character. Of course, there are a few exceptions to this, as there are as well with otherwise perfectly orthodox believers, who do not practice a "private prayer language." At the same time, while I recognize that sincere, godly interpreters of the Word of God take the view that certain supernatural gifts ceased at some time in the past, it seems to me that other equally sincere, godly, and objective interpreters of the Word of God have come to different conclusions.

I personally do not see how putting this new limitation upon Southern Baptist missionary service is going to make a positive difference in our faithfulness to Christ or in our effectiveness in carrying out His Great Commission. It does concern me, though, that some otherwise perfectly qualified candidates for missionary service might be disqualified because of this, especially in light of the previously existing policies limiting public expression of *glossolalia* and the "persistent emphasis of any specific gift of the Spirit as normative for all or to the extent such emphasis becomes disruptive to the Baptist fellowship."

I also feel that the new policy stating that "baptism must take place in a church that practices believer's baptism by immersion alone, does not view baptism as sacramental or regenerative, and a church that embraces the doctrine of the security of the believer" and that "a candidate who has not been baptized in a Southern Baptist church or in a church which meets the standards listed above is expected to request baptism in his/her Southern Baptist church as a testimony of identification with the system of belief held by Southern Baptist churches" does not have scriptural justification and goes beyond what Southern Baptists have traditionally accepted. Others have already written eloquently, exposing the flaws in Landmarkist ecclesiology. I imagine most, if not all of you, are well familiar with the arguments on both sides of this issue.

I would like, however, to point out the biblical example of the baptism of the Ethiopian eunuch, which leaves the question of any local church "sponsorship" or "supervision" of the baptism very much up in the air. We also have the testimony of the roots of the Anabaptist movement, in which the initial "baptizers" had not yet been scripturally baptized themselves.

I am not saying that those who approved the new policy change on baptism are necessarily sympathetic on the whole towards Landmarkism. However, I do recognize the policy as reflective of at least one "plank" of Landmarkist argumentation, and a "plank" for which I believe there is no biblical basis. And, it concerns me that we, as a denomination, may be making steps in that direction.

Another related issue that is on the minds of all involved has to do with the proposed dismissal of Wade Burleson from the Board of Trustees. Since I was not present during Trustee meetings in order to personally observe Mr. Burleson's behavior in that setting, I must reserve judgment regarding that. At the same time, I have carefully read through Mr. Burleson's "blog," and reflected deeply both upon the ideas expressed therein, as well as the tone in which they are expressed. My opinion is that, while Mr. Burleson, just like any of the rest of us, is not perfect, and may here or there say things which might be able to be expressed in a more circumspect manner, what I have read there written by Mr. Burleson is a long way from amounting to, in and of itself, "slander," "gossip," "broken trust" or "resistance to accountability."

It would seem to me that if the Trustees are indeed accountable to the Southern Baptist Convention as a whole, and to the churches which comprise it, then Mr. Burleson acted in good faith making known to those who have the bottom line responsibility for decisions made something of the issues involved behind those decisions. Before the "conservative resurgence," it was frequently argued that many of the various boards and committees of the SBC were out of step with what the majority of Southern Baptists believed, and thus, it was necessary to make Southern Baptists aware of what was going on. In my concise but humble opinion: "what's good for the goose is good for the gander."

At this point, I must reiterate it is impossible for me to know exactly how my father would have addressed each of these points. Each of us is our own person. However, having grown up under the wings of this great man of God who has been so influential in Southern Baptist life, I can honestly say I think that he would be in general agreement with the gist of what I am saying here.

How each of you respond to this is between you and God, taking into consideration your accountability to the SBC as well. I pray God will give you the grace and wisdom to act in a way glorifying to His name and advantageous to the advance of His kingdom.

Your co-laborer in the Harvest, David Rogers[2]

Notes

1. Rankin's letter, with Floyd's handwritten notes, is posted online in my article, "Pulling Back the Curtain on SBC Politics," http://kerussocharis.blogspot.com/2008/04/pulling-back-curtain-on-sbc-power.html.

2. See the Appendix for the complete letter.

Chapter 7

DISCOVERY

Taking Action
November–December 2005

When the International Mission Board trustees passed the two new doctrinal policies on November 15, 2005, the next step in the natural progression of voicing dissent over this action was to make my opposition known to the Southern Baptist Convention as a whole. My objections to the policies had been voiced to trustee leadership repeatedly, consistently, and graciously. Public forums in which opposition was allowed were rare, and questions pertaining to the need for the doctrinal policies that exceed the 2000 *Baptist Faith & Message* were considered out of order by trustee leadership. On a couple of occasions, trustees Rick Thompson, Alan McWhite, and I were able to voice our opposition to the policies during public meetings, and the press picked up some of my comments, leading other Southern Baptists to contact me to express their opposition to the new policies.

However, once the majority of trustees voted to approve the new doctrinal policies, and I was shown officially to be on the minority side, the forum for dissent became the convention as a whole. Trustees have accountability to the entire convention. I knew on the evening of November 15, 2005, and told trustee leadership, that I would not be seeking a reversal of the policies at the next IMB meeting. I would be addressing the entire convention. This is where the rub comes. Many trustees are under the impression that dissent should become silent when a measure or policy is passed by a majority of trustees. "Majority rules!" they adamantly cry. I agree that the trustee on the losing side of a vote should acquiesce to the majority, except if the dissent is based upon a violation of conscience or Scripture. Then, as Luther would say, "My conscience is held captive by the Word of God. Here I stand. I cannot do otherwise. God help me."

The issue for me after our November meeting in Huntsville was clear. How do I let the SBC as a whole know about these new doctrinal policies that exceed the 2000 *BFM* and exclude otherwise qualified Southern Baptist missionaries from serving on the mission field? I decided that I needed to do two things: (1) First, I would get to the bottom of why trustee leadership violated IMB President Jerry Rankin's desires and brought these two new doctrinal policies before the board, and (2) I would find some way to inform Southern Baptists of what was happening at the IMB board, particularly since missionaries from our Southern Baptist churches were being disqualified.

To figure out why the trustee leadership brought the doctrinal policy changes before the board, I began writing e-mails and letters to various people between Thanksgiving and Christmas 2005. It was common knowledge among the trustees who had served on the board prior to 2005 that Paige Patterson, then the president of Southeastern Baptist Theological Seminary, and Patterson's professor of missions, Dr. Keith Eitel, had sought to influence the IMB trustees by casting doubt on the theological acumen and leadership skills of IMB president Jerry Rankin.

The Baptist grapevine is alive and well. In response to hearing that I was raising questions about the need for the new doctrinal policies that exceeded the *Baptist Faith & Message*, several former trustees and IMB employees sent me copies of a letter Paige Patterson had written to every IMB trustee in fall 2003, along with an eight-page critique of IMB operations written by Keith Eitel in that year. The critique was a blistering indictment of the International Mission Board, but particularly of President Jerry Rankin. Eitel accused the board of neo-orthodoxy, neo-charismaticism, and a host of other theological aberrations—particularly the establishing of baptistic churches on the mission field rather than Baptist churches. According to Eitel and Patterson, the only true church is a Baptist church, or more precisely, a Baptist church as defined by their narrow Landmark ecclesiology.

I was floored when I began receiving these papers from people to whom they had been sent a few months earlier. I couldn't imagine the president of one Southern Baptist Convention agency (Dr. Patterson) seeking to turn a board of trustees of another SBC agency (the IMB) against her president (Dr. Rankin). But this is precisely what Patterson was attempting to do in the years leading up to the adoption of the new doctrinal policies. It was Patterson who instructed his missions professor to send the critique, titled *Vision Assessment: The International Mission Board of the Southern Baptist*

Convention, to all the IMB trustees. The indictment of Dr. Rankin, without first going to Rankin with concerns, irritated Dr. Rankin, who in response sent a letter, dated October 30, 2005, to Dr. Keith Eitel and carbon copied all the IMB trustees and Paige Patterson. He opens the letter acknowledging that Eitel sent the critique to the IMB trustees at the request of Patterson and then writes,

> I cannot understand why we [the IMB administration] were not made aware of this analysis, why it was given such widespread circulation, and why no effort was made to confirm your premises and perceptions. We always welcome objective feedback and outside insights that help us see beyond our perspective within the organization, recognizing that periodic assessments and evaluations are essential to effectiveness. However, I fail to understand the rationale for disseminating your unfounded perceptions and these inaccurate implications without bringing them into an open forum of dialogue that should be representative of the partnership we have presumed to have with you and Dr. Patterson.[1]

The partnership Dr. Rankin mentions was the 2+2 mission partnership between the IMB and Southeastern Baptist Theological Seminary. SEBTS students who were interested in a career in missions entered this program and partnered with the IMB for training, special missions assignments, etc., all with an eye toward being a future career IMB missionary. One such Southeastern seminary student, Ben Cole, who later served on the staff at Emmanuel Baptist Church, Enid, Oklahoma, was asked by Paige Patterson and Keith Eitel to enter the 2+2 program at the IMB in order to "spy" on the IMB, particularly Dr. Rankin, by sitting in on training for the 2+2 program, recording the lectures, and culling out any "charismatic heresy" and turning it over to Eitel and Patterson. Ben later apologized to Dr. Rankin for partic- ipating in this plan to spy on the IMB and undermine Rankin's leadership, although the damage was being done not by young seminary students, but by Eitel and Patterson, who were encouraging these students to "keep a daily journal and log of events" of their training at the IMB.[2] The students were specifically instructed by Eitel to keep a log of "date, time, place, and person involved in teaching those things you know to be incorrect."[3] In the e-mail to the Southeastern students being trained by IMB administrators, Dr. Eitel listed three specific problem areas at the IMB:

(1). There seems to be a series on Church Planting Movements (CPM) in which a highly questionable ecclesiology is presented. The ordinances, in particular, may be an issue, i.e., the way they will be conducted or taught, and the role of ladies in places of house church leadership.

(2). Likely you will, in a session or two, be made to feel like a second rate candidate for having "wasted time" attending seminary. The fact that you've studied theology, reasoned through the great doctrines of the faith, and have a set of theological convictions, may be spoken ill of during your time there by some at the Missionary Learning Center.

(3). Apparently, even raising questions in various sessions has caused some to be interviewed by staff and reexamined as to whether or not they will be "divisive" on the field.[4]

Eitel sent a carbon copy of the above e-mail to Bill Sanderson, IMB trustee from North Carolina, who is close friends with both Patterson and Eitel. An attorney contacted me in fall 2005 and told me that he participated in meetings with Sanderson, Eitel, and Patterson in the back room of a restaurant in Wake Forest, North Carolina, called The Border, which was a popular hangout for faculty and students at Southeastern. A round table that seated eight to ten people was brought into the stock room where The Border kept paper goods, and the business of the Southern Baptist Convention would be discussed. At this restaurant, individuals discussed the theological "problems" in the SBC (i.e., everyone is not interpreting the Bible the way we do), stacking the IMB board with like-minded trustees, and eventually removing Dr. Rankin from his position as president of the IMB.[5]

Former Southeastern Seminary employee Ben Cole (the seminary student who had been asked to spy on the IMB and who was a disciple of Paige Patterson) later wrote about Eitel and Patterson's attempts to undermine Rankin's presidency at the International Mission Board in his June 8, 2006, blog entry titled "The FBI and the SBC":

> On July 3, 2003, an e-mail was sent out to all Southeastern Seminary students preparing for six weeks of intensive training at the IMB's Missionary Learning Center in Rockville, VA. In that e-mail, the director of Southeastern's mission program (Dr. Keith Eitel) requested that young missionary candidates collect information and record in detail what they saw and heard during their training and report back to him. In the e-mail, he disclosed that he was working with IMB Trustee Bill Sanderson of Wendell, NC, to prepare a dossier in order to address the "problems" at the

International Mission Board. Within a few months, Paige Patterson was circulating to all IMB trustees a "white paper" written by Eitel and which contained severe criticisms of the Rankin administration. During the time, I myself was involved in several conference calls with a caucus of trustees at the International Mission Board where plans were discussed to bring an end to Jerry Rankin's tenure. Among the participants in those calls were Diane Reeder of Louisiana, Albert Green of Texas, and Wyndham Cook of Texas, and others. Moreover, I was personally offered a job working at Southwestern Baptist Theological Seminary in February 2004 to listen to multiple hours of audio-recordings of Jerry Rankin, collected by the seminary president's office, and cull them for suspicious theology, potential instances of charismatic teaching, or questionable statements that could be interpreted as contrary to the *BFM*2000. Of course, I refused to accept the job or the payment of Cooperative Program dollars that came with it. Adding to the problems are the stacks of e-mails I have received, most of which are from Russell Kaemmerling of TX, that detail a strategy to block candidates for top IMB administrative posts and replace Rankin's choice with Patterson's stalking horses.[6]

I was discovering these attempts to force the removal of Dr. Jerry Rankin in fall 2005, and though it was becoming more and more obvious to me that the doctrinal policies were the fruition of months of effort by Dr. Paige Patterson, Keith Eitel, and several IMB trustee leaders with connections to Patterson to force Dr. Rankin to resign, I was not quite ready to make these attempts known.

I have never been concerned with defending Jerry Rankin personally. Though I appreciate his love for missions and his genuine concern for his missionary staff, I have sometimes been unimpressed with the manner in which Dr. Rankin will push hard *privately* for those things that will benefit the IMB or the SBC, only to display publicly, for the benefit of politics, a totally opposite view. For instance, it was Dr. Rankin who privately pushed me hard for the 2006 SBC motion that recommended an official investigation into the actions of the IMB board of trustees. Rankin told me privately at the 2006 convention that the trustee leadership must not be allowed to do their own investigation; he said I must push for an independent panel. Later, he publicly defended trustee leadership's ability to investigate themselves. Likewise, as I will explain in chapter 25, it was Dr. Rankin who privately pushed hard for the 2007 Garner Motion, only to vote against it at the Southern Baptist Convention. When I later asked him about the incongruity of his vote, he assured me it was not because he was seated beside IMB trustee leadership at the time of his vote.

There is a dark region in Central Asia, a place where missionaries and trustees have been praying for a gospel presence for the past three years. This dark place is dangerous for anyone who says the name of Christ. In 2005, just before the IMB trustees adopted the new doctrinal policies, a young Southern Baptist couple felt God's call to serve in this dangerous region of Central Asia. They would never be recognized for their service because of security reasons. Their lives would be in constant danger, and frankly, there would be no guarantee they would ever make it back to the States alive. They passed all the candidate interviews with flying colors, impressed the IMB staff and trustees, and brought a surge of excitement and anticipation to the Central Asia region as an answer to many prayers. When the new policies were passed by the trustees November 15, 2005, the candidate consultant approached the young couple and asked, "Do either one of you have a private prayer language?"

The wife, unbeknownst to her husband, had prayed privately in tongues for years. With full integrity she answered, "Yes." Her husband, though surprised to learn of his wife's *private* prayer life, was shocked that the candidate consultant was probing into private matters—at the demand of trustees.

The couple was rejected as missionaries. Many tears were shed. The candidate consultant was heartbroken. The Central Asia region was shocked. Why were they declined? The trustees, not the staff, declined them. I propose that a dark region in Central Asia is still dark because certain IMB trustees lost sight of the gospel and our mission, and went way beyond Scripture, the 2000 *BFM*, and our duties to keep an eye on world missions and evangelism.

That's the issue. The fact that IMB trustee leadership went beyond the 2000 *Baptist Faith & Message*, the only consensus Southern Baptist doctrinal statement, and disqualified an otherwise qualified (not to mention outstanding) missionary couple, makes me sad, just as the baptism policies make me sad.

Because the issues of narrowing the doctrinal parameters of missionary cooperation and seeking to remove Dr. Rankin as president of the IMB are interconnected, I wrote my first convention blog post on December 10, 2005, and dealt with them both. This post was titled "Crusading Conservatives vs. Cooperative Conservatives: The Battle for the Future of the Southern Baptist Convention," and in it I detailed, without names, the struggle going on in our convention to remove people from SBC leadership who do not agree with a narrow doctrinal viewpoint—one that goes beyond the 2000 *BFM*. (The full text of this post is printed in chapter 8 below.) I did not mention Dr. Patterson or anyone else by name, but two days later I received an e-mail from Dr. Patterson. In it he reminded me that "There are some powerfully precious folks" who serve as IMB trustees, and he expressed his hope that one day I might come to the place where I would be able to say, "I might have misread some folks."[7]

I responded to Dr. Patterson by e-mail and assured him I felt confident that I accurately stated the predicament our convention faces, but since I did not mention him by name (or even referenced anything about him) in my post, I wondered why he felt the need to e-mail me. I then took the opportunity to ask Dr. Patterson directly, "Are you seeking the termination, early retirement, or forced resignation of Dr. Jerry Rankin?"[8]

Patterson responded with these words: "Do I believe the IMB would be better with a retirement [of Dr. Rankin]? Yes, if we do not end up with tragedy, I do. But this is a belief that I will share with my friend Jerry only if he asks."[9] I laughed when I read his response because I am not sure that, after the reams of material I had read that was penned or sent by Paige Patterson to all the trustees with the purpose of castigating Rankin's administration, Jerry Rankin would call Paige a friend. When Patterson would later suggest to Rankin via e-mail that it was time for Rankin to step down as IMB president, any bluff about friendship was exposed.

What still baffles me as a Southern Baptist is how a man such as Paige Patterson can serve as president of one of our seminaries and feel it necessary to manipulate the trustees of another agency. I still cannot understand why the average Southern Baptist, not to mention pastors and leaders of the Southern Baptist Convention, are all remaining silent as they watch a small nucleus of Southern Baptists rotate from one trustee board to another—all placed there by an oligarchy of Southern Baptist leaders led by Paige Patterson.

Again, the main issue for me is the rip in the fabric of cooperation that is caused by passing doctrinal policies that exceed the 2000 *BFM*. But the tangential issue remains that certain leaders of the SBC, led by Paige Patterson, are allowed to manipulate processes so that trustees of an SBC board will narrow the doctrinal parameters of cooperation beyond the 2000 *BFM* and possibly remove from the presidency of the IMB a man who is not "one of them." I felt it was time to tell the Southern Baptist Convention what was going on. Unknowingly, I had stepped to the plate for the first pitch of hardball religion.

Notes

1. Jerry Rankin to Keith Eitel, 30 October 2003, author's personal files.

2. Keith Eitel, e-mail to Southeastern 2+2 students, 3 July 2003, copy in author's personal files, forwarded by Southwestern students.

3. Ibid.

4. Ibid.

5. Ben Cole, conversation with Wade Burleson, January 2006.

6. Baptist Blogger, "The FBI and the SBC," http://baptistblog.wordpress.com/2006/06/08/the-fbi-and-the-sbc/, 8 June 2006 (site now requires access via password).

7. Paige Patterson, e-mail to Wade Burleson, 13 December 2005.

8. Wade Burleson, e-mail to Paige Patterson, 13 December 2005.

9. Paige Patterson, e-mail to Wade Burleson, 13 December 2005.

Chapter 8

GRACE AND TRUTH

The Blog
December 2005

In December 2005, six months after I attended my first International Mission Board meeting and not quite one month after the adoption of the two new doctrinal policies that exceeded the 2000 *BFM* and excluded otherwise qualified Southern Baptists from serving on the mission field, I began a blog. As has been stated, the word "blog" is an abbreviation for the phrase *Web log*. A blog is simply a personal log of a person's thoughts or life, posted on the Web (or Internet). It can be used as a diary or journal. In my case, it became a tool through which others can be informed of what is happening in the Southern Baptist Convention. It is a form of communication readily accessible by anyone. The power of communicating via the Internet is not dissimilar to that experienced by people in the 1500s when the printing press made communication possible to the masses. The difference between the Internet and the printing press is that Internet postings can be read instantly by people halfway around the world, whereas in the 1500s it took much time (sometimes months) to print, distribute, and read what others had written. I knew nothing about beginning a blog, but knew it would be the perfect tool to use in order to inform Southern Baptists of what was taking place at the International Mission Board and the effect that adopting the new doctrinal policies would have on the entire SBC. I titled my blog *Grace and Truth to You* and began posting some of my writings on December 6, 2005. My first few posts were thoughts on God's providence and other doctrinal matters, but it was my post of December 10, 2005, that allegedly made trustee leadership at the IMB so upset.

What is interesting about that particular post is that it resulted from a lengthy phone conversation I had with Morris Chapman on December 9 about the new doctrinal policies. Morris Chapman is the executive director of the executive committee of the Southern Baptist Convention in Nashville, the highest-ranking executive in the SBC. Dr. Chapman is an astute man, and he had been warning our convention for years that we had best stop fighting one another and learn how to cooperate in spite of our differences as conservatives. In his 2004 executive director's address to the SBC, an address titled "The Fundamentals of Cooperating Conservatives," Dr. Chapman exhorted the Southern Baptist Convention with these prescient words (emphasis mine):

> There's a road wrongly taken by many on our left, the road of liberalism. But there is also a road wrongly taken by many others on our right side. It may not be as treacherous as the road of liberalism, but it is just as disabling to the Convention.
>
> What is this road? It is the road of separatism—an ecclesiastical methodology that devalues cooperation in favor of hyper independence. In the past, we have avoided this road as fervently as the road on the left. If Southern Baptists steer too sharply toward the right, we will end up on the road of separatism.
>
> Southern Baptists have never embraced the methodologies of separatism. We can be both conservative and cooperative. It is our distinctive heritage. It is the genius of our success. It is our spiritual destiny.
>
> We must never cease to be vigilant against heresy. This is always the task of faithful Christians. However, crusades cannot last forever. Again and again we have debated vigorously that the conservative resurgence was theological, not political; that our objective was doctrinal purity, not political control.
>
> If this is true, the crusade phase of the conservative resurgence has passed. The stated goals have been achieved. The battle has been won. Now there are other tasks at hand. We cannot linger at the base camp of biblical authority. We are a people who not only believe the Book; we are compelled to live by the Book. Biblical concepts such as surrender, sacrifice, righteousness, and holiness must consume our hearts and minds. We must plant churches on almost every corner of every block in this nation. And we must take the gospel to the ends of the earth. This is our biblical mandate. This is our commission . . . .
>
> While each SBC president has conscientiously sought out Southern Baptists who had never served as a trustee of an SBC entity or on a committee of the Convention, we have never executed to the fullest extent that

promise to "enlarge the tents, lengthen the cords, and strengthen the stakes." Why is it important to this day? It is because the Convention is a convention of churches and their members. There is no hierarchy. You who attend the Convention as messengers are the authoritative and final word in Convention business. That is our theology. That is our ecclesiology. That is our polity. Therefore . . . it is to be our practice. There are thousands of our people, young and old, who, as we do, need to be enlisted and encouraged to see that this old ship Zion is still an effective witness for our Lord. She's still afloat. She's still seaworthy. She may be in need of a tune-up. She may be in need of paint and polish. But she's still strong, and sails the seas with grace. Cooperating conservatives believe our Convention is at its best only when rank and file Southern Baptists are pulling together and on the move. And we need every possible person who loves our Lord Jesus Christ and believes He died for the church to hear and heed the call of God to go to the ends of the earth, empowered by His Holy Spirit.

It is imperative that our Convention return to some sense of normalcy in the operation of the Convention. May I suggest one way to begin the process? Southern Baptists now agree that our trustees should be inerrantists. We believe they should embrace the *Baptist Faith & Message* (there is only one, you know . . . the last one). Most believe that trustees and their churches should be faithful in giving a significant amount through the Cooperative Program. We believe our trustees should have a heart for lost souls and be affiliated with churches that evangelize at home, and support missions around the globe. And finally, but most importantly, our trustees should be people who have a close daily walk with our Lord Jesus Christ.

Anyone with these characteristics of devotion to the Lord, His church, and our Convention qualifies to serve Southern Baptists in these positions. *We should elect trustees who attend trustee meetings with the freedom of conscience to pray about decisions facing that board, and vote accordingly. We cannot let this Convention be driven by politics.* It must be driven by passion for our Lord Jesus Christ and for the unsaved and compassion for those who are persecuted for Christ's sake around the world. In a practiced democracy, politics, the art of influence, is always an ingredient. But the passion of a trustee should be born from deep within in an encounter with the Living Christ, and then he is free to enthusiastically persuade others of the burden God has laid upon his heart. This is how it should be in the church, the association, the state convention, and the Southern Baptist Convention. This Convention deserves to be led by trustees who listen to God's Spirit on the way to making decisions, not trustees who are susceptible to political agendas. Politics for the sake of control by a few is not how our forefathers envisioned the operations of our Convention. But I must warn you. Politics do not die easily. Do you know why? It is because the death of politics in a spiritual environment only comes after we die to self . . . .

The example of lifeless orthodoxy parading as true faith is found in the Pharisees of Jesus' day. How ironic that these defenders of supernaturalism—the miracles, angels, and the resurrection of the dead, all the right beliefs—were out of touch with the kingdom of God. The Pharisees had the right doctrines but the wrong measures, the wrong motives, and the wrong means. They measured their righteousness by their rule-keeping and their affiliations. They were motivated by selfishness and ambition. They believed the end justified the means. Thus, they employed subterfuge, slander, false witnesses, and murder conspiracies to get rid of Jesus. They congratulated themselves and despised everyone else. They intimidated all who dared to oppose them, threatening them with a first century form of excommunication. But in the end, they missed God and all who followed them missed God. They had the vocabulary of the people of God but they did not have the character of the people of God.

Jesus' rebuke of the Pharisees is a lesson for us. Simply holding the right doctrinal beliefs doesn't mean that our behavior is righteous. Christianity should be known not only by its biblical convictions, but also by the life and testimony these convictions inspire. A zeal for the Bible should result in a zeal for "living" for Christ, i.e., treating others with dignity, telling the truth, and insisting upon one's own integrity. A mistake of some Fundamentalist movements in the past has been the belief of the adherents that to be right with doctrine is to be right with the Lord. True righteousness was too easily discarded in favor of a type of dogmatism that was stifling and demoralizing to other Christians. In other words, right doctrine was equated to righteous living. They are not one and the same.

Contemporary shibboleths are employed to exclude people. It is the sin of Pharisaism when good people, whose theology and ministry are above reproach, are slandered, discredited, or ostracized simply because they refuse to blindly follow particular political posturing. Innuendos, unfounded rumors, sly winks and nods are as deadly as an assassin's bullet and usually as ungodly.

Could Southern Baptists fall into the error of Pharisaism? Could we ever, while priding ourselves on orthodox beliefs, be out of fellowship with the Living God and the true saints of God? The threat is real. I am concerned . . . now that we have affirmed by vigorous endeavor that Southern Baptists are people of the Book, that we will develop a censorious, exclusive, intolerant spirit. If this occurs, we will be the poorer for it. It will not only result in narrower participation in denominational life, a shallower pool of wisdom and giftedness in our enterprises, and a shrinking impact upon the world, but we will be in the unenviable position of being right on doctrine but wrong with God.[1]

The phone conversation with Dr. Chapman, initiated by me, was an encouragement to me. I understood that there was someone in denominational life who understands the danger of a demand for all Southern Baptists to conform to the narrow theological shibboleths of certain Southern Baptist leaders. I considered the demand for a "qualified" administrator of baptism and the prohibition of a "private" prayer language such narrow shibboleths. Dr. Chapman also confirmed to me that it was well known in denominational circles that there was animosity between Dr. Paige Patterson and Dr. Jerry Rankin, and that Patterson had sought to orchestrate the placement of trustees on the IMB who would be sympathetic with bringing about an end to Rankin's tenure as president.

I was still frustrated that trustee leaders at the IMB refused to answer my questions as to why they were pushing for new doctrinal standards that were opposed by the president of the IMB, and also growing more disconcerted by what I was discovering about Paige Patterson's and Keith Eitel's involvement in undermining the staff and administration of the IMB by seeking to turn IMB trustees against Rankin. In particular, I was grieved by the growing number of Southern Baptists who were now being disqualified from serving on the mission field because of the implementation of these new policies. Finally, I decided to make known the problems arising at the IMB. On December 10, 2005, less than one month after the doctrinal policies were adopted, I wrote and published "Crusading Conservatives vs. Cooperating Conservatives: The Battle for the Future of the Southern Baptist Convention." A month later, Jerry Corbaley and trustee leadership pointed to this post as the basis for their recommendation to the trustee board that I be removed for "gossip and slander." Read for yourself what I wrote:

> Crusading Conservatives vs. Cooperating Conservatives: The Battle for the Future of the Southern Baptist Convention, December 10, 2005
>
> Twenty years ago liberalism in the Southern Baptist Convention experienced her Waterloo in Dallas, Texas, as 45,000 messengers set the course of our beloved SBC for the next two decades. We are all grateful to the leaders of the conservative resurgence including my friend Paul Pressler, current Southwestern Theological Seminary President Paige Patterson, and the late Adrian Rogers for their foresight, courage, and wisdom in snatching the SBC from the clenched jaws of dead neo-orthodoxy and restoring

our seminaries, agencies, and institutions to an unapologetic adherance to the inerrancy of God's word, the sufficiency of Christ's work, and the evangelical missionary zeal which has marked the SBC since her formation in 1845.

I have stood side by side with my fellow conservatives and toe to toe with liberals in our convention over the years. When the Cooperative Baptist Fellowship organized in Oklahoma I nailed on the door of their organizational meeting "95 Theses Against the Formation of the CBF," an act which marked me forever as an opponent of the CBF, and resulted in a caricature of me by the unofficial artist of the CBF in Oklahoma.

My forefather, Dr. Rufus Burleson, was president of Baylor University and twice served as president of the Baptist General Convention of Texas in the late 1800s. I myself recently completed a second term as president of the Baptist General Convention of Oklahoma. I bleed Southern Baptist blood. I have personal battle scars as a result of the war against liberalism within our convention.

I am glad and I rejoice over the conservative resurgance. I am a conservative. I love my convention.

But sadly, a new war has begun. It is a war initiated by fellow conservatives; conservatives who have forgotten how to put their swords in their respective sheaths. It is a war that technically may not have just begun, but one that simply never ended.

Conservatives who loved the battles of decades past have fallen victim to a crusading mentality of bloodthirst. Since all the liberals are gone, conservative cruasaders are now killing fellow conservatives.

A clear understanding of how this war is proceeding may be seen in the recent actions of the International Mission Board, an agency that I now serve as trustee. New policies were recently approved by the Board of Trustees of the IMB regarding the appointment of missionaries. The new policies forbid the appointment of any missionary who uses a private prayer language or one who has not been baptized by a "qualified administrator" of baptism.

I personally and publicly opposed the proposed new policies of the IMB not because I do not believe we need standards for our missionaries— we do! *I opposed the new policies because we already had excellent policies on the books regarding tongues and biblical baptism.* My objections to the new policy on baptism are well documented on my blog, so I will not go into them here, but I will use the new policy on "glossolalia" to show how crusading conservatives are killing other conservatives.

The former policy of the IMB regarding tongues stated that if you practiced tongues publicly on the mission field you would be fired. But the new policy narrows the restriction to preclude a *private* prayer language. Our own Bertha Smith of South Carolina, one of the finest missionaries we have ever had as Southern Baptists, professed to be gifted with a private prayer language. Dr. Jerry Rankin, before being hired to be president of our International Mission Board, made known he had experienced a private prayer language, but agreed contractually to abide by the policy of the IMB as president and to never publicly practice "glossolalia." Some of the greatest men and women of God throughout the centuries have disagreed over the issue of a private prayer language, but have cooperated in the work of spreading the gospel.

Why have some conservative crusaders now insisted on new policies at the IMB regarding tongues? Again, it seems clear to me that some conservative crusaders have yet to learn how to sheath the sword, and rather than cooperate with fellow conservatives in reaching the world with the gospel of Jesus Christ, they have gone after the head of Dr. Jerry Rankin. I have been told by an authority in the crusading effort that there are some trustees who will settle for nothing less than Dr. Rankin's "head on a platter."

A conservative killing a fellow conservative. What a shame.

It is not my intention to defend Dr. Rankin. The issue is much larger than one man. This is not about Dr. Rankin, Dr. Draper, Dr. Crews, Dr. Chapman, or anybody else in leadership of the SBC.

The issue is much more. The future of our convention is at stake.

When are people in the Southern Baptist Convention going to stand up and say enough is enough?

If we are not careful we are going to lose a younger generation of pastors that are disillusioned with the SBC because all they see is the continuing narrowing of the parameters of fellowship within our convention. These young pastors don't see eye to eye with the conservative crusaders, but they themselves are conservative, seeking to reach their generation with the gospel. Where, they are asking, do we fit within the SBC?

Again, I think if people are not careful they will see arguments against the new IMB policies on tongues and baptism and believe the problem is simply a theological one. If that's the case, the real issue at hand, the issue that is so disturbing to many of us, will never be grasped by SBC laypeople at large. The Southern Baptist Convention, through trustees of boards and agencies, is narrowing the parameters of fellowship and cooperation to the point that real, genuine conservatives are being excluded as unfit for service in the SBC.

Our convention hated liberalism twenty years ago and we expelled it from our midst, but at this hour we better hate legalism and

Fundamentalism as much as we did the former liberalism or we will find ourselves so fractured and fragmented that we no longer have the ability to cooperate about anything, including missions. We all agree on the inerrancy of Scripture and the nature and work of Jesus Christ our Lord, but we must not be Fundamentalists when it comes to our convention. Fundamentalism with a capital F is known for her independence, separation, schism-making, and her "I'll do it my way without your help because you don't qualify to work with me" attitude.

I believe if God does not intervene in the Southern Baptist Convention by raising up men and women in the SBC who are more concerned about conservative cooperation than we are conservative conformity, we are headed down this road of religious Fundamentalism.

In closing, allow me to explain what is happening in our convention in crystal clear terms.

The war that is now taking place with crusading conservatives attacking cooperating conservatives is following the same battle plan conservatives used to defeat liberalism.

Trustees of agencies are being "vetted" or cleared by men and women who are of the opinion that no conservative is worthy of leadership that does not toe the party line. That line is no longer the nature of Christ and Scripture, but has moved rapidly toward a specific *interpretation* of Scripture related to eschatology, ecclesiology, soteriology, missiology, etc.

Crusading conservatives are using private meetings at trustee meetings, an unethical violation of all agencies' guidelines, to cram their agendas through. Crusading conservatives are influencing nominating committee members of various states to place on the different boards and agencies of the SBC those who are in lock step with crusader goals. Agency heads who are not the appointed leaders of crusaders, i.e. elected by the crusaders themselves, are being forced to resign or simply removed.

Crusaders gather to elect chairmen of the boards and appoint committee chairmen. Crusaders have an agenda and if anyone steps in their way they become vicious. Ask someone who has dared to speak out against a crusader.

Conservatives throughout the centuries have had differing interpretations regarding what Scripture teaches, but have been, and are today, united regarding the nature of Scripture. Our cooperation historically has been built upon our belief in the inerrant word of God and the person and work of Jesus Christ, and we have joined hands in cooperation to advance the kingdom. But sadly, the Southern Baptist Convention is now moving toward a time when everyone must look the same, talk the same, act the same, believe the same on the non-essentials of the faith, or else you will be removed as "not one of us."

God forbid.

I am a Southern Baptist. I will be a Southern Baptist until the day I die. I am a conservative. I will cooperate with other conservative evangelicals until the day I die. I fought one war to rid our convention of liberalism. I am prepared to fight another war to rid our convention of legalism.

I, and others, are now being attacked by conservative crusaders who want to rid our convention of fellow conservatives who don't interpret Scripture as they do. These crusaders refuse cooperation in favor of conformity, and I really think it is because they have forgotten how to minister in the power of the Spirit through prayer, humility and cooperation. If the crusaders sheath their sword, I promise, I will sheath mine. I do not want to fight my fellow conservatives. I want to cooperate with every conservative to win the world to Christ.

However, the stakes of this war are too great to roll over without a fight. This war is about the future of our convention. I promise you I will ask the Lord for grace and mercy for us all. But I cannot stand by and watch our convention die. Today it is "glossalia" vs. cessationists and the "proper administrator" of baptism vs. biblical baptism. Tomorrow it might be Calvinism vs. Arminianism or Dispensationalism vs. Preterism. Where will it end?

Why can't it end *now*. We need cooperating Baptists instead of crusading Baptists. I believe, as did Spurgeon, there is a time to draw a line in the sand for the cause of Christ.

That time has come for the Southern Baptist Convention. My line has been drawn. How about yours?

Wade Burleson[2]

I think any rational human being would be hard pressed to identify gossip or slander in my December 10, 2005, blog post. The facts are evident. Any board that passes a policy that would exclude their own president from serving as a new missionary in the very agency over which he allegedly presides has a great deal of explaining to do to the constituency that elected them—the Southern Baptist Convention. I felt it was my responsibility, yes, even my duty to let the SBC know what was taking place at the IMB.

The next couple of posts I published on my blog compared the old policies of the IMB with the new doctrinal policies adopted on November 15, 2005. I asked questions in my blog that I had already repeatedly asked trustee leaders. Why did we need new "doctrinal" policies when the old ones served us well for decades? Is anyone else bothered that these new "doctrinal" policies go well beyond the 2000 *BFM*? Is there any anecdotal field evidence that shows us these policies are needed to correct theological aberrations on the field? Why are trustee leaders implementing a new "doctrinal" standard for our missionaries, in direct opposition to President Rankin's wishes, and why are trustees, staff, and others who disagree not given opportunities to speak? I simply posted on my blog these questions that I had already raised within the trustee meetings. Had trustee leadership given me answers that showed the reasons why the new policies were needed, I would not have started the blog. But because my questions went unanswered, I felt it was time for the SBC to know what was going on at the IMB. Little did I know at the time that I had taken a stick and stirred up the hornet's nest.

Notes

1. Morris Chapman, *The Fundamentals of Conservative Cooperation,* address to the Southern Baptist Convention, 15 June 2004.

2. "Crusading Conservatives vs. Cooperating Conservatives: The War for the Future of the Southern Baptist Convention," 10 December, 2005, http://kerussocharis.blogspot.com/2005/12/crusading-conservatives-vs-cooperating_10.html.

Chapter 9

TEACHING THE "ROOKIE" A LESSON

The Back Story
Christmas 2005

By Christmas 2005 I had received enough e-mails and correspondence from people across the Southern Baptist Convention that I knew a concerted attempt had been underway for the previous two years to undermine and possibly remove Dr. Rankin from his position as president of the International Mission Board. I also knew that IMB trustee leaders, including Bill Sanderson of North Carolina, Bill Sutton of Texas, along with Tom Hatley of Arkansas, Chuck McAlister of Arkansas, John Floyd of Tennessee and other trustees, had been successful in removing Dr. Curtis Sergeant from his position as associate vice president for Global Strategies. Curtis Sergeant's story was one of the first of many I would become familiar with regarding conservative Southern Baptists who were being forced out of their denominational positions of leadership because they could not agree with the Fundamentalist ideologues who were serving as trustees.

Curtis Sergeant left the International Mission Board to become missions pastor at Saddleback Community Church in 2004, just shortly after Keith Eitel's and Paige Patterson's distribution of white papers that called into question the ecclesiology of church-planting movements. Curtis Sergeant had been an IMB missionary in the Far East who saw genuine revival occur in his place of ministry, with thousands of "house" churches springing up all over the country where he was serving. Most, if not all, of these house churches did not have "Baptist" in their name; many were led by women (in some cases, there were no converted men in the house church); and the Lord's Supper was being distributed and baptism performed by indigenous (native) women as others in their community came to faith in Christ. These kinds of practices became a sore point among Paige Patterson, Bill Sanderson, and Keith Eitel and eventually led to their meeting at The Border restaurant to discuss how to orchestrate the appointment of trustees to the IMB who would help remove Rankin and other staff who allowed such poor ecclesiology to occur on the mission field. Of course, "poor" ecclesiology was the subjective opinion of Patterson, Sanderson, and Eitel—an opinion based upon their firm belief that the only true church is a Baptist church, and that men alone (i.e., "the leaders of this Baptist church on the mission field") should dispense the ordinances.

However, the success of church planting movements (i.e., indigenous house churches) in seeing tens of thousands of people come to faith in Christ became the impetus for a paradigm shift at the International Mission Board called "New Directions," where the stated goal of the IMB in the mid-1990s became reaching "the unreached people groups of the world" rather than concentrating on areas and people where the gospel had already made an impact. Curtis Sergeant and IMB missionary David Garrison became the spokesmen for this new emphasis on church planting movements. Both men are sharp, articulate, and highly respected missiologists in the evangelical world. Unfortunately, in the climate of the Southern Baptist Convention, and particularly with the mood of Fundamentalist trustees at the IMB, both Curtis Sergeant and David Garrison became targets of wrath. David Garrison has survived and continues as a regional leader for the IMB. Curtis Sergeant left the IMB due to what he told me were threats, personal harassment, and an untenable relationship between him, trustee Bill Sanderson, and other IMB trustees, then Southeastern Seminary president Paige Patterson, and then SEBTS missions professor Keith Eitel.

Curtis told me that in 2003 trustee Bill Sanderson approached him in what he would characterize as "a threatening manner," accusing him of being "a heretic" and of teaching "heresy."[1] The alleged "heresy" was later documented in writing for Curtis by Sanderson's friend, Dr. Keith Eitel. According to Eitel, Paige Patterson, and trustee Bill Sanderson, Curtis Sergeant was guilty of three things: (1) First, Curtis taught that the Great Commission gives *all* believers the authority to perform *all* the duties of reaching the world with the gospel of Jesus Christ, rather than the "officers" of the church whom, according to Eitel, Patterson, and IMB trustee leadership, were the only ones to whom Jesus gave the Great Commission. (2) Second, Sergeant was accused of allowing some women in the indigenous house churches to be viewed as "ministers." Eitel, Patterson, and IMB trustee

Sanderson accused Curtis Sergeant of the "heresy" of advocating women pastors on the mission field. (3) Third, Sergeant was accused of a lack of orthodoxy and orthopraxy by not transporting "Southern Baptist" churches onto the mission field. He was too sensitive to the cultures in which he served, to the point of not even placing "Baptist" in the name of the house churches that were being planted. Eitel closed his letter to Sergeant with a threat: "Do you find yourself working for a convention that is so misaligned with your own convictions that you're working to "reform" it by undermining the biblical convictions of the Convention? If there is a hint of doubt in your mind about whether you work for the Convention with a clear heart and mind and fully support it's [*sic*] convictions, then you really ought to resign as an act of integrity."[2]

I was shocked when I read that last sentence. An employee of a Southern Baptist seminary (Dr. Keith Eitel), under the direct orders of his president (Dr. Paige Patterson) and through private communications with IMB trustees favorable to their "doctrinal convictions" (Bill Sanderson and the "caucus" group of trustees that included Patterson's pastor, Patterson's hunting buddy, Patterson's security guard's wife, Patterson's brother-in-law, Patterson's . . . well, you get the idea), was orchestrating the removal of high-ranking IMB employees. Sergeant was by no means the last denominational employee I discovered to be treated in this manner. As vice president of the International Mission Board, Curtis Sergeant was accountable to the full board of trustees at the International Mission Board. Yet what angered me when I became an IMB trustee was learning about the interference of seminary president Paige Patterson and his staff at Southeastern Seminary in the affairs of the International Mission Board. That interference had climbed all the way to an attempt to remove President Rankin.

In 2004, both Patterson and Eitel transferred to Southwestern Baptist Theological Seminary in Fort Worth, Texas, and the harassment of Curtis Sergeant continued. Sergeant's dissertation—which was supposed to remain under restriction, including lock and key, at Southwestern due to the danger its public release would bring to the leaders of the house churches where Sergeant ministered—was copied and distributed by Patterson. Faculty members at Southwestern called Sergeant and informed him of the latest diatribe against him. Eventually Sergeant resigned "out of frustration that the staff leadership of the IMB was not willing to do anything that involved a level of risk on the field because they were so concerned about *protecting their positions*, their authority to continue serving on the board."[3]

This small group of IMB trustees (I call them a "caucus" group) that was receiving directions from Patterson, Eitel, and other like-minded ideologues had been in the habit of meeting privately for at least three years when I joined the board. This group vetted me before I was contacted by the Southern Baptist Convention's nominating committee to serve as a trustee of the IMB.[4] When Eitel or Patterson would send this caucus group of trustees or their 2+2 seminary students e-mails and letters to update them on attempts to "correct" the errors of the IMB, they began this correspondence with the greeting "Dear Team."

The Backlash
December 2005–January 2006

By the time I wrote my first SBC blog post on December 10, 2005, I was frustrated with the caucus group's blatant violation of the IMB trustee hand-book on policy (commonly called the "Blue Book" because of its blue cover) by meeting in secret subgroups during regularly scheduled IMB trustee meetings. IMB trustees were strictly forbidden by the Blue Book to meet in such caucuses. I was also horrified that another Southern Baptist agency head felt he had the power not only to serve as president of the seminary to which he had been called, but also to control the International Mission Board, and even had the gall to seek the removal of high-ranking administrators and the president of the IMB. But most of all, I had personally experienced the manipulations of this caucus group as they subverted the processes of the Southern Baptist Convention to place trustees on boards of SBC agencies who reflected their own narrow doctrinal viewpoints, which, as I've said, exceeded the 2000 *BFM*. Southern Baptists are a cooperative body, and these demands for conformity threatened our cooperative nature. This caucus group met to try to prevent anyone with differing views from coming onto the trustee board. My December 10, 2005, post was my first attempt to let Southern Baptists know what was going on behind the scenes.

Dozens of Southern Baptists , including Dr. Morris Chapman, called or e-mailed me with encouragement after reading my posts about the IMB and the state of the convention in December 2005. Interestingly, Dr. Chapman expressed his disappointment that my "Crusading Conservatives vs. Cooperating Conservatives" post was no longer on the front page of my blog. Since I had written several other posts, it was now archived and diffi-cult to find. At his encouragement, I put a link on my front page that connected people to that particular post. From December 2005 until the present, that post is on the front page of my blog, thanks to the encouragement of the executive director of the SBC.

My first inkling that my blog posts regarding the new doctrinal policies had caused heartburn among trustee leadership was an e-mail sent to all IMB trustees by Chairman Hatley on Wednesday, January 4, 2006, about a week before our January trustee meeting in Richmond, Virginia. Dr. Hatley wrote,

> Hey Team!
>
> I hope you had a great holiday and have more joy in this year than ever before.
>
> The root word of the [*sic*] trustee is "trust." Many of you have expressed some serious concerns over how some trustees have reacted to the conclusions we reached on the doctrinal issue after our last meeting (November 15, 2005). I too am very concerned that protocol and deportment and perhaps issues of integrity have been breeched on a level I have never known before on this board.
>
> Whatever conclusions we reach in the future will be meaningless unless we address our own lack of accountability as trustees. Perhaps we need a refresher course or two on what we are as a board elected by the Convention. I'm not sure we all understand the authority granted and entrusted to us by the SBC and our relationship to other agencies and to the executive committee. Matters of polity and parliamentary procedure must be followed and that is not optional by we who are trustees. We live within those guidelines or we resign. Those are our only options.
>
> We left our last meeting discussing the need for us to hold each other accountable in matters of trustee behavior. (And that was in relation to an entirely different matter). I have asked our legal counsel to be ready to brief us on such and hope we can use much of the forum for constructive discussion on how to move forward from here.
>
> So, I call on all of us to come prayed up. Come to the meeting ready to love each other no matter what. Come ready to set concerns for particular personalities aside in favor of just "doing right." Right behavior will always be best for everyone, even if it hurts for a moment.
>
> Again I state my own humble opinion that until we resolve our own issues on how we will behave as trustees after a vote we will not have the ability for any vote to resolve any controversial issue.
>
> I look forward to seeing each of you . . .
>
> For His Glory,
> Tom Hatley[5]

It was obvious that Hatley's e-mail was a shot at me. It was also revealing on several fronts. First, the "lack of accountability" he mentions in the third paragraph is the same phrase he used with the media as he sought to explain the recommendation for my "removal" from the board. The only issue that made trustee leadership upset in December 2005 was my blog and my *public* opposition to the new "doctrinal" policies. That was *the* issue and the *only* issue. Later Hatley would seek to defend the motion to remove me, saying that it was needed because of "broken trust and resistance to accountability, not Burleson's opposition to policies recently enacted by the board."[6] Since the vote to adopt the new doctrinal policies at the IMB had occurred on November 15, 2005, I had not spoken to a single IMB trustee other than my friend Rick Thompson. We had no trustee meetings during the 2005 Christmas holiday season. The only thing I did was begin my blog on December 10, 2005. The "lack of accountability" referred specifically to my posts that questioned the rationale and need for the new doctrinal policies.

However, having received during December 2005 reams of material from former trustees, former IMB staff, former missionaries, and current high-level SBC executives—all of whom confirmed what I already knew, that a small group of IMB trustees loyal to Paige Patterson were seeking to control the direction of the IMB and even remove high-ranking IMB officials—and after experiencing myself the manipulative and controlling tactics of this trustee caucus group, I decided I'd had enough. One can read my blog posts for December 2005 and see that every post was supportive of the work of the International Mission Board, respectful, and focused on issues, not people. I did not give names, but I was determined to stop the manipulation, coercion, and demands for "doctrinal" conformity over minutiae matters that far exceeded the 2000 *Baptist Faith & Message* and put an end to the excluding of highly qualified Southern Baptist denominational employees and missionaries who disagreed with trustees demanding conformity. I responded to Hatley's e-mail at 6:15 p.m. on the same evening trustees received his e-mail. I sent the following e-mail to Tom Hatley and all the trustees of the International Mission Board:

> Hey Team!
>   I am definitely looking forward to our next trustee meeting. It is exciting to hear that we will address polity and parliamentary procedures. I look forward to the discussion. When I first came on the Board, I was invited to attend a caucus meeting of trustees dissatisfied with the current direction of the IMB. It seems I am not the first trustee to whom this has happened,

as evidenced by the following excerpt of a letter from Pam Blume, a former IMB trustee, sent to Marty Duren, editor of the *SBC Outpost*:

> It is commonly known among the IMB trustees that there is a group that meets outside the authorized sessions of board meetings. This is in violation of the policies contained in the trustee orientation manual *Ordered of God*. During my tenure on the trustee orientation committee, we sought advice as to the applicability of this document to board governance, and were told that, since the document had been requested by, crafted by, and approved by trustees, it did have the weight of set policy. Several trustees, at several times during my term of service, reminded trustees of the inappropriateness of "unauthorized subgroups." The exhortation was always ignored. One trustee responded, "If I want to get together with friends for coffee, no one has the right to tell me I can't." But what goes on is not a coffee klatch. Each year, new trustees are recruited to attend these meetings. A new trustee was told "we need your e-mail address because we plan our agenda ahead of time." Another new trustee was invited to attend and he said he would not go back again because Dr. Rankin was excoriated during the meeting. Others have had the same experience. They are invited to discuss "issues of concern to the board," and then realize, by the tone of the meeting, that this is something that they want no part of. Several trustees have been blessed to have had a hotel room near the one where this group meets, and have overheard some of the discussions. Trustees that are deemed supportive of Dr. Rankin were called "bleeding heart conservatives," or just "bleeding hearts." A comment was made "We can accomplish whatever we want as long as the bleeding hearts don't perceive it as attacking Jerry Rankin." After Dr. Rankin had announced he had written some new books, it was said in one of these caucus gatherings that "We need to go over those books with a fine-tooth comb and look for fire-able offenses." The height of audacity occurred several years ago when the group actually rented space in a separate hotel from the official board meeting in order to meet.

I appreciate the accountability that we will bring to bear to those who have, and continue, to participate in this caucus. As you might can tell, I was shocked to be invited to a similar meeting as a new trustee and was just wondering if other trustees were equally approached when they came on the Board. Though I am saddened this is happening, I am equally delighted to know that our Chairman is wanting to do something about it.

I would also be very interested in knowing who the people are who made the alleged statements, referred to by Pam Blume, regarding Dr. Rankin and "the bleeding hearts." I have been told who it was, but it may be important for that person to identify himself to the group as a whole. I will, as you suggest, love him regardless, as I am sure others on the Board will as well.

Frankly, Mr. Chairman, I think it is a little harsh to request the resignation of those trustees who are violating Board policy by caucusing together to undermine the work of the IMB. I do, however, believe a public reprimand is in order, and a personal apology to Dr. Rankin for undermining his leadership.

Yes, it may be painful, as you suggest, but I am sure it will be for the benefit of our Convention as a whole. Obviously, I have other concerns, articulated at length at our meetings, but rather than rehashing them here I would suggest that all the IMB trustees read my blog at www.kerussocharis.blogspot.com.

Here's wishing everyone a safe landing in Richmond. See you Tuesday.

In His Grace,
Wade Burleson[7]

Of course, it was at the IMB trustee meeting the following week, January 10, 2005, that trustee leadership recommended I be removed from the board. It was obvious to me that trustee leadership was not happy with this "rookie" trustee who was unafraid to challenge their stranglehold of power. They were ready to teach me a lesson, and that lesson was a hardball attempt to ruin my reputation and my ministry. They would not succeed, but in the process, they would reveal their true colors. My only desire was that the outside manipulation and control of the IMB trustees cease, and that the demands for "doctrinal" conformity on matters not addressed by the 2000 *Baptist Faith & Message* end.

After I sent the above e-mail to all the trustees, President Rankin, and other high-ranking IMB staff, I received the following e-mail from Gordon Fort, vice president for Overseas Operations, on January 6, 2006. Gordon, as all our staff at the International Mission Board, is a highly qualified missiologist. He wrote,

Thanks Wade—Good letter. You lay the issue squarely on the table and now you give each trustee the opportunity to address it and decide how best to respond and work together for the future benefit of the purpose for which we exist—world evangelization.

Your brother, Gordon[8]

While I am not sure Gordon understood at the time that nothing comes before the IMB board unless trustee leadership allows it, his e-mail does prove that it was common knowledge among staff that a caucus group of trustees were meeting to undermine the direction of administrative staff. One of the reasons IMB chairman Tom Hatley would never allow a "bleeding heart" discussion is because, according to Pam Blume,[9] he was the one who made the original statement. There was no way there would be a discussion of a "caucus" group of trustees who were meeting together to undermine Dr. Rankin. The caucus was in control of the board and the board agenda for business meetings. All of them were in leadership positions of the IMB. That's not to say that *all* trustee leaders were part of the caucus group, but the vast majority of them were. I arrived in Richmond, Virginia, on Sunday, January 8, 2006, intending to blog for the first time all that happened at the IMB meeting. I would abide by all confidentiality rules, knowing them by heart, but would ensure that every Southern Baptist was made aware of what was taking place at their missions agency.

Little did *I* know that trustee leadership would work hard to make sure that January 2006 trustee meeting would be my last. Little did *they* know that those kinds of hardball tactics only gave me more resolve.

Notes

1. Curtis Sergeant, transcribed phone interview, 5 December 2005.

2. Keith Eitel to Curtis Sergeant, 13 September 2003.

3. Curtis Sergeant, transcribed phone interview, 26 July 2006.

4. See chapter 3, "The Phone Call."

5. Tom Hatley, e-mail to IMB trustees, 4 January 2006.

6. Baptist Press, "Mission Board Trustees Seek Removal of Trustee Burleson," 11 January 2004.

7. Wade Burleson, e-mail to Tom Hatley, et al., 4 January 2006; "Former IMB Trustee, Pam Blume, Speaks Out," *SBC Outpost*, 16 December 2005, http://sbcoutpost.iemissional .com/2005/12/16/former-img-trustee-pam-blume-speaks-out/.

8. Gordon Fort, e-mail to Wade Burleson, 6 January 2006.

9. Pam Blume to Wade Burleson, 2 January 2005. Pam Blume later reaffirmed Chairman Tom Hatley as the author of the "bleeding heart" statement in a phone interview, 23 August 2008.

Chapter 10

CLOSED DOORS

IMB Trustee Meeting
Richmond, Virginia
January 2006

I flew to Richmond, Virginia, on Sunday, January 8, 2006, to attend only my fourth IMB trustee meeting. I changed planes in Memphis, Tennessee, and boarded with other IMB trustees also on their way to Richmond, including personnel chairman John Floyd and his wife, Helen. John's position as chairman of the personnel committee placed him as the key figure in the drive to get the new doctrinal policies adopted. It was no secret that John Floyd had little good to say about Dr. Rankin. The two men had served together as regional leaders of the IMB before Rankin was chosen to become president of the IMB in 1993, and John Floyd had publicly opposed Rankin's first new board initiative called "New Directions." I always found it curious that former high-ranking employees of the International Mission Board, men who left the IMB with ill will toward Rankin, could end up serving as trustees (John Floyd, Louis Moore, David Button, etc.). If one didn't know better, someone might think these people were being placed on the board *because* of their feelings toward Rankin.

The atmosphere in the airport terminal and on the plane was tense. I knew that the IMB trustee leaders were upset because of my blog and the articles I had posted opposing the new doctrinal policies. Baptists have a peculiar way of saying, "How you doin', brother?" all the while giving you an icy stare that could kill. I experienced many such greetings on the way to Richmond. I had posted on my blog that I would be reporting on what occurred at the meeting. My rationale for blogging about the meeting was simple: no longer did I want IMB trustees to pass "doctrinal policies" that exceeded the 2000 *BFM*, terminate high-ranking IMB administrators, violate agreements with missionaries, or conduct business in secret without

Southern Baptists at least knowing what was being done. Baptist Press is neither an independent watchdog nor a free press. Baptist Press printed what
Southern Baptist leaders told it to print. I believed there needed to be a voice
that was not beholden to anyone and who kept Southern Baptists informed
about the largest missions organization in the world. In explaining my decision to blog about the trustee meetings, I gave four primary reasons:

*1. To bring more understanding and support for the cooperative program, the
Lottie Moon Offering, and the work of the IMB among younger pastors and
church leaders.* There is a generation of young pastors who are feeling disenfranchised from the Southern Baptist Convention. Many of them pastor
churches that are nontraditional in most areas of church polity and practice.
I want to let these young pastors see that the Southern Baptist Convention is
composed of many pastors, including me, who do not walk lockstep with
the current trustee leadership of the IMB. I want these young pastors to see
that at the heart of the polity and practice of the Southern Baptist
Convention is the tremendous privilege of disagreeing, yet cooperating.
Doesn't it make sense to let these young pastors see the inner workings of the
IMB to help them feel involved?

*2. To allow missionaries around the world a peek inside the board meeting that
holds all missionaries accountable.* I have received several e-mails from missionaries around the world who are grateful that they can find out about the
IMB trustee work through my blog. The following is an excerpt from just
one of the letters I have received:

> There are many here, due to their isolation that are only now finding out
> about what has been happening in Richmond. It is imperative that you
> continue to stand for all of us here. I have yet to find a single worker
> among our 450 people that serve in Central Asia that is supportive of the
> new policy. What is utterly amazing is that apparently decisions are being
> made without our knowledge and no one is bothering to ask those of us
> who are out here whether we even have an opinion or not.
>
>   Again, thank you for your words of encouragement and mostly for the
> prayers that sustain us all.
>
> Sincerely in Christ,
STG
Central Asian Region, IMB

3. To bring support to the IMB staff from trustees through calling attention to any undermining influences. I have felt for some time that there are a few trustees who are dead set on opposing the direction, vision, and leadership of Dr. Jerry Rankin. It is impossible for IMB staff and Dr. Rankin to set and implement vision if trustees continue to oppose him. For our organization to run effectively, we must hold Dr. Rankin accountable and either fire him for cause or give 100 percent support to his vision for the IMB. We must never undermine him. I can assure you this godly man cannot be fired for cause. As a result, we trustees MUST support him—period.

4. Most importantly, I am blogging during the IMB meeting to ensure we stop narrowing the parameters of cooperation in missions and evangelism. Some people misunderstand the purpose of this blog. I am not trying to convince anyone that I am right and they are wrong about the new policies. I am trying to convince everyone that if we continue to disqualify people because of specific interpretations of Scripture on nonessential doctrines, we will soon so fragment and isolate the SBC that there will be very few dollars to support a shrinking pool of SBC missionaries, because everyone who is told, "You don't qualify" will leave the SBC. I am attempting to keep people in the SBC and stop people from leaving.

This comment from Gordon Cloud articulately expressed my feelings:

> Bro. Wade, I think that you are on track with your concerns. Having several friends in the independent Baptist ranks, I have seen what the progression of legalism has done to them. Eventually they reach a point of not only independence but also isolationism. I hope that our convention leadership will keep a broad perspective: that is, that Satan is our enemy, not man, and if he cannot defeat us with persecution from without then he will most certainly try to subvert us from within with useless divisions. Let us pray for them and one another that we will all run the race looking unto Jesus.[1]

One of the first things IMB trustees do when they arrive at an IMB meeting is to go to what is called the trustee forum. This particular trustee meeting is held behind closed doors, and though the bylaws of the IMB state that no business can be conducted in the forum, trustee leadership used this closed-door meeting of the full board to set the table for the next day's plenary (public) business session. Ostensibly, the reason for "closed-door" meetings is to be able to come out into the public eye and present a "unified" front, but invariably, closed-door meetings are used to hammer anyone trustee leadership does not like, whether it be administration, dissenters from within the trustee body, etc. One of the things that should change at every Southern Baptist agency, in my opinion, is the use of trustee forums. There ought to be none—ever. What Baptists say ought to be said publicly. If business needs to be conducted in private for security reasons, go behind closed doors, but those occasions should be rare. If Southern Baptists involved in Christian ministry cannot say something publicly, then it ought not to be said. What bothered the IMB trustee leadership is that I was saying publicly what I had been saying to them all along privately. They wished that what I said would remain private, and my resistance to their accountability meant I wouldn't do what they wanted. The idea that I was "breaching confidentiality" was absurd. I wasn't writing on my blog what others were saying; I was writing what *I* had been saying. I was the one speaking, and it was my message that they did not want heard by others.

I entered the trustee forum in Richmond on Monday afternoon, January 9, 2006, knowing that I would be the recipient of verbal abuse. It was worse than I could have imagined. I sat through a two-hour meeting during which certain trustees felt led to call me every derogatory name in the book—and some that may have been brand new. One trustee compared blogging to Internet pornography. Comments made by Southern Baptists on my blog were read as if I were the author of them. I learned that most trustees had not even read my blog, but had been sent an e-mail by Jerry Corbaley that contained my posts and the comments that Southern Baptists were making on my blog. What upset trustees most were the comments. When I reminded the trustees that I did not write the comments, and thus, could not be held responsible for them, they retorted that I had begun the blog and Southern Baptists now felt free to express their negative views regarding the new doctrinal policies in a forum that I had created.

One trustee, Skeet Workman, launched into a verbal harangue against me, accusing me of taking a "private" e-mail from her and posting it on my blog. Skeet had written the e-mail to me on Saturday, January 7 (the day before I arrived at the meeting):

Dear Wade,

Well, I have been listening to you rattle on and on. I guess I am ready to talk a little. You say you do not want trustees to visit with each other in any location because it is bad and against policy. Are you going to bug all our rooms like they do in China? Do you think women don't talk? We talk all the time! Do you have committees in your church and do you have a policy that they cannot discuss church issues at any time? Do Sunday class members (have a policy) about whether or not they can discuss church issues on Sunday mornings? Do you have policy that your deacons cannot discuss anything going on or decisions made at your church? How do you police this? Do you control members this tightly? What are you afraid of them saying?

I think any trustee who is a blogger on the internet and gathers in blogger groups and discusses IMB policies in writing for others to read and pass around is much worse than a group of trustees verbally visiting in private. In fact, it is much worse in that your mail has been published on the Baylor website which is much more harmful to the cooperative program and the IMB than the visiting of that a small group [*sic*] of trustees might do privately. You are guilty of a much bigger infraction in my opinion. I would never get on the internet and discuss IMB business with those who are not trustees. You are calling the kettle black! I find you a very arrogant young man who has no respect for those who have come before you.

Skeet Workman[2]

As Skeet waved a copy of the e-mail she had sent me and chastised me before the trustee board for placing her e-mail on my blog, she artfully neglected to mention several things. (1) I did not identify the author of the e-mail on my blog, but simply complimented this unnamed trustee for taking the time to write me and express his/her concerns. (2) Skeet had already told the trustees that she had never read my blog—despite complaining of listening to me "rattle on" in my blog postings. (3) Skeet confessed that another trustee had told her earlier in the day, "Wade Burleson published your e-mail!" I laughed out loud at Skeet's unwitting acknowledgment before the trustees that she had sent her "private" e-mail to the entire caucus of trustees. (4) The trustees who were in the practice of meeting privately to undermine Rankin, including Skeet, were nervous about my e-mail of a week earlier that called our board to deal with the caucus issue.[3]

It was obvious to me that trustee leadership was launching into an all-out offensive to discredit me. It is impossible to transcribe all that was said in that closed-door meeting on January 9. To summarize, what follows are a few excerpts from trustee Jerry Corbaley's letter to me and about a dozen other SBC leaders, sent in that same month. These comments were made about me because I began a blog and publicly opposed the new "doctrinal" policies they pushed.

"Mr. Burleson is a willful gossip."

"I am appalled that the work of the Board is publicly disparaged at Mr. Burleson's blog site. It has over 28,000 hits since December 10, 2005. This is similar to one individual gossiping on 28,000 phone calls."

"You are responsible for the entire contents of your blog site, including the comments of others."

"Your technology has outstripped Christian ethics."

"The Constitution of the United States grants you the right to freedom of speech, but combined with man's sinful nature the freedom of speech becomes the freedom to gossip."

"You are slandering the integrity of the board."

"Your method of impatient, emotional anarchy [blogging], contrasts poorly with the proven effectiveness of current policy."

"You are arrogant: full of unwarranted pride and self-importance; giving oneself an undue degree of importance, haughty, conceited. Synonyms include: overbearing, presumptuous, imperious, proud, rude."

"You are ignorant of Board procedures."

"Your arrogance combined with your ignorance creates a pattern."

"You have no skill . . . ."

"You do not seek cooperation, you seek submission."

"Few trustees have met someone like you, and they are temporarily daunted. However, they will rise to the occasion."

"The passion behind your ministry is not joy, nor compassion for the lost. Your passion is anger."

"You often express your love, respect for the board, and your cooperative nature verbally, but dear brother, what motivates you is the praise, adoration, and submission of men toward you. I fear for you."

"You habitually attempt to daunt people and wear them down with your persistence. You do it on purpose."

"You, sir are divisive. It is very clear who the Wade Burleson faction is. They are the blogging congregation you are cleverly encouraging to come to the Southern Baptist Convention."

"Titus 3:10 says 'Warn a divisive person once, and then warn him a second time. After that, have nothing to do with him.'"[4]

I left that Monday discouraged over what I had experienced. Yet, during dinner with fellow trustee Rick Thompson, and through some careful reflection over why trustee leaders were making me the issue rather than dealing with the issues I was raising, I went back to the hotel to prepare for the Tuesday IMB business meeting.

Later that night, as I waited for the elevator at the hotel, I overhead the caucus group meeting, in violation of IMB policy. There in the lobby, at about 11:30 p.m., they were discussing their strategy for the IMB plenary session the next day. I determined then and there that I would break up the caucus group of trustees once and for all.

What happened next is something that I will never forget.

Notes

1. "Richmond IMB Meeting, January 9–11, 2006," http://kerussocharis.blogspot.com/2006/01/richmond-imb-meeting-january-9-11th.html.

2. Skeet Workman, e-mail to Wade Burleson, 7 January 2006.

3. See chapter 9, note 7.

4. Jerry Corbaley to Wade Burleson, Dr. Chapman, Dr. Hatley, Dr. Rankin and others, 26 January 2006.

Chapter 11

THOSE WEIRDOS FROM OKLAHOMA

Hotel Lobby—Trustee Caucus
January 2006

As I waited for the elevator that Monday night, I tapped my fingers on the door and waited for the bell to ring. It was late and I was tired, both emotionally and physically. The barrage of verbal attacks from trustee leaders during the trustee forum had taken its toll. I assumed everyone was in bed, but I heard a chorus of laughter around the corner and knew someone had just told a joke. I looked over a set of raised potted plants and saw a group of International Mission Board trustees sitting around the center of the lobby, empty pizza boxes littering their tables. There was no lobby traffic, and seats were configured so they had a clear view of the front door. The garage entrance, however, where I had entered, was out of their sight. I paused.

After the laughter subsided, I heard someone say, "What are we going to do about those weirdos from Oklahoma?" I could not identify who asked the question, but I assumed that the "weirdos" were Rick Thompson and myself. I later discovered that an attorney from Oklahoma, who preceded me on the board as a trustee, had resigned a couple of years earlier, frustrated over the attitude of trustee leadership and the inability to effect any change. The attorney contacted me in 2006 by writing a letter to offer me moral support. He detailed the treatment he had received by trustee leaders as he sought to help implement the plans of IMB administration and staff. He was so disillusioned by the actions against him that he seriously considered leaving the Southern Baptist Convention after his resignation from the board. I now believe the "weirdos" from Oklahoma included this attorney, Rick Thompson, and me.

Another trustee, also unidentifiable, followed up the query with this statement: "Yeah, we need to let Alan Day know that he needs to stop giving us the names of turncoats." My eyebrows involuntarily rose at this statement simply because several things began to click for me. Alan Day is the pastor of First Baptist Church, Edmond, Oklahoma, and a friend. He has been heavily involved in "conservative resurgence" leadership at both the state and national levels. He is friends with Paige Patterson, Al Mohler, and Judge Pressler, and was in the running for the presidency of New Orleans Baptist Theological Seminary before Patterson's brother-in-law, Charles Kelley, was chosen for the job. Alan had suffered a severe brain tumor a few years earlier and almost died. A remarkable recovery had enabled him to continue his pastoral and preaching ministry at FBC Edmond, but he had curtailed his Southern Baptist political activities since the tumor, so the mention of his name surprised me. I later learned that he had been an IMB trustee during the same time Paige Patterson and Paul Pressler served as IMB trustees.

Alan's name, however, revealed to me that International Mission Board trustee leaders—and the caucus of trustees who met secretly with them— were using Alan to "vet" those they wanted to see elected to serve with them on the board. The process worked this way: (1) Trustees who were interested in bringing Southern Baptists on board as "like-minded" IMB trustees would call Alan and say, "Alan, there is a position open for IMB trustee from Oklahoma. Who would you recommend join us?" (2) Alan would give them a name, and IMB trustees would select one of their own to call that person and "vet" him. (3) If the person Alan recommended (in this case me) passed the standard the IMB caucus of trustees set, then the trustees themselves would contact the SBC nominating committee representatives from Oklahoma and "recommend" that the committee get "so and so" to serve on the IMB board of trustees. All of the above is a violation of Southern Baptist bylaws, which state that the nominating committee is to work independent of the input of sitting boards.

Alan Day had recommended me. Winston Curtis had been assigned to "vet" me. After I passed muster in Winston's mind, Winston and the caucus of trustees contacted the SBC nominating committee and explained why they needed me on the board (i.e., "he's conservative, he's an inerrantist, he's not afraid to make tough decisions," etc.). The nominating committee contacted me in spring 2005, and I was nominated at the 2005 Southern Baptist Convention to be the next Oklahoma trustee for the International Mission Board. It made perfect sense to me. And it bothered me. Conservatives were acting as if they were still at battle with "liberals." It was as if the reformers got in charge and didn't know how to lay down their swords and work. They had to keep acting as if there were an imaginary enemy.

I recognized the next voice immediately. Winston Curtis chimed in and said, "Yeah, guys, I now know what Ronald Reagan felt like when he appointed Sandra Day O'Connor to the Supreme Court." I almost fell over when I heard Winston say this. The bold admission that the trustee caucus was appointing the IMB trustees to serve on the very board on which *they* served was incredible to me. The tight control these men felt they deserved and held at the IMB, as if the IMB couldn't function without them, was the essence of arrogance in my mind. It was also a violation of every bylaw at the IMB and SBC that was designed to bring impartiality and fairness to agencies. Cooperation was being killed by closed-door attempts to "appoint" only trustees who saw eye to eye on tertiary matters. I knew then that I would say something to the entire group before I went to bed. I started to go and confront them when I was stopped in my tracks by what I heard next.

Bill Sutton, a good friend of Paige Patterson and the granddaddy of all trustees on the IMB, having served an extraordinary sixteen years as IMB "doctrinal watchdog" for the conservative resurgence leaders, declared, "We must do something about Wendy Norvelle. She's a woman in a slot reserved for men, and Rankin's pushing her for the permanent vice presidency position. She's incompetent. Tomorrow I am going to make a recommendation that we terminate Wendy. Who'll second the motion?"

Wendy was the acting vice president of Communications. She was the official IMB spokesperson, and after the November 15, 2005, trustee vote on the new "doctrinal policies," a vote taken by the simple raising of hands, Wendy reported to the press that the vote total was 25 trustees voting "for" the new policies and 18 trustees "against" the new policies.[1] The trustee leaders were infuriated that there was a discrepancy in the vote totals over the passage of the new doctrinal policies. Louis Moore, the trustee with a reporter's background and self-proclaimed purveyor of all things "truth," contacted the Associated Baptist Press and said, "After the vote was taken, my wife and I were with Tom Hatley, IMB trustee board chairman, so I asked him what the actual vote had been. Tom said the vote was 50-15 [reflecting far more votes cast and a much smaller percentage of dissenting votes]. He should know . . . more than anyone else in the room, Tom was the most authoritative."[2]

It seems IMB trustee chairman Tom Hatley had tallied the vote on a napkin after being consulted by trustee leaders who were allegedly given the assignment to "count." The trustee caucus never forgave Wendy Norvelle for what they perceived as an intentional attempt to alter the vote total to reflect a far greater division over the proposed policies than trustee leaders wished to represent. I believe Wendy was just doing her job, and as the official spokesperson for the IMB, she and IMB staff simply counted the votes they saw with their own eyes. Many trustees were unsure of how to vote and simply didn't vote, but the caucus couldn't bear that thought, so they added 25 more to the "for" vote. Tom Hatley began issuing "official" statements to the press in January 2006, snatching this responsibility from the Wendy, whom Southern Baptists pay to perform the service.

The conversation I was overhearing at the late-night meeting of the trustee caucus, particularly the proposed motion to terminate Wendy, violated the code of conduct for trustee behavior found in what was commonly called the "Blue Book." I decided I needed someone to witness what I was about to do, so I went to the room of Georgia pastor Marty Duren and his youth director Joey Jernigan. They were both up late working on their computers, and I asked them to come down to the lobby with me in order to be witnesses. They asked what was going on, and I told them to follow me and they would soon discover why I needed them.

Arriving back in the lobby at 11:45 p.m., I went straight to the caucus group. Two or three trustees who saw me coming immediately got up and left before I even arrived to speak with them. By the time I crossed the lobby and breached the boundary of the chairs circled together so that the trustees could discuss their plans for the next day's plenary business sessions, about a dozen trustees remained. I began by saying, "I have wondered why it is that the Lord would have me serve as a trustee of the IMB. I didn't ask for it. I didn't seek it. Now I know why he wants me to serve. It is to break up this caucus group that is undermining the vision and leadership of Dr. Rankin and his staff. Who was it that recommended Wendy Norvelle be fired?"

After I asked this question, fully knowing what the answer would be, Bob Pearle, Paige Patterson's friend and pastor, angrily stood up and said, "What are you doing? Were you secretly listening to our conversation? I've had enough." Bob waved his hand at me as if to dismiss me, and he angrily left the lobby. Bill Sutton remained seated, and to his credit said, "I said that about Wendy. Why?" I told Bill and the other trustees that our Blue Book code of conduct states that no group or subgroup of trustees shall caucus together during official IMB meetings for the purpose of conducting IMB business. The basis of such a policy was to prevent a small group from seeking to control the entire board. If a motion had merit, it should be discussed with all trustees, not only a few, having the advantage of hearing the pros and cons of such a motion. Then I asked the question, "And, by the way, who are those weirdos from Oklahoma?" It got really quiet.

Then I said what I had come down to say. "Listen, fellows, I like you guys. I consider you to be my friends. But I will not—I cannot—allow you to continue to meet like this. You guys are undermining our mission work by making everything personal and political . . . ." As I was speaking I noticed a trustee from Texas, Albert Greene, reach into his pocket. In the 1980s, I had gone through training at the Tulsa Police Academy in order to serve as chaplain for the Tulsa Police Department. We were taught always to sit with our backs to the wall at restaurants so that we could face the entrances, always to know the number of people in the room at all times, and to watch the hands of people when in a tense environment. Albert pulled a folding knife out of his pocket and opened it. He clenched the handle with a closed fist and put the base of his fist on his knee with the open-ended knife pointing in my direction. I stopped what I was saying and said, "Is that a knife?" Albert, a big man with a country Texas drawl, grinned, and slowly said "Yep." He then raised the knife and began to clean his fingernails.

It was obvious he was trying to intimidate me, and later he apologized, but I said to him and the others, "Listen, you guys can't intimidate me. We are called by the SBC to do the work of missions, and this political maneuvering, using the board to undermine Rankin and others that you don't believe are 'Baptist' enough, and all the other nonsense I've experienced the last six months as you have sought to control the board is the very reason I believe God has placed me on the board. It's to break up this kind of behavior. Listen to me carefully. If I hear so much as a whisper of this motion to terminate Wendy Norvelle tomorrow, I will reveal everything I know about you guys and what you are doing." I can't say it was one of the more articulate speeches of my lifetime, but it certainly was one that "crossed the Rubicon." As General Caesar took his soldiers back to Rome to claim the throne, he had to cross the Rubicon River, a point at which he told his soldiers that there would be no turning back. If they followed him, they would either be put to death as traitors or would eventually win the battle and reform Rome and the Senate. I knew my Rubicon had been reached. I was now considered an official "traitor" of the conservative resurgence, and I and others would have to succeed at reforming the IMB and SBC to be a cooperating group of independent autonomous churches, or we would see a small, ideological group of men demand conformity on all tertiary matters.

The trustees eventually grumbled their way out of the lobby and back to their rooms. Bill Sutton and I stayed in the lobby and talked for another 10 or 15 minutes. Bill is a likeable guy, but he truly believes the SBC is in danger of collapse through the influence of liberals, though he would call anyone left of Attila the Hun a liberal. Bill respected the fact that, like him, I speak my mind when I think something is wrong. I reminded Bill that it was wrong to conduct IMB business in small caucus groups outside the regularly scheduled plenary trustee meetings and that I meant what I said about shutting down the movement to terminate Wendy Norvelle and get rid of Jerry Rankin.

I went to bed that Monday night, January 9, 2006, knowing I had experienced one of the most difficult days of my life. The character assassinations against me from behind closed doors had been intense. Skeet Workman, Jerry Corbaley, Tom Hatley, Chuck McAlister, Bob Pearle, and a handful of other trustee leaders had no problem publicly voicing their dislike of me. Other, more tactful trustees, such as Louis Moore, Bill Sutton, Bill Sanderson, Joe Hugley, and others, never said anything publicly, but angrily denounced me in private to anyone who would listen. Most trustees did not know me, but the fifteen or twenty trustees who both knew me and agreed that the "doctrinal" policies were horrible for SBC cooperative missions were supportive. I slept soundly that night, not because I knew I had a majority of trustee support, but because I knew that the issues we faced in the SBC were not personal. Southern Baptists were now in a real battle for the future of our convention. What would we look like twenty years from now? Would we be a diverse, cooperating group of churches that focused on missions and evangelism, or would we be a small, ideologically narrow group of conforming churches led by Fundamentalist pastors who wished separation from any evangelical who disagreed?

The next morning I went to Wendy Norvelle and told her about the confrontation the night before. I told her that if trustees came after her, I and others would try to protect her. She looked a bit rattled as I explained what had happened, but she is a classy lady and thanked me for standing up for her. I then met Jerry Rankin in the foyer before the trustee meeting and told him what had happened. His exact words to me were, "Wade, those guys don't stop, do they? They'll do anything." I have often said that I do not know how Jerry Rankin has stood up under a barrage of verbal assaults by the trustees who were supposed to encourage and help him. He has often said that he has silently endured because the issue is getting the gospel to the world, and God has given him influence to help take the message of Christ to the uttermost parts of the earth. Maybe so, but sometimes the way to "handle" trustees with agendas is to resist them openly. That was the path I chose.

We went through the day conducting routine business until the end of our afternoon plenary session. It was then that Wendy Norvelle stood before the trustees, emotional and crying, and apologized several times for her "mistakes." She kept repeating the phrase "I'm sorry . . . I'm sorry . . . I'm sorry." Finally, Tom Hatley interrupted and said, "Look, lady, one apology is enough." I thought that statement from the chairman was particularly rude, both with the use of the word "lady" and the attitude in which it was delivered. After Wendy Norvelle sat down, Jerry Corbaley stood up and asked that we move into executive session. I leaned over to trustee Rick Thompson, whom I had told about the meeting the night before, and said, "Here we go, Rick. The caucus is going to go after Wendy. They are going to move she be terminated and use her public apology for mistakes as the excuse. Get ready. I'm not going to let them go after her."

I asked Hatley why we were moving into executive session. He ignored me. I asked him again. He ignored me again. I was seated in the front of the room. Tom was on the raised dais seated behind a table with Jerry Rankin. After all guests and reporters were removed from the room and the door was shut, Jerry Corbaley stood to make his motion.

"I move that Wade Burleson be removed from the International Mission Board of Trustees . . . ."

Talk about being blindsided. The thing that continues to amaze me to this day are the attempts by trustee leaders who wanted me off the board to try to make the reasons for their recommendation point to my actions or attitude on the board. In reality, I had simply withstood trustee leadership's demand that everyone conform to their ideology. It had nothing to do with my behavior and everything to do with my blog. It had nothing to do with poor treatment of trustees, and everything to do with the poor view Southern Baptists were having of trustees who pushed the IMB to approve "doctrinal" policies that exceed the 2000 *BFM*.

One week after the recommendation for my removal on January 15, 2006, I wrote the following on my blog:

[T]he major issue for me is not so much the new policy forbidding the appointment of missionaries who have a private prayer language, or even the policy that rejects prospective missionary candidates who are not baptized in a Southern Baptist church or in a church that teaches eternal security. Sure, I believe both new policies go beyond Scripture and the *Baptist Faith & Message*, but they are only symptoms of a deeper problem. If we don't stop the demand that people conform to specific interpretations of the Bible in "doctrines" that are not addressed by the Convention in the 2000 *BFM*, we will rip the fabric of our cooperation away.

That is the real problem.

We are continuing *to narrow the doctrinal parameters of fellowship and cooperation* in the area of missions and evangelism by demanding conformity and agreement on nonessential doctrines. Now you must be a cessationist and very close to a Landmark in order to be a Southern Baptist missionary.

We have lost sight of the gospel.

The gospel is Jesus Christ and Him crucified. The gospel is the good news that God saves sinners through the work of His Son. We are called to preach Christ. We are commissioned by Christ Himself to be ambassadors of this good news. We are to go far and wide, or at least support those who do go far away, in the sharing of this good news that God saves sinners through Jesus Christ His Son. . . .[3]

As far as I can tell, this was the first time the phrase "to narrow the doctrinal parameters of missionary cooperation" had been used to describe the SBC. It eventually became an often-quoted mantra during the reformation in the Southern Baptist Convention that began at the IMB and eventually swept through the SBC with the election of Frank Page as president.

Notes

1. Associated Baptist Press, "Conflicting Reports on IMB Vote Tally Raise Questions about Board's Intent," 9 December 2005, http://www.abpnews.com/index.php?option=com_content&task=view&id=834&Itemid=118 (accessed 11 January 2006).

2. Ibid.

3. "Never Forget It Is About Missions," 18 January 2006, http://kerussocharis.blogspot.com/2006/01/never-forget-its-about-missions.html.

Chapter 12

MEET ME IN ST. LOUIS

St. Louis, Missouri
February 2006

Considering that in 160 years no Southern Baptist Convention board had ever recommended that a trustee be removed, it was deemed prudent by Morris Chapman and those who serve on the executive committee of the Southern Baptist Convention to convene all parties to try for a resolution before the SBC met in Greensboro, North Carolina, in June 2006. Bobby Welch, president of the SBC, feared his infamous bus trip across America would be overshadowed by controversy and so his office initiated contact with Morris Chapman's office and arrangements were made for a meeting to take place.

Those invited to this meeting in St. Louis in February 2006 were IMB chairman Tom Hatley and IMB trustee vice chairman Lonnie Wascom (a director of missions from Louisiana); IMB staff attorney Matt Bristol and SBC attorney Augie Boto; IMB president Jerry Rankin and IMB vice president Clyde Meador; SBC president Bobby Welch; Tom Elliff, chairman of the SBC executive committee; Rob Zinn; and myself. The only way I could be removed from the board was if the SBC voted to remove me, and before they could do that, I would receive an opportunity to explain what I had been saying from the beginning of my service as an IMB trustee.

I agreed to attend this meeting in St. Louis on two conditions. First, trustee Rick Thompson would accompany me. Rick had been with me at every single meeting of the IMB. He had seen my responses to everyone who talked with me. He knew that I had always been kind and soft-spoken to those who had verbally attacked me. Tom Hatley, Jerry Corbaley, and other trustee leaders often outright lied to others about my alleged "behavior" in trustee meetings in order to justify their over-the-top recommendation for my removal. Rick sat beside me, heard all the conversations, and was the one person on the board with enough courage to stand up to those who sought to smear my character. Morris Chapman and Bobby Welch readily agreed to my request for Rick Thompson's presence.

The second request was that I be given an hour, uninterrupted, so that I could present why I had started my blog and why I opposed the policies that had been passed in November.

Previously I had asked Tom Hatley to allow me to speak to the IMB board regarding my concerns about trustees seeking to undermine the direction and vision of President Jerry Rankin. I had requested the opportunity to speak to the board expressing my concerns that trustees were being influenced by an outside agency head, "vetting" future trustees and seeking to appoint IMB trustees themselves, narrowing the doctrinal parameters of missionary cooperation by proposing policies that exceeded the 2000 *BFM*, and were meeting privately in a caucus to undermine the vision and direction of President Jerry Rankin. I had requested to speak to the entire board several times in 2005, and the last request reached Hatley via e-mail a few days before the January 2006 board meeting. Hatley never responded to my requests. I wanted the opportunity for him to hear my concerns. My requests to speak to the entire board of trustees were in writing, and they all were denied. In fact, Tom Hatley never responded, verbally or in writing, to my requests. He was obviously angry that a "rookie" trustee had the gall even to request to speak to the entire board.

This time, Morris Chapman and Bobby Welch granted my request for an hour of uninterrupted time to speak before the St. Louis group. Rick Thompson and I flew together to St. Louis on Monday, January 30, 2006. We rented a car and made our way to the hotel where the meeting would take place. The meeting was scheduled for early afternoon, with a dinner to follow. Then the group would convene for a second and hopefully final meeting at night. If we could not reach a resolution, we would convene the next morning, though Bobby Welch explained that he had to fly out late that night. We were all hopeful that matters could be resolved by late Monday night.

We gathered in a hotel conference room on the ground floor at tables arranged in a square. Brief introductions were made, since most everyone had met before. Then SBC president Bobby Welch began the meeting with an opening statement. Bobby read prepared remarks. He is a former colonel in the United States armed forces and is best known for the creation of FAITH, the evangelistic tool used by many Southern Baptist churches. At the time he was SBC president, Bobby also was pastor of First Baptist Church, Daytona Beach, Florida. He is a polished speaker, well dressed in all environments, and not used to anyone questioning his decisions. In his opening statement, he simply emphasized that the request for my removal needed to be resolved prior to the Greensboro convention so that the SBC would not be in the news for controversy. Then he called upon Tom Hatley and Lonnie Wascom to present their rationale for my removal.

Basically, Tom said I was a new trustee (he had abandoned his favorite word "rookie"), and trustee leadership resented the fact that I would not listen to them since they had served on the board for years. This matter of the new doctrinal policies, he said, had been decided within the IMB personnel committee at the meeting before I even came on the board. The policies would never have become a full board controversy had I not complained about the "new guidelines" as a member of the personnel committee. He said the way Southern Baptist agencies worked is that the majority rules and when someone is in the minority, they either submit to the desires of the majority or resign. Tom said I had made my dissent public and had refused to resign. Therefore, the board had no choice but to remove me. Tom spent about five minutes defending trustee leadership's decision to recommend my removal.

Then it was my turn. I had two notebooks in front of me, one white and the other black, filled with e-mails, letters, notes, and even an affidavit that I had collected over the previous seven months. I started at the beginning. At every point that required documentation, copies of the documents were passed around, with the request they be returned to me at the end of the meeting. I related my background as a Southern Baptist pastor, showing that I was both a conservative and a loyalist to our denomination. I gave a brief history of my denominational service and explained that I had not sought to be a trustee for the IMB. Then I detailed what I have shared in the first eleven chapters of this book. The men listened carefully and quietly.

The major complaint of IMB trustee leadership is that I had alleged in my blog post "Crusading Conservatives vs. Cooperating Conservatives: The Battle for the Future of the Southern Baptist Convention" that IMB trustee leadership were using the doctrinal policies as a backdoor attempt to embarrass Jerry Rankin and possibly remove him from the presidency of the IMB. When I detailed the connections with Paige Patterson among those in trustee leadership, Tom Hatley began to interrupt me, but was told to be quiet until I finished. I then voiced my objections to the International Mission Board trustees being used by an outside agency head to undermine or undercut President Rankin and his work at the IMB. I said I believed that a handful of trustees pushed the "private prayer policy" and "baptismal policy" as backdoor attempts to accomplish the goal of removing Rankin from the IMB. I admitted that a handful of trustee leaders pushed the policies not to remove Rankin but for ideological reasons. However, they were simply pawns for those who knew precisely what they were doing—all of it leading back to Paige Patterson at Southwestern Baptist Theological Seminary.

I explained how we were told that the conservative resurgence was a battle for the Bible, and I believed it, but that what I saw happening now in the Southern Baptist Convention was unconscionable. Conservatives were going after conservatives since there were no longer any liberals in the convention. Worse, they were manipulating the trustee system at all our agencies to accomplish their goal of removing anyone who did not carry their definition of "Baptist identity," or, as they would say, those who were not "one of us." Unfortunately, their definition of Baptist identity was unique to their Fundamentalist interpretations of Scripture, and was never approved by the Southern Baptist Convention. The attempts at demanding conformity from all Southern Baptists to their interpretations of Scripture, which went beyond the consensus 2000 *Baptist Faith & Message*, were made through the backdoor adoption of doctrinal policies at Southern Baptist agencies through the trustee boards of those agencies.

I then documented and explained how those in charge sought to destroy anyone who challenged them about their manipulative and controlling tactics. When the subtle, behind-the-scenes attempts to stifle opposition failed, then the tactics would become vicious and public. I documented how I had sought to oppose the passage of the doctrinal policies, using the processes afforded me as a trustee, and how trustee leadership sought to discredit me with the entire board. I then explained my reasons for taking my objections to the new doctrinal policies public, and showed them how I had sought on my blog to deal with the issues. I gave them copies of what I had written, and showed them I had not identified any person publicly, had dealt with the issues and not personalities, and was in no shape or manner guilty of "gossip and slander." In addition, I detailed how nobody in trustee leadership had come to me prior to the extraordinary removal motion to tell me what they intended to do. I showed how the motion was made with "gossip and slander" as the basis for my removal in order to turn against me the trustees who had never read my blog. Then, when trustee leadership made the motion public, they changed the basis for the motion to "resistance to accountability and loss of trust." I detailed how trustee leadership came to me during the twenty-four hours before they made the motion public to try to entice me to resign.

I explained that I understood our convention to be a convention of independent, autonomous churches who agreed to cooperate for the purpose of missions and evangelism. In my understanding of the role of SBC agencies, they exist to facilitate and serve SBC churches in missions and evangelism. The idea that a Southern Baptist agency would take an "authoritative" role over an autonomous church by insisting one of that church's *members* who applied to the IMB to serve as a missionary be "re-baptized" in the candidate's home church—even though the church had already accepted the member's baptism—was to me absurd. Then, for the IMB to refuse to appoint that missionary if the church refused to "re-baptize" sounded to me as if the church was serving the agency rather than the agency the church. If trustees did not have the ability to object to this violation of Baptist autonomy, and if a trustee *supportive* of agency administration and staff was treated by trustee leadership as pariah, and if a trustee could not report to the people who elected him to the board (the Southern Baptist Convention itself) the reasons why he was doing what he was doing, then we had lost our understanding of what it means to be a Southern Baptist.

I explained that I was confident of the positions I had taken, had no regrets for anything I had said or done, and was willing to go before the Southern Baptist Convention and defend why I should remain as a trustee of the International Mission Board. If the *convention*, not trustee leadership, felt I should be removed—so be it. I would not only comply, but I would willingly step down, for the convention was my authority. Unlike trustee leadership, who pushed policies for an agenda not approved by the convention, I would take my instructions from the convention.

When I finished, you could have heard a pin drop. Everyone sat in silence for a few seconds. Then Tom Hatley made his biggest mistake. He said, "Wade, I didn't know all this. Why didn't you tell me?" I pulled several sheets of paper out of my notebook, passed them around, and said, "Tom, I tried. Here are the e-mails. I told you a great deal of this in our private meeting with IMB attorney Matt Bristol in Tulsa, but not the details. I asked you if I could speak to the entire board—my preference would be in public, but I would consent to speaking behind closed doors if trustee leadership demanded—in order to express my concerns to the full board. Here are the e-mails where I requested you to allow the board to address these issues." Tom grew quiet.

Then—and there is no other way to say it—Tom Hatley and Lonnie Wascom were both taken behind the proverbial woodshed and verbally thrashed by the leaders of the meeting. Then, surprisingly, several people spoke about the incompetent leadership of the board to allow this issue to become such a fiasco. At one point I felt sorry for Tom Hatley and Lonnie Wascom; I explained to the group they did not have the real authority on the board. The trustees who put them in their positions held the power. I knew within five minutes that there was no way the recommendation for my removal would be allowed to come before the SBC at the 2006 Greensboro convention. Before our meeting was over, Tom Hatley promised all who had gathered that he would ensure that the motion was withdrawn.

During a break, Tom Hatley, almost looking contrite, spoke to Rick and me in the hallway. I expressed my belief to Tom, again, that he had neither the power nor the authority to get the motion reversed by all trustee leaders. His response, witnessed by Rick Thompson, was clear, and I remember it verbatim: "Those guys will do exactly as I ask. I have too much dirt on them for them to do anything different." I have since wondered what "dirt" Hatley meant, but having seen enough mud with my own eyes, I didn't pursue it.

After the meeting, Rick asked me how I felt. On one hand, I was thrilled that the issue would be put behind us at the next trustee meeting in March 2006. On the other hand, I regretted being unable to speak to the entire Southern Baptist Convention. The damage to me, my family, and my ministry had already been done. The ability to repair it was being taken away, but in the end, I felt it was best for Southern Baptists as a whole to resolve the situation before the convention. The only concern, which later proved justifiable, was that Tom Hatley would kowtow to the demands of others on the trustee board. Trustees such as Chuck McAlister, Jerry Corbaley, and Joe Hugley would never understand Hatley's demand for a reversal of the motion for my removal.

The next morning, Jerry Rankin, Rick, and I ate breakfast together. Jerry suggested that, when the board met in March to rescind the motion, I apologize to the board in order to get in good graces with trustee leadership. I asked Jerry why I needed to apologize. Typically, he said to apologize for upsetting them. When the trustees accused him of financial misappropriation, he apologized—not for the misappropriation, but for his lack of communication. When they accused him of charismatic heresy, he apologized—not for heresy, but for not being more aware of their doctrinal concerns. When they accused him of fudging numbers to make New Directions look good, he apologized—not for fudging numbers, but for not meeting their expectations in board meetings. Jerry's modus operandi is to be a peacemaker and apologize in order to make people feel better. I swallowed a little harder than usual and told Jerry that I would only apologize for the things for which I was guilty. In the March 2006 trustee meeting, this personal conviction would infuriate trustee leadership.

Chapter 13

TRUSTEE LEADERS
TRY TO SAVE FACE

Marty Duren and SBC *Outpost*

When trustee leadership of the International Mission Board recommended my removal in January 2006, a pastor from Atlanta, Georgia, named Marty Duren was at the meeting. Marty is the grandfather of Southern Baptist bloggers, having started his own blog, called *SBC Outpost*, a full year before any other Southern Baptist pastor began to blog. I owe a great deal to Marty Duren because in those initial days, Marty raised the ire of IMB trustee leadership by letting the entire SBC know what was going on. No longer could trustee leadership control the flow of information through IMB communications staff or Baptist Press. Now they had to deal with Marty Duren. For instance, as Tom Hatley was figuring out how to get those trustees "he had dirt on" to reverse their recommendation that I be removed, Marty Duren was posting on his blog about the absurd sequence of events at the IMB. The following is a timeline of events at the IMB, along with his comments, that Marty posted on *SBC Outpost* that accurately reflect the changing positions of IMB trustee leadership.

> **November 15, 2005**—IMB Trustees approve new policies regarding private prayer language and baptism.
> **December 6, 2005**—Wade Burleson begins blogging.
> **Jan 10, 2006**—IMB Trustee Jerry Corbaley (CA) moves that the board enter executive session, during which time he makes the following motion: "I move that the trustees request the Southern Baptist Convention remove Wade Burleson from the International Mission Board as soon as possible; that the trustees reprimand him for gossip and slander that hurts the work of the board; that the chairman make public the nature of the reprimand in the manner of the chairman's choosing; and that Mr. Burleson be

removed from all trustee committees until such time as the Southern Baptist Convention rules otherwise."

Jan 11, 2006—IMB Trustee Chairman releases a statement, informing Southern Baptists that the trustees are seeking the removal of Wade Burleson for "broken trust and resistance to accountability." Chairman Hatley also insisted that the board had exercised "due deliberation," exploring "other ways to handle" the matter before taking such a "difficult measure."

Jan 13, 2006—The Oklahoma Baptist Convention's Executive Director, Anthony Jordan, releases a statement supporting Wade Burleson. The statement reads: "While the Baptist General Convention of Oklahoma is not privileged to firsthand knowledge regarding the actions taken by the IMB board of trustees concerning Wade Burleson, we can speak to the outstanding service Wade Burleson has and continues to provide to our state convention. As a current member of the BGCO board of directors and as a past state convention president, Wade has demonstrated excellent leadership and integrity while exemplifying a passion for reaching the world with the Gospel of Jesus Christ."

Feb 3, 2006—IMB Trustee Bob Pearle (TX) explains in the *Southern Baptist Texan* that the move to oust Wade Burleson was grounded in alleged "distortions" of facts on Burleson's blog, and only after "every effort" was taken to get Wade Burleson to correct the "misinformation." Pearle continued by denying that illegal caucusing exists, calling the notion "ridiculous." The action taken against Burleson, according to Pearle, was, in the end, about Wade Burleson's "attitude and arrogance and running roughshod and just some stuff that's inappropriate."

Feb 15, 2006—IMB Chairman Tom Hatley grants an exclusive interview with the *Southern Baptist Texan* to report the actions of the board's executive committee. His interview precedes his statement, which he assures everyone is forthcoming. The original article reports that Burleson had "improperly opposed the board's action to establish a new missionary candidate criteria." Yet Hatley, oddly enough, states that "the decision to seek removal was based on broken trust and resistance to accountability, not Burleson's opposition to policies recently enacted by the board.**"**

In contrast to Hatley's earlier assertion (Jan 11) that "due deliberation" had been exercised and "other ways" of handling the matter were considered, he now tells Southern Baptists that " the committee determined the matter of disciplining a trustee could be handled internally." Just what kind of due deliberation is that? And are we to assume that they explored all ways except the best one? Strange. Very strange.

Feb 16, 2006—The *Southern Baptist Texan* story is "updated," and the words "disciplining a trustee" in the second paragraph are changed to say that the committee determined that the board has the authority to 'handle the matter internally without the necessity of making a recommendation to the SBC."

Feb 16, 2006—Baptist Press runs its own story on the IMB Executive Committee recommendation to reverse course. In it, Hatley is quoted as saying that "We have determined that we have the ability to seek management of these issues through internal processes that were not known during our January meeting. We have never reached this stage of conflict before and did not know of all our options until recently." First, he wants to remove Wade after exercising "due deliberation" and exploring "other options." Then he wants to "discipline" Wade internally. Then he wants to "handle the matter" internally. Now he wants to "manage" the issues through internal processes because they "did not know" all their options in the January meeting. Again, "due deliberation"? How many different reports will Hatley make until he finds language that works? How many approaches will he take before everybody realizes his incompetence?

Feb 16, 2006—In yet another interview, Hatley breaks ranks and talks to Associated Baptist Press. In this article, he gives the impression that Tammi Ledbetter, his first choice to break the news of the Executive Committee's decision to rescind the motion against Wade Burleson, mischaracterized his comments. Hatley parses the difference between the conflicting stories: "Hatley told ABP that the line was not a direct quote, but the author's characterization of what he had said. Hatley also said the term 'disciplining' was not directed specifically at Burleson, but intended more generally to refer to conflicts among trustees. 'It would be more than "discipline"— it would be any conflict; it would be [dealing with] interpersonal relationships' needing repair, he said. 'I'm hoping that cool heads and smart people can get together and pray and love each other and find ways to get things done for the Kingdom.'"

Hey Tom, better find another reporter to massage your message if Tammi Ledbetter was so far off base. Surprising, really. She's always been known for accurate, clear, and concise reporting. Wonder why she botched your interview? Or maybe, she got it right and you changed course again?

Feb 16, 2006—In yet another story running in Baptist Press, Tom Hatley confirms the phraseology of Tammi Ledbetter's story in the [*Southern Baptist*] *Texan*: The BP article states, "The discussions were prompted in part by a statement in Baptist Press Feb. 15 that 'the committee determined that the matter of disciplining a trustee can be handled internally.'

Hatley confirmed the phraseology to Baptist Press but clarified that he was speaking about the proposed accountability guidelines."

Hatley goes on to tell Baptist Press that he is "very optimistic that our relationships will be more harmonious in the future."

Feb 25, 2006—In an interview with the Arkansas Democrat Gazette, Tom Hatley states that nobody on the board of trustees was "against [Wade's] blogging or anyone else's communication in public." The problem, according to Hatley's latest take on things, was how Wade Burleson behaved "toward his fellow trustees . . . just a general approach to his relationships on the board."

So here you have it. We've gone from gossip and slander to broken trust and resistance to accountability to arrogance and attitude and running roughshod to Wade's general approach to his relationships on the board. We've gone from "due deliberation" and exploring "other options" to "oops, we forgot one." We've gone from "remove Wade Burleson at the convention because he's unfit for trusteeship" to "let's not remove Wade and just handle it internally." We've gone from "remove Wade" to "discipline Wade" to "manage the issues." We've gone from "the evidence of Wade's wrongdoing is forthcoming" to "expect nothing further from the IMB BOT on this matter." We've gone from Wade's blog being a source of "misinformation" that must be corrected to "we are not against Wade's blogging."

Two thoughts in conclusion:

1. A double-minded man is unstable in all his ways. —James 1:8

2. Does anybody else remember the following interviews, or the man who gave them?

"I did not have sex with that woman, Miss Lewinsky."

"Indeed I did have a relationship with Miss Lewinsky that was inappropriate."

Or what about these:

"There are weapons of mass destruction in Iraq . . . mobile laboratories that we must find and destroy before they destroy us. We've exhausted every diplomatic means. The inspectors are being kicked out. Let's go in there and make the world safe again."

"It seems that information we had at first—which seemed reliable—has been proven false. Inspectors were not being duped, because there was no enriched Uranium in Baghdad. But since we're in Iraq anyway, let's just finish the job. I mean, c'mon, these are evil people."[1]

Marty's quick wit infuriated trustee leadership. The time line put into black and white the fumbling attempts to remove a trustee who disagreed with trustee leadership. At the time, Marty did not know about the secret meeting in St. Louis on January 30–31 where Hatley swore he would get the trustees to reverse the recommendation. He did not want me to have the opportunity to speak to the entire SBC. So, to fulfill his vow, Hatley convened a trustee leadership meeting at the end of February in preparation for the full March board meeting and the delicate process of rescinding a recommendation to remove me. It's not easy to take off the table something that you insisted was needed just a few weeks earlier. How do you explain your double-minded ways?

When Hatley convened IMB trustee leadership in Atlanta at the end of February, other trustees were unaware of the secret meeting he had participated in at St. Louis a month earlier. Neither had he made them aware of his pledge to SBC leaders that he would get the motion for my removal reversed. Now he had to fulfill his vow. He had to convince trustee leaders to reverse the motion. Hatley knew I would not apologize, for I had done nothing wrong. Yet, he was now being pressed to answer how and why a rescission should take place.

In one of the most memorable and funniest moments of my tenure as a trustee for the IMB, my wife and I gathered in my Oklahoma office while trustee leaders gathered in Atlanta to try to figure out how to "resolve" the growing controversy of dealing with their recommendation that I be removed from the board. My conversation with Hatley and the other trustees occurred over a speaker phone so my wife could hear it, and a tape recording began about one minute into the conversation when I knew individuals were hedging on promises made to me. There were some hilarious moments in the conversation as trustee leaders began to realize that the motion for my removal was being rescinded without any retraction of my blog posts. Hatley was pressing for motion to be rescinded, and in his odd but roundabout way, he was begging me to help by apologizing for my blog. I wouldn't do it. Frankly, I had become aware of Fundamentalist trustee leaders' tactics, who would charge anybody they didn't like with all kinds of false things only to try to extract an apology for something completely different from the charge. This happened to Rankin when Patterson and Pressler led a charge to allege he misappropriated funds. Rankin was cleared of all charges, but trustees said it would be "good for the board" if Rankin would apologize for "miscommunication." Rankin did, and later some trustees used his apology as proof that Rankin had admitted to misappropriation; for if he hadn't done it, why did he apologize? I told my wife that I would be prepared to defend myself before the entire SBC, but they might as well try to extract turnip juice from a turnip as to extract any apology from me. They were the ones who were backing down, not me.

Here is the transcript from the recorded portion of our conversation:

Tom: The more we've thought about it [the motion for removal from the board], the more that we're inclined to go to our next board meeting and just suggest to our trustees that we withdraw the request of the Southern Baptist Convention. We are going to just take that off the table altogether; not contingent on anything from your end at all. This is just something that we ought to do.

Wade: Well, I'm appreciative. . . . Tom, let me ask a question. I understand that you have said there is nothing that needs to be leveraged or brokered in order to rescind the motion to remove me. I need to know how many IMB trustee leaders are sitting around the table listening to our conversation.

Tom: Okay, we've got the nine that are on the executive committee, which is the standing committee chairman and the officers. Then we have Dr. Rankin and Clyde Meador here.

Wade: All right, I need some wisdom from you. In Oklahoma your efforts to remove me have been pretty big news; the Associated Press, my church, and my hometown newspaper have all made it pretty big news. I guess what I need is wisdom on what will be said when you take your recommendation for my removal off the table. Will there be an explanation as to why you made it in the first place and then remove it so quickly?

Tom: Well, we, that's what this conversation is about. Even after we get off the phone with you we're gonna work on that. We do need some kind of a news release about this and we want it worded well. I've worked on a statement that I might could just put out as chairman that would be constructive. It would probably [be] something such as, "It is my intention to request of our board that we rescind our action in January to recommend to the SBC in June that Wade Burleson be replaced as an IMB trustee. We have found workable options to resolve conflict that were not known during our January meeting. I've consulted with my board officers and with our standing committee chairman and they agree with me that we should move forward with a motion to withdraw our request for SBC action." It's a statement of fact, in other words.

Wade: All right. I'm not sure what you mean by you "found" workable options to resolve the conflict since the January meeting, but I guess it is allowing me to express my concerns to the full board instead of removing me, right?

Tom: Do you have anything working in your heart or head right now that you want to do as far as addressing the board in the March meeting?

Wade: Well, you know, Tom, like I've written to you in e-mails in months past, e-mails I sent to all the trustees, at some point, and again I leave the time to your discretion, I would like to share with the entire board what you heard me share in St. Louis. Our board needs to work to end the undermining of our administration. We cannot function properly as a board if we allow trustees, even some of you men seated around that table, to continually undermine our president. I'll express my concerns to the full board at your discretion; but from the beginning I really feel like folks need to know the story that you now know. We need as a board to deal with the issues I laid out to everyone at St. Louis. I realize that there's disagreement over some things and I understand that. But you have seen the documentation that I have. I think some things must be dealt with if we're going to function as a board that supports our president and staff. If we don't feel like we can, I think we need to remove him, but we can't continue this secret, outside-the-board-meeting attempt to undermine the work of the IMB.

Tom: Yeah, well, I agree with that. I think everybody here now agrees with that as well. I just think that your commitment to doing it within the board instead of making it public is the proper approach.

Wade: Absolutely. . . .

So if I understand you correctly . . . is it your intention is to remove "gossip and slander" from the official record of the IMB?

Tom: The motion to rescind will supersede the motion to remove you. We will withdraw this whole issue from the convention. The original motion is being taken off by this new motion. And basically this new motion rescinds the motion by replacing it.

Wade: Hmm. Tom . . . and forgive me for pressing here, but I just need to be clear for my wife's sake, for my sake.

Tom: Sure.

Wade: The "gossip and the slander" language will not be in the minutes so that one hundred years from now people who read the minutes will not read "Wade Burleson is being recommended for dismissal for gossip and slander."

Tom: I'm not sure; I will have to double check that, but we, you know, I will work on seeing how that can be accomplished.

Wade: I appreciate that, Tom, because that's the issue for me. That's why I can't apologize; because "gossip and slander" is the basis for the motion.

For me to apologize acts as if I am agreeing that I gossiped and I slandered; and I totally deny that. So I guess my spirit is this: I do want reconciliation and I do want to work within the board and I do want to do whatever is possible to make the IMB better, but I cannot issue an apology."

Tom: That's all right. Listen, would you do me a favor and consider this: As I'm thinkin' through this parliamentarily I think all we can do is that we could, in the minutes, we could amend them to have in those minutes in parentheses: "this motion was left moot by a new motion that was adopted at the next meeting." You know what I'm saying? . . .

Wade: Let me reiterate: There will be no apology from me in the statement. There will be an expression of gratefulness for the rescission of the motion and there will be from me an expressed desire to continue to work with my fellow IMB trustees and perform all my duties as a trustee as I have done from the beginning, within the parameters of the Blue Book that guides trustee conduct and behavior.

Tom: Well, that's between you and Jesus, brother. Good point; we're just leavin' that between you and him.

Wade: Okay, my wife wishes to ask a question.

Tom: Yeah.

Wade: She said what about you apologizing to me? What about an apology from trustee leadership for allowing the recommendation for my removal to come before the board in the first place?

Tom: I don't know . . . you want us to apologize to you for making the motion?

Wade: I guess I'm just wondering why I'm being asked to apologize when, if you are the ones retracting the motion . . . ."

Tom: . . . I'm not asking you to apologize, brother.

Lonnie: Wade, the officers and the chairmen, we put no conditions on what—this is Lonnie, by the way— . . . but please, we never have asked for an apology. When Tom first began the conversation today, he said that what we have been discussing is doing this within the trustee family where it needs to be handled to begin with. So what we're going to recommend to our board is not contingent on what you do.

Wade: Lonnie, thank you. I guess we were getting a little confused just because we felt like we were getting off track and I'm sorry. . . . I think you and Tom both can understand that if there's a charge that is floated, say for instance like embezzlement or misappropriation of funds, or slander or gossip, or whatever it may be, and then an apology is issued from the person being falsely charged, and that apology has nothing to do with the charges, then people get really confused as to whether or not somebody is guilty of what he is being charged with doing. . . . The issue before us is a recommendation for removal for gossip and slander, and I know I am not guilty. Nobody even had the Christian decency to point out what they thought was "gossip and slander" behind closed doors, and then you guys removed the language when you went public. I have a hard time apologizing for anything until the recommendation for gossip and slander is off the table.

Tom: It's gonna be off the table.

Wade: Okay, I hear you. I really appreciate that. You have my commitment to work within the process to do what I can to correct the problem of trustees undermining administration in violation of the Blue Book. God bless you guys.

Tom: Yeah, thank you and I appreciate your precious wife as well. I know I'm always better with my wife at my side. Would you do me a favor? Do you have the little blue book "Ordered of God" handy?

Wade: Yes, sir.

Tom: Okay, would you look at page 33? And I'm not gonna read that to you, but just . . . number 18 under 33. If you would just review that and look at it. It's just a statement in there about, you know, what we expect of trustees as far as being positive in public. It is a part of our . . . you could almost make that fit the blog, it requests, that you were talkin' about. If you wanted something to cite to say to your readers, you know, I really need to quit blogging because it's outside of an adopted board policy. You could cite that number 18 if you needed to. If you're looking for a way out, to quit blogging and cite it as a board policy, then that would be a spot where you could pick that.

Wade: Okay, well, in my view I've always been positive about the SBC and our mission work . . . . Of course, I'm not positive about the doctrinal changes. As you know, I believe they violate our convention's understanding that only the convention can establish the doctrinal parameters of our cooperation through the *Baptist Faith & Message*. . . .

Tom: Okay, God bless, brother.

Wade: God bless you.

Tom: Bye-bye.

Wade: Bye.[2]

The above conversation, behind closed doors, shows the utter ridiculousness of trustee leadership's logic in trying to remove me from the board. The desire to get rid of me was pure politics. Southern Baptist Fundamentalist leaders are not used to people opposing them—and getting by with it.

Notes

1. *SBC Outpost* is no longer online.

2. See the Appendix for a complete transcript of the conversation.

Chapter 14

A UNANIMOUS REVERSAL

IMB Trustee Meeting
Tampa, Florida
March 2006

The next International Mission Board trustee meeting was scheduled for Monday through Wednesday, March 20–22, in Tampa, Florida. I arrived in Tampa on Monday to attend the trustee forum. I had not spoken with Tom Hatley since the February meeting in St. Louis, and since that meeting was held in secret at the request of Bobby Welch and Morris Chapman, the trustees of the IMB did not know it had taken place. But all of trustee leadership knew that Hatley was pressing that the motion for my removal be reversed, and this did not make them happy.

The trustee forum is a closed-door meeting where trustees are free to say whatever they wish with impunity from the SBC. I cannot stand these meetings because cowards use them to say what they refuse to say in public. At this particular trustee forum, Chuck McAlister and Jerry Corbaley let it be known that they were furious that the motion for my removal was being reversed. They demanded that I apologize. I silently sat as they addressed me in the third person in order to influence the board.

McAlister's speech behind closed doors was probably one of the most humorous I've ever heard. He said he would vote for the rescission of the motion to remove me from the board if he could be guaranteed four things: (1) I would never be allowed to speak into a microphone during my entire tenure as a trustee; (2) trustee leadership would contact the nominating committee and demand that I not be given a second term; (3) I would not be assigned to a committee; and (4) I would pay my own way to all trustee meetings.

I leaned over to Rick Thompson and told him I would vote for Chuck's recommendation. He raised his eyebrows at me. I then told him I'd be the richest man in the SBC because every lady involved in the WMU and concerned about international missions would send me money to pay my way to be at the meetings. Rick laughed and probably didn't hear Chuck say he would vote for the rescission if his proposal were approved. Jerry Corbaley agreed with Chuck, and said the thought that I would serve another eight years as a trustee on the IMB, outlasting all other trustees, made him sick. None of the other trustees supported Chuck's proposal.

I listened to about two hours of trustees discussing the pros and cons of reversing their motion, and by the end of the forum, when everyone seemed resigned that the motion to rescind would need to happen or I would be given a platform at the convention to speak when the time came for a vote. Right before the trustees were called upon to vote, a pastor from a small church in Oklahoma, Mike Butler, stood up and asked if I would apologize to the board for my blog. Mike is a good guy, mild-mannered, and possesses a sweet spirit. However, Mike doesn't seem to understand what it means to stand on principle and not waver. My blog was designed to stop what I believed to be violations of Baptist principle, and I refused to apologize for it. So, in response to Mike's request that I apologize, I stood before the trustees and said, "Not only will I not apologize for my blog, I stand behind every word, sentence, and paragraph ever written on it. And for those of you who have not read my blog, the address is www.kerrussocharis.com."

This, of course, infuriated trustee leadership, but I wanted trustees to know that when this motion was rescinded, it was being rescinded without me giving one inch on the issues that troubled me in the first place. When the trustees voted on the motion to rescind their request that I be removed, the motion passed unanimously. I guess Chuck and Jerry had second thoughts about Chuck's four-part proposal. I can honestly say that any respect I had for trustee leadership was lost at that moment. To push hurriedly for a motion to remove me in January 2006, to tell trustees that the "evidence" for the need for my removal would come later, to refuse in the intervening days to give any evidence for the motion, and then to rescind the motion unanimously less than sixty days after it first passed—without me giving an inch—signifies that they don't know what it means to stand on principle. Their approach to "deal" with me was both political and personal.

Corbaley kept writing tomes to trustees in which he called me every name in the book. He had informed everyone that he was writing a book titled *The Most Excellent Way* that allegedly encouraged Christians to treat people with love. Every time I received a carbon copy of Corbaley's diatribes about me, sent to all the trustees, I would tell my wife that Jerry was up to his most excellent ways. Corbaley and McAlister are two men cut from the same emotional cloth. Both possess the ability to spiritualize their anger while justifying their angry actions. Many trustees had a knack for calling people "gossips," "slanderers," "liars," and other such names, all the while attempting to maintain the spiritual façade.

Associated Baptist Press reporter Greg Warner gives an excellent example of this. Warner was present at the March 2006 IMB trustee meeting and accurately described the attack on Jerry Rankin by several of his own trustees, led by former IMB employee and then current trustee David Button. Warner wrote,

> In the board's first plenary session, Rankin showed trustees a videotape of his chapel address to employees delivered soon after trustees approved new policies in November defining a proper baptism for new missionaries and prohibiting their use of a "private prayer language" (a form of speaking in tongues).
>
> Some IMB trustees have said privately the new policy prohibiting "private prayer language"—which applies only to new missionaries—was an attempt to embarrass Rankin, who has acknowledged using the practice, or force him to resign.
>
> The videotaped message has become a point of controversy between Rankin and some trustees, including one who was denied a copy of it before the board meeting.
>
> On the tape, Rankin said he "did not agree with these policies," which are "more restrictive." Nonetheless, he said, he will enforce the policies because God has placed him under the trustees' authority.
>
> "I can't control the actions of our board or the statements that others make," Rankin said. "There is only one thing I can control and that's my heart. Whatever is happening around us, whatever it is, however harmful or hurtful or painful it might be, or however untrue or slanderous it might be, we don't lash out. We can't attack. We can't defend ourselves. That's the fleshly nature. All we can do is guard our heart.
>
> Rankin said such differences, which "can disrupt our focus" on spreading the gospel, are evidence of spiritual warfare. "The spiritual nature of our task of reaching a lost world is so critical and important to the heart of God that our enemy is not just going to roll over and relinquish the dominions of darkness and power becoming the kingdoms of our Lord," he said. Rankin added, "It's not our trustees [causing the disruption]. These are men and women who love the Lord."

After the videotape was shown, Rankin said he was "compelled" to add: "We are not aware, on the field, of any doctrinal problems" with missionaries. If there are problems, he said, they are dealt with swiftly through an established process. "You screened them," he told trustees. "You examined their denominational loyalty, their faith, their church background and commitment, their affirmation of the '*Baptist Faith & Message.*' And our [staff] regional leaders are in touch with them, monitoring them. If there were any problems of doctrinal aberrations, of charismatic influences or practices, or even tolerance, or anyone not [properly] practicing baptism, or contributing in any way to ecumenical-type practices, we would know about it and deal with it.

"It is disrespectful to missionaries, those giving their lives and sacrifices and taking their families and laying their lives on the line, that anyone, without identifying and verifying facts, would spread rumors and innuendoes about doctrinal issues on the field. I want to make a public comment and stand for our missionaries in defense of their faithfulness."

Trustee Jerry Corbaley told Rankin his statement that there are no doctrinal problems on the field "seems to be in direct conflict with the fact we are dealing with several such instances now."

Rankin said the two controversial policies were adopted in part because of accusations that the IMB was sending out missionaries who were "not truly Baptists" or who were supporting ecumenism or charismatic practices.

"I've asked for evidence, for verification," he said. "If that is so, then tell us who and where, and we'll deal with it. But I have yet to have anyone document where there is a problem that we aren't dealing with or haven't dealt with when we became aware of it."

"That's not true," trustee chairman Tom Hatley shot back. "We've done that in several instances."

When those problems have been identified by trustees, Hatley said, the staff has dealt with them appropriately. But to say no doctrinal problems have been identified is an overstatement, the chairman added. "My point is," Rankin said, "we do have a process and are dealing with the [problems]."

Hatley, a pastor from Arkansas, said trustees have avoided naming names in their accusations because of the need for confidentiality in trustee proceedings, not a desire "to cover up fact." "We must speak in generalities," he said. Earlier in the meeting, after Rankin showed his videotaped address, trustee David Button of New York complained that his request for a copy of the tape in early February was denied four times by Rankin.

"I never once questioned your motives," said Button. "As a trustee, I think information that comes out of the board ought to be information we ought to have as trustees. . . . I believe the request of this tape was a reasonable request."

"I wasn't making a public statement," Rankin said. His message to employees was an internal communication "on a very sensitive subject," he said. "I felt I had the prerogative of how that is to be distributed."

Rankin said that he was worried excerpts from the message could be taken "out of context" and that it was best to show the full speech to all trustees at the same time.

"Trustees are not to involve themselves in administration," he reminded the board, adding later, "I do not have accountability to 89 trustees" but to the full board.

Several trustees said Button's request for the tape should have been honored, while others said Rankin handled the situation "prudently."

Button is one of at least three former IMB employees elected in recent years as trustees of the agency. A former vice president for public relations under Rankin, Button left the IMB in 2000 under strained relations with the administration.

Button, a local radio-TV executive, brought up the videotape request two other times during the trustees' meeting. "I don't believe that a trustee should act unilaterally on any information they receive, but a trustee should receive everything they ask for," he said.

Near the end of the meeting, Button made a motion that the IMB staff "shall honor all trustee requests for information, subject to the discretion of the chairman."

"How do we prevent the egregious overuse of privilege like we have seen in the last few months?" he argued. He accused Rankin's administration of "arbitrary and excessive" control "to keep trustees from receiving the information that they request."

After the board's lawyer warned such a policy might present "a host of issues" and encroach "somewhat on the prerogatives of the president," chairman Hatley referred the motion to the trustees' administration committee for study.

"We don't want to limit information at all," Hatley said, but a review of the motion would be "advisable."[1]

Warner's written account of the trustee attack on Dr. Rankin is accurate and impartial. It would be difficult for Baptist Press to report with such honesty on the proceedings of that trustee meeting because of the SBC's desire to portray everything as wonderful. This, again, is one of the reasons I believe it is always best to have independent news agencies in the Southern Baptist Convention rather than an arm of the executive committee. Warner's account of that meeting is one of the rare times when the animosity of trustees toward Rankin bled over into the public meetings. Chairman Hatley called Rankin a liar. Corbaley, in essence, said the same thing publicly. Button accused Rankin of a lack of integrity. Multiply these things said publicly by a hundredfold and I imagine it will be close to what was being said about Rankin privately.

The March 2006 IMB trustee meeting in Tampa Bay allowed the trustees to correct the egregious mistake of rashly requesting my removal before they would have to answer for their actions to the Southern Baptist Convention in June. But the meeting also afforded the trustees the worst policy ever adopted by any Baptist agency in the history of the Southern Baptist Convention.

Note

1. Greg Warner, "IMB Trustees Clash with Rankin over Doctrinal Charges, Information Access," Associated Baptist Press, 24 March 2006, http://www.abpnews.com/index.php?option=com_content&task=view&id=1013&Itemid=119 (19 January 2009).

Chapter 15

KEEP YOUR MOUTH SHUT
AND YOUR PEN SILENT

The "Burleson Guidelines"
March 2006

When the trustees of the International Mission Board voted unanimously to reverse their recommendation to remove me from the board at the March 2006 Tampa Bay, Florida, IMB meeting, they approved a new set of "trustee accountability" policies that replaced the former set of trustee guidelines known as the "Blue Book." When I confronted trustee leadership in January 2006 regarding their violations of Blue Book policies, such as convening in private caucus meetings to conduct IMB business, they were furious. When they sought to remove me from the board as retribution, the attorney for the International Mission Board told them there was nothing in my blog that violated the Blue Book, which guides trustee conduct and behavior. I had been informed during the February 2006 phone call with trustee leadership that changes to the Blue Book were coming. However, I was led to believe the changes were such that would give me an opportunity to take appropriate action against any trustee who violated rules of conduct and went about to undermine the people we were called to support, namely Jerry Rankin.

However, trustee leadership took a different approach. Trustee leadership wrote what some called the "Burleson Guidelines," in essence a total rewrite of the Blue Book that formerly governed trustee conduct. These new trustee accountability guidelines were pushed through at the same March 2006 IMB meeting where the motion for my rescission was reversed, in order to prevent any criticism of their actions. The four-page proposed document on trustee accountability, delivered to all trustees Tuesday night, March 21, 2006, at the conclusion of the plenary session, ended with the following statement: "Note, this policy supersedes the document, Ordered by God, Manual for

Trustees (The Blue Book), which now becomes a reference document." The statement was large and in bold letters. However, trustee leadership later removed that statement (without informing trustees), before we trustees voted on the new policies. We were told at the time of the vote that the new trustee guidelines were "additions" to the Blue Book.

That is why Baptist Press eventually reported that the new trustee accountability policies "add to, but [don't] replace, the older policy, dubbed the "Blue Book."[1] I did not recall hearing that said in business session, and I'm sure the reporter received this information from trustee leadership after the meeting. There is an old saying that attempts to cover one's mistakes only lead to more mistakes. The new trustee conduct policies pushed through by trustee leadership in this March meeting are the worst policies any board of the Southern Baptist Convention has enforced in the history of the SBC.

The Blue Book had stated, "A trustee is to bring (his/her) voice to the meetings when serving, but is to also take (his/her) interpretations back to the people after adjournment" (p. 33). We are called to put in a good word for the organization (the IMB). But the new trustee accountability policies document states, "Individual IMB trustees must refrain from public criticism of board-approved actions."

Any public interpretation of the board-approved actions may now not include criticism from individual trustees. In 1987 IMB trustees adopted the well-written fifty-page policy manual that governed our trustee responsibilities and accountability (the Blue Book), but in March 2006 IMB trustees were asked to adopt this four-page document that would supersede (or add to) the Blue Book, and that prohibits any dissension or criticism of board actions. Ironically, if this "trustee policy on conduct" had been in effect in the 1980s, there never would have been a conservative resurgence. Trustees appointed by conservative SBC presidents made their concerns public—over and over again. These new policies to "control" trustee conduct were rushed through for approval by IMB trustee leadership. Again, in my opinion, they were the most poorly conceived, poorly written policies ever adopted by any SBC board. Baptist Press gave an accurate accounting of the trustee debate before the vote.

> Trustee Allen McWhite of South Carolina spoke against the recommenda-
> tion, specifically the document's provision that says "individual IMB
> trustees must refrain from public criticism of board-approved actions. . . .
> Freedom of expression must give way to the imperative that the work of

the Kingdom not be placed at risk by publicly airing differences within the board."

McWhite voiced concern that any trustee who felt a board action was not in the best interest of the larger Southern Baptist constituency would not be able to express that concern to fellow Southern Baptists.

"I want to draw a great distinction between being critical of this board, which I would never do, and expressing disagreement, honestly, based upon personal conviction with a board policy or action," McWhite said. "I would hope no trustee would ever want to be put in the position where he or she could not share with the larger constituency. . . . The possibility exists that this may really tie our hands in some matters."

McWhite also said, "I believe my trusteeship primarily is to the Southern Baptist Convention. They are the ones who have given me that trust. Out of trust, I must relate to my other trustees in a trustworthy manner."

But trustee Randy Davis of Tennessee, referencing the ability to speak out against board policy, said, "[W]hen we become trustees we give up some things, and that's one of the things that we give up. . . . The first thing we learn is that we do not campaign against the board that we are serving on. . . . I especially appreciate the accountability built into [the document]. That's new, and that's different, and that's been needed a long time."

Another comment in favor of the motion came from trustee John Schaefer of Georgia. He said trustees have opportunities to voice concerns or disagreements at the time a board action is being discussed.

"The key point we all need to recognize is that once this board has voted and spoken that your personal opinion or preference or concern does not go to head of the line," Schaefer said. "Our . . . missionaries are far more important than your one mindset. And we have to put the greater good of our mission force before your own personal opinion. You have an opportunity to voice your concern or criticism prior to that approved policy, so I suggest you pay attention to proposed policy changes and make yourself heard."

Trustee David Button of New York added: "Ephesians 4:3, 'maintaining the unity of the spirit in the bonds of peace,' trumps our constitutional desire to protect our free speech after a decision has been made. We've not seen that over the past couple of months. We've had things that are tearing our board apart. . . . It's a good policy [that] adheres to those biblical maxims."[2]

I wonder if David Button would argue that the conservative resurgence "tore boards apart"? I wonder if Randy Davis has the ability to comprehend the illogic of his statement, and whether or not he believes Martin Luther in the sixteenth century in his struggle against the Roman Catholic Church, or seventeenth-century English Baptists imprisoned for their refusal to submit to secular authorities, or World War II German Baptists such as Dietrich Bonhoeffer would all agree with him and his bizarre views about dissent? Trustee leadership only wanted to still the pens and silent the mouths of those who disagreed with them.

The Arkansas *Democrat-Gazette* ran an article a few days after the March 2006 trustee meeting in which the reporter quotes Chairman Hatley talking about the unanimous action of the board to rescind the recommendation for my removal. The reporter wrote that Hatley said to her,

> Burleson is in a "status pending" and cannot serve on any International Mission Board committees until issues between him and other board members are reconciled. We're going to deal with some of those problems we've had in relationships with him under these new guidelines. Burleson aired information and criticism that is not proper for a trustee to engage in a public forum, and his blog is a public forum. The content of Burleson's blog is the issue.[3]

Hatley's comments to the reporter from his home state make obvious what trustee leadership was attempting to do to me. There had been no public distribution of the basis for the charge that my blog contains information and criticism that was *not proper*. Proper by whose standards? The Blue Book's standards? The IMB attorney's standards? Or by trustee leadership's standards, which were now made official by the adoption of what Hatley called "these new guidelines"? Of course, it was the latter.

I had followed the Blue Book meticulously as I began to blog in December 2005 and through the middle of March 2006. I followed all policies that were in effect at that time. Therefore, any criticism or information on my blog about board-approved actions or board-approved policies was perfectly legitimate and proper and within trustee guidelines. Of course, the new March 2006 policies that forbid criticism of board-approved actions made my old posts improper, but the new policies were not retroactive. So when Chairman Hatley said to the Arkansas newspaper in March 2006 that my blog contained "information and criticism that is not proper for a trustee to engage in a public forum," he and other trustee leaders did what anyone who abuses authority always does. If they don't like what you are saying, but you are abiding by the rules, then they change the rules.

The ridiculous policy that passed in March 2006 forbade "individual IMB trustees . . . from public criticism of board-approved actions." I guess Southern Baptists have forgotten that it is possible to criticize without disparagement and that it is entirely Christian to dissent without bitterness. For whatever reason, IMB trustee leadership felt that anybody who disagreed with them was not Christian enough, not Baptist enough, not "one of us." If that policy is allowed to stand, it is the end of the Southern Baptist Convention as we know it. Therefore, I voted against it, and continued to express my dissent over the passage of the new doctrinal policies and any other decision that I felt was detrimental to the fabric of Southern Baptist cooperation.

Though, on the whole, the new trustee guidelines regarding conduct were terribly written, I wholeheartedly agree with a few things added under the section called "General Responsibilities" in terms of our conduct: "Trustees are to refrain from speaking in disparaging terms about IMB personnel and fellow trustees." To disparage is to speak of in a slighting or disrespectful way or to belittle. I fully affirm that statement, and every one of my previous posts while serving as a trustee would have met that standard. But it is interesting to me that trustee leadership came out of that March 2006 meeting with a disparaging statement against me, violating their own new policies. Again, it's all right for trustees in control to criticize anyone who threatens that control, but it is not all right for anyone to criticize them.

The official recommendation for my removal in January stated that I was being removed for "gossip and slander." But when trustee leadership released to the press and the public the reason for my removal shortly after the vote, they said the reason was "resistance to accountability and loss of trust." Trustee leadership hid the wording of the official recommendation from the public. Even when they unanimously voted to rescind the official motion, they hid the official minutes from the public. The January 2006 IMB meeting minutes were not approved until a closed-door session in March and weren't released until June. I was told by a reliable source that the fear of those minutes being released publicly resulted from the danger of possibly being sued for alleging "gossip and slander" without offering proof. Trustee leaders were fearful of defamation charges.

Though I had no intention of suing anyone, it felt like mud-slinging when "gossip and slander" were charged against me with no written substantiation. When Hatley, Corbaley, and others were pressed to provide evidence of their charges, they claimed that they did not wish to make public things that would embarrass me. Anyone who thinks through that ludicrous logic would understand that everything I have written is already public—it is on a blog. Matthew 18 commands a Christian to address offense privately before making a charge publicly. Show me the improper content and I will vigorously defend it according to policy and documentation, or I will "repent" if I can be shown I am wrong. The reason that was never done is because they knew they couldn't prove "gossip," and they couldn't prove "slander." I was open, public, and truthful.

Because I had adhered to trustee conduct policies from the beginning of my service as a trustee in 2005, what makes the content of my blog, as Hatley says, "not proper"? This is the heart of the issue. I believed I was fulfilling my duty according to IMB trustee policy. Even more, I felt compelled to write my blog because of what the Blue Book demanded of IMB trustees. The Blue Book reminded me that I had a fiduciary responsibility to the entire convention, not just to my fellow trustees.

That I wouldn't stop blogging despite the insistence of trustee leadership is what became "resistance to accountability" and their "loss of trust" in me. Trustee leadership said, "Wade won't do what we say." Wade said, "I will do what the policy demands." Impasse. When trustee leadership decided in March 2006 that they couldn't defend to the entire convention their motion for my removal (because my blog met all trustee conduct policies) they decided to adopt new policies to solve the impasse.

I debated whether or not I should stop blogging after the March 2006 IMB trustee meeting, but I chose to continue for the good of the convention and my personal insurance against spurious attacks by trustee leaders. I also had seen trustee leadership go back on their word to me on several occasions, and I felt the blog was my only protection against trustee leadership saying one thing to me one day, and then reversing themselves when speaking to others the next. It was my intention to focus on missions, raise awareness of the needs of our missionaries around the world, and increase Cooperative Program giving through my blog. But, unfortunately, events forthcoming at the next trustee meeting in Albuquerque, New Mexico, in May 2006 caused me to realize I had to take this battle against Fundamentalism all the way to the Southern Baptist Convention.

My church, my family, and my friends will tell you that I am easy to get along with and gracious to those who have failed. But I can be a bulldog when I see an injustice, and I will not back down to bullies. What Tom Hatley did at our May 2006 trustee meeting gave me clarity as to what I needed to do to help turn around the ship we call the SBC, and it gave me a much sharper pen in my attempts to correct it. But from March 2006 to May 2006, I used my blog simply to articulate the problems we faced in the Southern Baptist Convention at SBC agencies and boards where Fundamentalist trustees sought to narrow the doctrinal requirements for cooperation. These backdoor attempts to change the SBC needed to be confronted, but I felt that, until the SBC understood the issues at stake, it would be difficult to rally Southern Baptists to turn the tide toward more cooperation and acceptance of diversity among conservatives. For that reason, I spent a couple of months in spring 2006 writing several posts that articulated the issues in the SBC.

Notes

1. Michael Chute, "Trustees at IMB Meeting Adopt New Document Regarding 'Public Criticism,' Formalize New Missionary Selection Process," Baptist Press, 23 March 2006, http://www.bpnews.net/bpnews.asp?ID=22898.

2. Ibid.

3. "A Move toward Transparency Is Needed," 4 March 2006, http://kerussocharis .blogspot.com/2006/03/move-toward-transparency-is-needed.html.

Chapter 16

RELIGIOUS LIBERTY AND BAPTIST FREEDOM

On March 30, 2006, I wrote a post on *Grace and Truth to You* that articulated my personal dream for the Southern Baptist Convention.[1] I stated that it included three visions for our convention. First, *I desired liberty for the people within the SBC.* One of the basic tenets of Baptists throughout the ages is liberty. Baptists in America, including the brilliant Isaac Backus, were influential in establishing the constitutional freedoms we enjoy as United States citizens.

I have a dream where we have a convention that is characterized by liberty; liberty of conscience, liberty of dissent, liberty of the soul. The privilege of dissent is especially vital for the health of our convention. It is possible for the majority to make decisions that are not healthy for the convention in the long run, but through patient, loving dissent, there is the real possibility that unhealthy decisions may be reversed.

Many are aware of the majority decision of Bethlehem Baptist Church in Minneapolis, Minnesota, where the elders voted to accept into membership those who had been baptized as infants. Not as many are aware that only one elder of the church opposed the new membership policy in the beginning, and that through the liberty granted that lone elder to dissent, even after approval of the policy, Bethlehem Baptist Church elders have since reversed the previous action and remained committed to the biblical view of baptism.

Liberty of dissent sharpens us. It strengthens us. I have a dream that we have a convention that is not fearful of dissent, but embraces it as part of our heritage, welcomes it as a vital member of our Baptist family, and sees it as a blessing and benefit. Frankly, that is why I love being a Baptist. I can disagree with my brother on the interpretations of nonessential texts (nonessential as it regards the salvation of the soul), and still fellowship and cooperate with my brother on the mission field and through the Cooperative Program as we seek to reach our world for Christ. Yes, we need our confessions. However, let's be slow to tamper with our confessions. We must absolutely not allow anyone to narrow the parameters of fellowship and cooperation beyond our confessions. And let's hold sacred the principles of liberty so that we do not become a creedal people, a denominational sect, and in the end, a people more concerned about jots and tittles than God and people.

The second part of my dream for the SBC includes *love for the world outside the SBC.* The kingdom of God is bigger than the Southern Baptist Convention. God's kingdom includes all the elect from every nation, tribe, kindred, and tongue, and it transcends any one denominational boundary. I have a dream that Southern Baptists see the hand of God at work in other evangelical venues and, where possible, join in the efforts of those of like faith to win the world for Christ. In many cases we will be the forerunners of the gospel, reaching nations, peoples, and lands where the gospel has little presence. Where we lead the charge, I pray that we will welcome the support of other evangelical witnesses who follow. The world is too big, the time is too short, and the lost are too many to believe that we Southern Baptists can do it alone.

I look forward to the day when a missionary for the Southern Baptist Convention can minister to his people group without concern of what others say of his partners, without fear of someone looking over his shoulder for heresy, and with the singular aim, seared into his heart, of reaching others for Jesus Christ. Great Commission churches and like-minded missions organizations are those with whom we can, and should, have great partnerships. When our missionaries are on the fields of the Far East, Middle East, Near East, and all lands in between, we must empower those missionaries to find like-minded evangelicals and work together to reach their people groups for Christ.

A generation of Southern Baptists is being raised in an evangelical culture different from the previous generation of Southern Baptists. These young, evangelical men and women not only want to support missions, but they want to *do* missions. Frankly, they are more concerned about a mission partner's love for Christ than they are their denominational affiliation. To the extent we capture and mobilize the hearts of these young Southern Baptists, we will also further expand our reach into a lost and dark world. I have a dream that when we speak of evangelizing the lost and winning the world for Christ, it is not simply the slogan of a new program, but the passion of the hearts of thousands of Southern Baptists being heard and felt as we join our hands together in cooperation to accomplish our task.

When we as Southern Baptists are more concerned for the lost than we are that we get the credit for the new church plants, then we will truly be kingdom minded. When we are more concerned for the lost than we are to separate from any evangelical who is not called a Southern Baptist, then we will be truly kingdom minded. God has called all his disciples to be Great Commission disciples, and to the extent that we participate with other Great Commission disciples all over this world to fulfill our Lord's command, we will also fulfill that commission given to us.

The final portion of my dream for the SBC includes *loyalty from the churches in the SBC*. I have a dream that every Southern Baptist church will be loyal and faithful to contribute to the Cooperative Program, and to all our agency offerings, particularly the Lottie Moon offering. I am of the opinion, however, that to demand loyalty without allowing freedom to dissent or exhibiting a love for others outside the SBC will be like putting the cart before the horse.

I received an e-mail from Pastor Chris Keathly in spring 2006. Chris is a doctoral student at Southern and a lifelong Southern Baptist. He related to me an incident where he and a fellow pastor were discussing issues related to the Southern Baptist Convention. Remembering a book he had been given years earlier that seemed to address some of the concerns they discussed, Chris went to his library and pulled from his shelves a commentary written by Dr. Hershel Hobbs, longtime pastor of FBC Oklahoma City, Oklahoma, and former president of the Southern Baptist Convention. Chris related to me what he read:

> As I reread the commentary I was given as a young man by Hershel Hobbs, I was encouraged that I had been taught correctly who we were as Southern Baptists. Hobbs stated that "in reality Baptists are the most broad-minded of all people in religion. They grant to every man the right that he shall be free to believe as he wants. But they insist upon the same right for themselves. The moment that a Baptist seeks to coerce another person—even another Baptist—in matters of religion, he violates the basic belief of Baptists." He continues to state that "in all likelihood the only thing that would divide Southern Baptists with regard to their faith would be for one group—to the right or left of center or even in the center—to attempt to force upon others a creedal faith. So long as they hold to the

competency of the soul in religion they will remain as one body in the faith."[2]

The *Baptist Messenger* in Oklahoma once ran a four-page article on the different soteriological views of salvation among Southern Baptists. I presented one view, and Dr. Hobbs presented another. Before Dr. Hobbs died, I interviewed him for four hours in the executive board room of the Baptist General Convention of Oklahoma headquarters for an article I was writing. Dr. Hobbs and I did not see eye to eye on all things, but I respected this man immensely. He represented to me what a Baptist should be in deportment and spirit. I think the words of the late Dr. Hobbs encapsulate the attitude that is required in the Southern Baptist Convention before my dream for the SBC is realized.

The Southern Baptist Convention seems to be in danger of being killed by disputes of minute doctrines. Charles Spurgeon, the great prince of preachers, articulates for us well the importance of having missionaries consumed with Christ:

> I do not know whether all our missionaries have caught the idea of Christ—"Go ye and teach all nations," but many of them have, and these have been honored with many conversions.
>
> The more fully they have been simple teachers, not philosophers of the Western philosophy, not eager disputants concerning some English dogma, I say the more plainly they have gone forth as teachers sent from God to teach the world, the more successful have they been.
>
> "Go ye, therefore, and teach." Some may think, perhaps, there is less difficulty in teaching the learned than in teaching the uncivilized and barbarous. There is the same duty to the one as to the other: "Go and teach."
>
> "But they brandish the tomahawk." Teach them, and lie down and sleep in their hut, and they shall marvel at your fearlessness and spare your life.
>
> "But they feed on the blood of their fellows, they make a bloody feast about the cauldron in which a man's body is the horrible viand." Teach them and they shall empty their war-kettle, and they shall bury their swords, and bow before you, and acknowledge King Jesus.
>
> "But they are brutalised, they have scarce a language—a few clicking sounds make up all that they can say." Teach them, and they shall speak the language of Canaan, and sing the songs of heaven.
>
> The fact has been proved, brethren, that there are no nations incapable of being taught, nay, that there are no nations incapable afterwards of

teaching others. The Negro slave has perished under the lash, rather than dishonor his Master.

The Esquimaux has climbed his barren steeps, and borne his toil, while he has recollected the burden which Jesus bore. The Hindoo has patiently submitted to the loss of all things, because he loved Christ better than all. Feeble Malagasay women have been prepared to suffer and to die, and have taken joyfully suffering for Christ's sake. There has been heroism in every land for Christ; men of every color and of every race have died for him; upon his altar has been found the blood of all kindreds that be upon the face of the earth.

Oh! tell me not they cannot be taught. Sirs, they can be taught to die for Christ; and this is more than some of you have learned. They can rehearse the very highest lesson of the Christian religion—that self sacrifice which knows not itself but gives up all for him.

At this day there are Karen missionaries preaching among the Karens with as fervid an eloquence as ever was known by Whitfield, there are Chinese teaching in Borneo, Sumatra, and Australia, with as much earnestness as Morison or Milne first taught in China. There are Hindoo evangelists who are not ashamed to have given up the Brahminical thread, and to eat with the Pariah, and to preach with him the riches of Christ. There have been men found of every class and kind, not only able to be taught, but able to become teachers themselves, and the most mighty teachers too, of the grace of the Lord Jesus Christ.

Well was that command warranted by future facts, when Christ said, "Go ye, teach all nations."[3]

I have believed that the Southern Baptist Convention is in danger of ending. Words are meaningless without definitions. I realize that vocabulary is the foundation of all communication, and unless the meanings of words are properly defined, effective communication is impossible. The word "Fundamentalism" needs to be defined.

John Piper's book *Contending for Our All* highlights the life of Dr. Gresham Machen, professor of New Testament at Princeton University in the early part of the last century. Dr. Machen was fired from Princeton and later stripped of his ordination in the Presbyterian Church USA for "insubordination." It seems he questioned various policies of the Presbyterian USA Mission Board, which led to his censure and eventually to the formation of an alternative missions-sending agency begun by Dr. Machen. He also founded Westminster Seminary just a few months before his unexpected death on New Year's Day 1936 at the young age of fifty-five. He died a hero of the Fundamentalists of his day because of his "insistence on defending great doctrines that had come under particular attack by vigorously defending the truth."[4]

However, Machen did not like being called a "Fundamentalist." Listen to his own words: "Do you suppose that I do regret my being called by a term that I greatly dislike, a 'Fundamentalist'? Most certainly I do. But in the presence of a great common foe [liberalism], I have little time to be attacking my brethren who stand with me in defense of the Word of God."[5]

Piper gives seven reasons why Machen never spoke of himself as a Fundamentalist. To Machen, Fundamentalism meant (1) the absence of historical perspective; (2) the lack of appreciation of scholarship; (3) the substitution of brief, skeletal creeds for the historic confessions; (4) the lack of concern with precise formulation of Christian doctrine; (5) the pietistic, perfectionist tendencies (i.e., hang-ups with smoking, drinking alcohol, etc.); (6) one-sided otherworldliness (i.e., a lack of effort to transform the culture); and (7) a penchant for futuristic chiliasm (or premillennialism).[6]

Machen was on "the other side" of all seven of these issues, yet God used him greatly to preserve conservative evangelicalism within his beloved Presbyterian denomination. He is the epitome of a conservative evangelical who could not be considered a "Fundamentalist."

I have been praying that God will grant the grace and wisdom needed to see that within our Southern Baptist Convention, there are thousands of pastors and people who share the same spirit of Machen—warmly conservative and fervently evangelical but not "Fundamentalist" as defined by Machen. The SBC is large enough for all of us who are conservative and evangelical to cooperate together. Will our Fundamentalist brethren within the SBC, with whom we sided in the liberal debates of yesteryear, stand willing to cooperate with those of us who disagree with them on periphery issues?

I was about to discover at the May 2006 IMB trustee meeting in Albuquerque, New Mexico, that some of our brethren would stop at nothing to get people out of the SBC who dare to disagree with them.

Notes

1. "I Have a Dream for the SBC," 20 March 2006, http://kerussocharis.blogspot.com/2006/03/i-have-dream-for-sbc_30.html.

2. Chris Keathly, e-mail to Wade Burleson, 30 March 2006; Herschel H. Hobbs, *The People Called Baptists and the Baptist Faith & Message*, The Herschel H. and Frances J. Hobbs Lectureship in Baptist Faith and Heritage (Shawnee OK: Oklahoma Baptist University, 1981), 28.

3. Charles Spurgeon, "The Missionary's Charge and Charta," in *Classic Sermons on World Evangelism,* comp. William Wiersbe (Kregel Academic & Professional, 1999). Spurgeon preached this sermon April 21, 1861, Metropolitan Tabernacle, Newington, England.

4. Ned B. Stonehouse, *J. Gresham Machen* (Willow Grove PA: Committee for the Historian of the OPC, 2004), 336.

5. John Piper, *Contending for Our All* (Wheaton IL: Crossway Books, 2007), 337.

6. Ibid., 127.

Chapter 17

"TURN OFF HIS MIC"

IMB Trustee Meeting
Albuquerque, New Mexico
May 2006

My wife, Rachelle, and I arrived in Albuquerque, New Mexico, via Denver about 6:00 p.m. Sunday night, May 21, 2006, for the IMB trustee meeting. We enjoyed a great dinner, and as we left the restaurant I had the pleasure of introducing Rachelle to Johnny and Margie Nantz, the pastor and wife of First Baptist Church, Las Vegas, Nevada. Johnny had served on the IMB for the term limit of eight years, and this was his last meeting. I have found Johnny to be a sincere, humble, and wise man. He is a person whom I quickly learned both to appreciate and admire. With Johnny and Margie was fellow IMB trustee Paul Brown and his wife, Ruth. The fellowship with these four was quite enjoyable and yet another confirmation to me that the SBC has some absolutely stellar people.

During dinner, Johnny and Margie shared with us the story of their thirty-one-year-old missionary daughter in Africa. Three weeks earlier, Muslim men had kidnapped her at gunpoint and driven her deep into the African jungle, where she eventually escaped. The vivid details of the kidnapping, the near death of the Nantz's daughter, her remarkable display of courage and faith, and the incredible providential events that led to her miraculous escape sent chills up my spine. It caused me to remember that the ultimate goal of our board is to be a lifeline and support team for those men and women God has called to proclaim the gospel of Jesus Christ on the front lines of spiritual darkness.

I left the restaurant realizing that no matter the personal costs for doing what I believe is right, they pale in comparison to anything 5,400 SBC missionaries do every day to serve our Savior. I know all the missionaries would say they enjoy their ministry and don't consider themselves paying a price, but the Nantz's story was a fresh reminder to me of what is important about my service to the IMB—protecting and supporting our missionaries. That support includes freeing and empowering them to fulfill completely the call of God upon their lives in the people group to whom he has brought them.

There were no public meetings of the IMB scheduled for Monday, but I did attend the closed-door forum. The forum was uneventful except for a debate over the recommendation of a "blue-ribbon panel" to evaluate the "new doctrinal policies." What happened after the closed door forum was far more interesting. Trustee leaders, led by Tom Hatley, were angry that I was able to attend the IMB trustee meetings while continuing to blog. They also felt embarrassed they had failed to remove me, so they were on point to attempt, once again, to embarrass me.

I had communicated on my blog my good-faith effort to continue working with all the IMB trustees before the meeting in Albuquerque. I shared that I did not harbor ill feelings toward any of the trustees who had worked to embarrass me into resignation or to recommend my removal from the board. My wife and I attempted to enjoy the fellowship in the hallways, meeting rooms, and around the dinner table with the trustees and missionary candidates of the IMB. We did our part to make the conversation enjoyable. We found the spirit to be warm, and the trustees in general to be some of the most wonderful people one could be around.

Only a small handful of trustees found it difficult to speak to me. But even among those who seemed to harbor ill feelings, I went out of my way to be friendly. Some trustees, according to Dr. Tom Hatley, were "hurt" by some things I said on my blog and wanted me to "repent" of what I had written. I continue to be amazed by these "anonymous" trustees who were "hurt," since I only dealt with issues on my blog, never personalities. My name was the only name mentioned in the press at the time. I reminded Tom that I had already said on several fronts that I stood by everything I had written because I was addressing *issues*. Could I have worded things more softly? Sure. I've said so.[1]

After the trustee forum, Tom Hatley met me in the hall and said some trustees were pressing him to "deal with me" before his final meeting as chairman of the board. Hatley's term of service as chairman of the International Mission Board would end the next day, and he informed me that he would be reading a statement regarding his final attempt at resolving "the Wade Burleson issue." This was news to me. I did not know what to expect from the statement, and Hatley didn't offer details. I had been led to believe the issue was resolved, so I was curious as to why it was coming up again. I encouraged Hatley to refrain from reading any statement, since he and trustee leadership would be returning to old news. I told him that nothing else regarding "the Wade Burleson issue" needed to be done, and if he and trustee leadership attempted to embarrass me publicly again, I would take my complaints against trustee leadership to the floor of the convention. Hatley was unconvinced, and when he walked away I knew that I was in for another rough meeting.

As I was to later discover, every IMB trustee meeting I would attend during my tenure would be about Wade Burleson. Trustee leadership had a hard time focusing on anything else. Every meeting would focus on "how can we embarrass Burleson." I was grateful that my wife was with me at this May meeting because she told me afterward that had she not been present, she would have a hard time believing Christians were capable of treating people the way trustee leadership treated me. Rachelle is a strong woman of extraordinary grace and character, but after she observed the shenanigans at this May meeting, I had a hard time justifying to her my continued support of the SBC.

Rachelle was beside me at the missionary appointment service when I went up to Jerry Corbaley, hugged him, and told him I looked forward to working with him in the future. Corbaley pushed me away and said he would have nothing to do with me. When I expressed my love for him and assured him that I would seek his forgiveness for anything I had done that offended him, he said, "Your forgiveness is not accepted." My wife saw the exchange and heard Corbaley's remarks. Later she asked me what he meant by "Your forgiveness is not accepted." I told her that as with most things Mr. Corbaley said, I had no idea what he meant. This was simply his most excellent way of relating.

In the first plenary session Tuesday afternoon, Rachelle sat beside me as one of the trustee leaders spoke to the entire 89-member board. This particular leader was rotating off, and it is a tradition for trustees rotating off the board to say a few parting words. This trustee, a person I am choosing not to name, took the microphone and then blasted "those who have a lot to say, but say nothing." He proceeded to use some colorful descriptive language to identify "those people." It was evident by those who approached me later that my perceptions of his remarks were on target. He was identifying me but didn't have the guts to name me. Yet, most everyone knew it. It got quiet (remember this is in public forum), and then he said, "That person reminds

me of that thing on Trustee Barnes's shirt! You see that! It's a Longhorn."
(Trustee Barnes was wearing a Texas Longhorn shirt.) He continued, "He
who says a lot but actually says nothing at all is like that Longhorn—there
are two points [stretching his arms out to show the two points] with a lot of
bull in between."[2] Rachelle blushed and leaned over to me and said, "Do
they do this to you in all the meetings?" I said, "Honey, this is nothing."

My patience, though, was stretched to the maximum at Wednesday
morning's plenary session when Tom Hatley, for his last act as chairman of
the board, read into the public record a report from the executive committee
of the International Mission Board regarding "the Wade Burleson issue." The
report was a blistering indictment of my personal character and integrity.
Neither Tom nor anyone else on the executive committee had shown me the
report in advance, talked with me about it coming before the board, or even
addressed me privately about what it contained. In fact, based upon their
communications with me, most of which I recorded, I was led to believe that
they were doing all they could to put the Wade Burleson issue behind us.
Yet, at every meeting they would pull another stunt designed to embarrass
me. Again, I was grateful that Rachelle was with me and that these things
happened in a public forum, for she told me later she would never have
believed such things could happen in the Southern Baptist Convention
unless she had seen them with her own eyes and heard them with her own
ears. Other friends were present at the Albuquerque trustee meeting in May
2006, including Clif Cummings, pastor of FBC Duncan, Oklahoma, who
had come to the IMB meeting to offer support for me and our missionaries.

Hatley began his report by reading statements from my December 10
post "Crusading Conservatives vs. Cooperating Conservatives" and said I
had not repented of the things I said. I must have hit a chord with this post,
because though it dealt with issues going on within the SBC and no names
were mentioned, trustee leadership kept returning to it as the cause for their
angst. I had already expressed regret that I used the militant word "crusade"
in the post, but I repeatedly stated that I stood by the content and facts of
what I wrote. Unlike what happened in January, Tom actually read from my
blog rather than simply saying "trust us," but unfortunately, he read mostly
the comments from other Southern Baptists who were free to write their
thoughts in the open comment section below my post. He said the words he
read to the trustee board, written by other Southern Baptists, should be my
responsibility because I gave the individuals a forum to criticize the IMB. I
was responsible, he reasoned, because I was the administrator of the post.

It is true that I have attempted to maintain a high standard on my blog regarding comments, but people must realize that I try to keep an open dialogue and do not always catch inappropriate comments because I don't read them all. The quotes Tom read from were not my words, and I didn't even agree with some of them, but Tom and trustee leadership felt that I should be held accountable for them.

These things were not new to me, but what Tom said at the conclusion of his report caused my blood to boil. Tom said I could not be trusted because of "multiple breaches of confidentiality." I am usually a calm, mild-mannered person. My blood pressure went through the roof on this one. I became angry. My wife patted my knee and told me to be gracious. I appreciated her counsel and I believe I was, as I will tell you what I did in a moment.

I knew that trustee leadership did not like what I was posting on the blog and that the charge they would most likely use would be "breach of confidentiality." They would go over everything I wrote with a fine-tooth comb trying to find a breach of confidentiality. This is why I have been fastidious to make sure I only give information that is available to the public. Not one time have I failed to abide by confidentiality rules. I knew this. Trustee leadership knew it. They were outright lying.

What infuriated me was that, once again, a charge was made in public without substantiation. That was not only unethical, not to mention anti-Christian, but it was a violation of the "new" policies on trustee accountability voted on at the last meeting in March. Trustee leadership was not interested in following the model of resolving conflict that they allegedly instituted with the new rules passed in March. Had they been, they would have confronted me privately. Once again, they simply desired to stifle my voice and influence by embarrassing me publicly. As my wife put it later, the average Southern Baptist would ask, "Why is this Wade Burleson such a troublemaker?" Well, the short answer is that trustee leadership was designing meetings that would portray me as one. Yet, as in January 2006, Hatley leveled the charge of "multiple breaches of confidentiality." I had no idea to what breaches Tom was referring.

As a consequence of my alleged actions, Tom Hatley said he was recommending as his final act as chairman that I not be allowed to serve on any committees of the IMB or be allowed to attend any forum or executive session of the IMB for the next year. He then closed his report and sought to move on with the agenda. However, I would not let him off the hook that easily. I went to a microphone to ask him the specifics of the charge.

When recognized, I asked this question: "Mr. Chairman, could you please explain to me the basis for these very public charges of breach of confidentiality? This is the first I have ever heard of this. If you tell me what it is I have done, and if it is a true breach, I will repent on the spot."

The chairman then said (the following words are my paraphrase), "I appreciate that and I think repentance is due, but I would not, even after revealing this, I would still not change my recommendation even with repentance because of the pattern of the breach of confidentiality demonstrated. Repentance needs to be shown by action and not just by words." Dr. Hatley never read from the blog regarding any alleged breach, never quoted for me or others the offending words, never gave specifics to the charge, and just happened to forget that he mentioned "multiple" breaches without supplying me or anyone else with a shred of evidence. Policy and Scripture state that I am to be approached privately first, and trustee leadership violated both—again. First it was "gossip and slander," then it became "resistance to accountability and loss of trust," and now it had morphed into "a pattern of breach(es) of confidentiality." I considered suggesting trustee leadership make up a charge and stick with it instead of making up charges and switching them every meeting.

I said, "Mr. Chairman, I don't understand, could you please explain—"

Dr. Hatley interrupted and said, "I'm sorry, you'll have to close that microphone." They shut off my microphone without giving me specifics, and I sat back down.

When I arrived at my seat, I was angered by the cowardice of trustee leadership, but I calmed down enough to ask Rachelle, "Sweetheart, was I gracious in my tone?" She said, "Of course." I said, "Was I respectful?" She said, "Absolutely." I said, "Then why in the world is the microphone shut off by the chairman when I am trying to figure out what they are accusing me of doing?" She said wisely, "It's because they don't like the fact that they cannot control you."

After the plenary session, I went up to Dr. Hatley and said, "Tom, will you please tell me the basis for your charges?" He said he would not talk to me. I asked him, "How could you make such public charges and not come to me privately?" He reiterated, "I will not talk with you." I was incredulous. Clif Cummings witnessed the exchange and later said the rudeness of the chairman would be incomprehensible to the average Southern Baptist.

I later discovered that trustee leadership was upset that I had reported on my blog the actual vote for John Floyd to be the next chairman of the board. It seems they were embarrassed that the vote was close, and I had reported the numbers, and the charge of "breach of confidentiality" was in retaliation for my reporting information they did not want known, though the vote occurred in a public forum and there was no "guideline" that this information not be given to the SBC.

I also think Hatley and the new chairman of the board, Dr. John Floyd, who was the 2005 chairman of the personnel committee that established the new policies, were extremely sensitive because of past and potential further criticism related to the two new policies within the convention. They wished to discredit me, the chief critic of the policies.

I determined then and there, at that IMB meeting in Albuquerque, that I would not be quiet until the SBC had turned away from her slide into Fundamentalism. Why in the world are we establishing doctrinal parameters at the IMB that exceed the 2000 *BFM*? Does every agency have the authority to determine what they will and will not believe? Can the IMB be Landmark? Can the IMB be anti-reformed? Can the IMB refuse to appoint godly, conservative missionaries who affirm the 2000 *BFM* but don't agree with new doctrinal requirements established at the whim of trustees without support of IMB administration? *Why is Christian dissent silenced?*

The only way the SBC could be turned around was through the election of a president. I made it my goal to ensure that the presidential election for the SBC and the problems associated with Paige Patterson seeking to control the IMB were addressed at the June SBC meeting in Greensboro.

I also visited with the IMB attorney about the recommendations of Hatley and trustee leadership that I not attend forums and executive sessions, and he told me they did not have legal authority to bar me. I wrote on my blog that I would attend all IMB forums and/or executive sessions in the future, regardless of trustee leadership attempts to bar me.[3] Counsel for the SBC executive committee also confirmed that it was illegal for a trustee to be barred from meetings at which all trustees are present.

Trustee Chuck McAlister from Arkansas went so far as to suggest in the trustee meeting that nobody blog about public meetings. Chuck doesn't seem to believe Southern Baptists should know what is happening. I take the opposite approach. Every Southern Baptist should know everything that is occurring in our cooperative missions efforts.

Too much is at stake for the future of our Southern Baptist Convention. We must discuss the issues freely. I vowed in Albuquerque to let all Southern Baptists know what was taking place at the IMB by bringing it to the Greensboro convention in June.

Notes

1. "Political Conservatives vs. Cooperating Conservatives," 4 February 2006, http://kerussocharis.blogspot.com/2006/02/political-conservatives-vs-cooperating.html.

2. "The Commissioning Service and Election of Officers," 24 May 2006, http://kerussocharis.blogspot.com/2006/05/commissioning-service-election-of.html.

3. "The Tipping Point Is Reached," 26 May 2006, http://kerussocharis.blogspot.com/2006/05/tipping-point-is-reached.html.

Chapter 18

THE IMB MOTION
AT GREENSBORO

Though all winds of doctrine were let loose to play upon the earth, so Truth be in the field, we do injuriously, by licensing and prohibiting, to misdoubt her strength. Let truth and falsehood grapple; who ever knew truth put to the worst, in a free and open encounter?
—John Milton's *Areopagitica*, 1644

After the debacle at the Albuquerque trustee meeting, and after listening to the advice of many trusted advisers, visiting at length with my wife, and both requesting and receiving from the Lord a peace in my spirit, I decided the week after the May 2006 trustee meeting to take the next appropriate step in my service on behalf of the Southern Baptist Convention at the International Mission Board. I made public my determination to present a motion to the Southern Baptist Convention in Greensboro, North Carolina, requesting messengers to authorize the executive committee of the Southern Baptist Convention to appoint an *ad hoc* committee in order to listen to, view evidence of, and possibly investigate further five concerns involving the International Mission Board. Further, the motion would request that the *ad hoc* committee report on its progress to the executive committee of the SBC with a final report and recommendation given to the 2007 Southern Baptist Convention in San Antonio.

The next meeting of the IMB was scheduled for July in Richmond, Virginia, a month after the June SBC in Greensboro. I was to begin my second year of service as an IMB trustee during that July meeting. Blogging was my attempt to energize and mobilize grassroots Southern Baptists in their understanding of and participation with the IMB's ministries through a greater comprehension and appreciation of the IMB's work, while at the same time making Southern Baptists aware of the backdoor narrowing of the doctrinal parameters of cooperation in our convention. Even after

Albuquerque, I desired to continue to seek to build relationships with every trustee of the International Mission Board, and I determined to confront my fellow trustees privately if I believed they were taking actions to the detriment of a greater cooperation among Southern Baptists. I knew I had seven more years to serve the Southern Baptist Convention as a trustee of the IMB. I also knew that a great many trustees would stop at nothing to get me off the board. So, to let them know that I meant business, I turned the tables on trustee leadership and revealed the specifics of the motion that I would make to the entire Southern Baptist Convention regarding the IMB at the June meeting in Greensboro.

The Greensboro IMB Motion

I move that the Southern Baptist Convention, in session, in Greensboro, North Carolina 2006, invoking Bylaw 26 B of the Southern Baptist Convention, authorize the Executive Committee of the Southern Baptist Convention to appoint a seven member Ad Hoc Committee to determine the sources of the controversies in our International Mission Board, and make findings and recommendations regarding these controversies, so that trustees of the IMB might effect reconciliation and effectively discharge their responsibilities to God and fellow Southern Baptists by cooperating together to accomplish evangelism and missions to the Glory of God; and

That this Committee listen to, view evidence of, and possibly investigate further, five concerns involving the International Mission Board which are not limited to, but include:

(1). The manipulation of the nominating process of the Southern Baptist Convention during the appointment of trustees for the International Mission Board.

(2). Attempts to influence and/or coerce the IMB trustees, staff, and administration to take a particular course of action by one or more Southern Baptist agency heads other than the President of the International Mission Board.

(3). The appropriate and/or inappropriate use of Forums and Executive Sessions of the International Mission Board as compared to conducting business in full view of the Southern Baptist Convention and the corresponding propriety and/or impropriety of the Chairman of the International Mission Board excluding any individual trustee, without Southern Baptist Convention approval, from participating in meetings where the full International Mission Board is convened.

(4). The legislation of new doctrinal requisites for eligibility to serve as employees or missionaries of the IMB beyond the 2000 *Baptist Faith & Message*.

(5). The suppression of dissent by trustees in the minority through various means by those in the majority, and the propriety of any agency forbidding a trustee, by policy, from publicly criticizing a Board approved action; and

That this Committee follow the 2000 *Baptist Faith & Message* Statement in regard to theological issues, and operate within the Constitution and Bylaws of the Southern Baptist Convention; and

That to accomplish the Committee's work all the trustees, officers, employees, and administrators of the International Mission Board, shall fully cooperate with the Committee to accomplish the purposes outlined in this motion; and

This Committee shall report on the progress of its work to the Executive Committee of the Southern Baptist Convention and the International Mission Board; and

That the Ad Hoc Committee make its final report and recommendation to the June 2007 Southern Baptist Convention and request that it be discharged.[1]

The motive for introducing this motion was simply to make the convention aware that the politics of destruction, as were taking place at the IMB, were coming to an end. No longer could the powers that be run roughshod over those who disagreed with them. Unlike others who leave the convention due to personal hurts, I decided to force the convention to deal with the actions of IMB trustee leadership so that the convention could decide what needed to happen to clean up the mess on the board. Some trustees, including Bob Pearle, Paige Patterson's pastor, were accusing me of using my position as trustee of the IMB to gain convention-wide influence. I laughed when I heard this and told my wife I could think of about a dozen better ways to gain influence. Even funnier, Jerry Corbaley wrote on his blog prior to the convention (he was to later erase it), "From Wade Burleson's first IMB meeting it has seemed as if trustee Burleson has had an agenda to hurl himself into the national limelight regardless of the consequences."

In the ever increasing ironies at work among IMB trustee leadership, trustee Corbaley had begun a blog himself, seemingly overturning any previous professed abhorrence to such a means of spreading "gossip and slander." Corbaley used his blog to denigrate me personally, constantly questioning my motives and character, as illustrated above. I had fastidiously sought to only deal with issues at the IMB, and to avoid mentioning any names or personalities, but it was beginning to seem to me that it was impossible for IMB trustee leaders, like Corbaley, to separate Christian issues from Christian fellowship. You either had to agree with them or you had better be prepared for vicious personal attacks.

Corbaley told anyone who listened everything that was evil about Wade Burleson. Bob Pearle participated as much as possible, through phone calls, e-mails, and hallway conversations where it was said I would destroy the convention. Interestingly, hundreds of people who actually read my blog jumped to my defense and began to challenge Corbaley and Pearle openly, as well as any other IMB trustee who tried to make me the issue. My wife and I appreciated those who came to our defense, but particularly IMB trustees Rick Thompson, Alan McWhite, John Click, Ken Kawahara, and others. In addition, several Oklahoma pastors who understood the craziness of Corbaley and his crew trying to make me the issue sent letters to all the trustees to help them focus on the real issues. One such Oklahoma pastor, Chuck Andrews, wrote a letter to all the trustees with the concluding pointed statement, "the 'Wade Burleson Issue' is much more about the 'issues' than about 'Wade Burleson.'"

Chuck hit the nail on the head. I had no desire to hold office at the SBC level. I had not sought to serve as a trustee of the IMB. Other IMB trustees contacted me requesting that I serve, and due to many family members and church members who are serving on the mission field through the Southern Baptist Convention, I felt that declining the invitation to serve would be letting go of a lifeline of support. When I agreed to serve, I did not come to the International Mission Board in a denominational vacuum.

As I've explained, there was within me a growing concern that the SBC had been moving away from the simplicity and power of biblical Christianity to a Westernized version of a surface morality that looks far more like that of the Pharisees of Jesus' day than Christ's disciples. A progression of events in the Southern Baptist Convention has aroused this concern in my heart—the boycott of Disney, the withdrawal of participation in evangelical alliances, including the Baptist World Alliance, the overemphasis on national politics, the often anti-reformed rants by a handful of "leaders" of the SBC, and the continuing insistence by some to label evangelical conservatives "liberal" simply because they do not conform to a specific, narrow ideology and morality.

When the Protestant Reformation began, its aim was to reform the church. However, the Roman Catholic Church and the Protestants ended up at war with each other. During the Wars of Religion in the sixteenth century and the Thirty Years War of the seventeenth century, neither Catholics nor

Protestants succeeded in bringing each other to their respective knees. The outcome of this stalemate was the doctrine of *cuius regio eius religio*, or "he who is the ruler, his the religion."

It would seem to me that there has been within the SBC over the last quarter century a "religious war" not dissimilar to the religious wars of the sixteenth and seventeenth centuries. And there seems to be a similar outcome—*cuius regio eius religio*. What started as a genuine concern for upholding the sufficiency, authority, and inerrancy of the Bible became much more about Fundamentalist leaders demanding that all Southern Baptists interpret the Bible the way they do.

In 1974, Broadman Press published Jimmy Draper's book *The Church Christ Approves*. This beloved pastor and statesman, who in the 1970s was the pastor of First Southern Baptist Church, Del City, Oklahoma, made this startling statement in his book:

> Fundamentalism is more dangerous than liberalism because everything is done in the name of the Lord, in the name of the Lord, the fundamentalist condemns all who disagree with him . . . he uses the Bible as a club with which to beat people over the head, rather than a means of personal strength and a revealer of God. To the fundamentalist, the test of fellowship is correct doctrine. If you do not agree with his doctrinal position, he writes you off and will not have fellowship with you.
>
> There is no room in his world for those who have a different persuasion. He feels threatened by diverse convictions and writes them off as sinister and heretical. As long as you support his position, he is with you. Cross him, and he has no use whatever for you . . . the fundamentalist tactic is simple: hatred, bitterness and condemnation of all whom they despise . . . in the name of the Lord they will launch vehement attacks on individuals and churches, in the name of the Lord they attempt to assassinate the character of those whom they oppose, they direct their attack most often on other Christian leaders with whom they find disagreement.[2]

I have been the pastor of Emmanuel Baptist Church, Enid, Oklahoma, for fifteen years. We have an incredible church. There is a love for Scripture among the people. We teach, live, and breathe grace. The people are missions minded. We practice loving church discipline for violations of biblical commands, but we are careful not to demand conformity on the personal convictions of some. The fellowship is sweet. The gospel drives all we do. Lives are changed through the ministries of the people of Emmanuel. I have learned that the convention is not where we are as a church—yet.

What drives me as a trustee of the International Mission Board is the belief that we must draw a line in the sand and stop narrowing the definition of what makes a "true" Southern Baptist. We must stop narrowing the parameters of cooperation in missions and evangelism by excluding people who do not agree with the doctrinal positions of those in leadership, yet affirm the *Baptist Faith & Message*.

By the time the 2006 Southern Baptist Convention in Greensboro rolled around, we already had rejected dozens of Southern Baptist Convention missionary candidates described by these qualities:

(1) They believed in the deity of Jesus Christ.

(2) They believed in the Triune God—Father, Son, and Holy Spirit.

(3) They believed in the sacrificial atonement of Jesus Christ for sinners.

(4) They believed in the physical resurrection of Christ from the tomb.

(5) They believed in salvation by grace through faith in Jesus Christ.

(6) They professed their faith in Christ as Lord through believer's baptism by immersion.

(7) They had been members of Southern Baptist churches for at least three years.

(8) They affirmed the 2000 *Baptist Faith & Message*.

But because missionary candidates either possessed a private prayer language or were baptized in a church that was not Southern Baptist, they were rejected as missionary candidates.

Lest some believe that I felt everything was wrong at the IMB, I posted a week before the 2006 convention in Greensboro several things I knew to be right with the International Mission Board. First, I pointed out the cooperation among our missionaries *on the field* with other evangelicals. Though some trustees wish to shut down this cooperation, missionaries from all over tell me how wonderful it is to cooperate with Southern Baptists and other evangelical missions organizations on the mission field. Missionaries from Youth with a Mission, Wycliffe, Samaritan's Purse, HCJB Radio, and other Great Commission evangelical mission organizations have written that Southern Baptists are leading the evangelical movement to reach unreached people groups. When you hear about the partnerships with the IMB that are occurring as we lead in taking the Scriptures through oral translations of Scriptural narratives, or the translation of the Word of God into the languages of people groups who have never heard the gospel, you can't help but marvel at what the IMB is doing. One high-level non-Southern Baptist missionary told me recently over lunch that there is a genuine move of God taking place all over the world, and Southern Baptists are at the leading edge with other evangelicals. He has been around a long time and said it is a new day of cooperation with Southern Baptists.

Second, I reminded all my readers that the administration of the IMB is professional. My undergraduate degree is in business administration and corporate finance. I considered an MBA before going into the ministry. I can assure every Southern Baptist that the administration of the IMB is on top of every aspect of the business end of missions. I have read diligently the public report of the problems at the North American Mission Board (NAMB), and I can guarantee you that there are not similar problems at the IMB. The work of the IMB is particularly complicated because of the countless countries with which we are involved, but the staff and administration do a tremendous job in their areas of responsibility, and the trustees actively demand accountability. When one looks at the leadership of Dr. Jerry Rankin, the assessment is stunning. There are more than 5,400 missionaries at the IMB. There is constant evaluation and implementation of different philosophies designed to take the gospel to as many unreached people groups as possible. I hesitate to list the numbers of conversions and new churches on the mission field because, frankly, I am more interested in people being faithful in fulfilling their calling than in determining success by numbers. Some fields will not have much harvest because of the conditions, but similar to William Carey's first two decades in India, the seeds planted will reap a harvest in centuries to come. The books are not closed on the Rankin administration, and with a possible five or six more years of his effective leadership at the IMB, I believe history will point to the last decade of the old millennium and the new decade of this millennium as a watershed moment in Southern Baptist history.

Third, giving to the International Mission Board set a new record in 2005. $137,939,677.59—that's what Southern Baptists gave to the Lottie Moon Christmas Offering for International Missions in 2005, making it the single most successful year in the offering's history. The $137.9 million marks a 3.03 percent increase over 2004's $133.9 million Lottie Moon offering, not to mention a 1.28 percent gain over the old record set in 2003—$136.2 million. More than 5,100 International Mission Board missionaries depend on the annual offering, of which every penny is used to support their work of sharing the gospel around the world. "This historic level of giving will enable us to send an increasing number of God-called missionary candidates moving toward appointment," said IMB President Jerry Rankin. "It will enable us to push forward in fulfilling the vision of bringing all peoples to saving faith in Jesus Christ. At a time of economic uncertainty, and a year in which massive amounts of funding have been directed toward hurricane relief and recovery, it is gratifying to see God prove His faithfulness through Southern Baptists."[3] Clyde Meador, IMB executive vice president, echoed Rankin's sentiments and acknowledged the critical role of the Woman's Missionary Union in the offering's success. "The IMB wouldn't be able to do any of this without the faithful support of our state and national Woman's Missionary Union partners."[4]

Fourth, there is vision on the International Mission Board. The administration of the IMB does an outstanding job of casting vision, selling vision, and then implementing vision. Of course, the trustees of the IMB must approve the vision and policies of the IMB, and I have not heard one trustee say publicly that he is not supportive of the vision cast by administration and Dr. Jerry Rankin. This is one of the reasons why I believe all business sessions should be in the public view of the Southern Baptist Convention. The International Mission Board is owned by the SBC. The trustees are elected by the SBC. We all need to see, hear, and affirm the vision established by Dr. Jerry Rankin or allow for the full, free debate against it to be *publicly* heard.

Finally, the IMB has a bright future. I believed in June 2006 that the best days of the International Mission Board were ahead. But for a new day to dawn at the IMB, new trustees with a cooperative mindset, an aversion to Fundamentalism, and a love for the gospel needed to be placed on the board. For that to happen would require the election of a like-minded president and the rise of like-minded trustees.

Notes

1. "The Decision—A Motion in Greensboro," 1 June 2006, http://kerussocharis.blogspot.com/2006/06/decision-motion-in-greensboro.html.

2. Jimmy Draper, *The Church Christ Approves* (Nashville: Broadman Press, 1974).

3. Baptist Press, "Lottie Moon Sets Record Missions Giving," May 2006, http://www.bpnews.net/bpnews.asp?id=23381.

4. Ibid.

Chapter 19

THE MOTION, AN ELECTION, AND THE BLOGOSPHERE

The Southern Baptist Convention
Greensboro, North Carolina
June 2006

Rachelle and I flew into Greensboro on Saturday evening, June 10, 2006, for the annual Southern Baptist Convention. On Sunday morning we ate breakfast at the Greensboro Sheraton Four Seasons, the convention headquarters hotel, with several other Southern Baptist messengers. Around the breakfast tables near us, we overhead a few conversations regarding blogging, with remarks such as "be sure and check the blogs" and "they will be blogging all day," etc. It was interesting to us how blogging had become part of conversations of everyday Southern Baptists.

On our way to the room after dinner that night, a sixteen-year-old from Washington, D.C., named Tim Sweetman asked me in the elevator if I was Wade Burleson. I told him I was, and he shook my hand and said it was an honor to meet me. In the morning, I read on his blog that he had met me in the elevator, and after hearing some of his thoughts about the convention, I realized again that blogging is a way to engage a generation of young people in SBC involvement; young people who, without blogging, would be oblivious to some of the issues at stake. To me this new generation's involvement in the SBC is one of the great blessings of the blogs.

Rachelle and I left at 9:30 a.m. Sunday morning to travel to the Calvary Baptist Church at McLeansville, North Carolina, where Terry Larson is the pastor. I had never met Terry before, but he is a reader of my blog and he invited me to speak to his congregation for a Greensboro Crossover Rally at 10:30. Several people had read on my blog the previous night that I would be at Calvary, and they came to the worship service. It was my privilege to meet for the first time a layman from Alabama named Bob Cleveland, who would become a lifelong friend and make SBC news himself in the following months. I also met a professor of North Greenville College who spoke words of encouragement to me, students from Criswell College in Dallas, and several pastors who came to the rally from around the country, including several of my good friends from Oklahoma, all of whom were encouraging in their support.

The religion editor for the Greensboro paper was in the audience and wrote a news piece (that appeared the next day) about the effects of blogging on the SBC. The reporter was a gracious Christian lady with a keen mind and a professional manner. It was the first of many interviews during the convention that helped me realize the SBC leadership often gave newspaper reporters an undeserved bad rap. After lunch, Rachelle took a nap and I visited with many pastors in the lobby of the hotel. It was good to visit with a few men whom I had not seen in many years and to renew acquaintances. I met several people whom I had not known previously, but they came up to me because they recognized me from pictures in Baptist Press news stories from the previous six months; they also spoke encouraging words. The vast majority of people were friendly, though I did see a few people glaring in my direction. Sometimes I felt I ought to ask when I shook hands, "Friend or foe?"; but of course, in the SBC we are all friends and family (wink).

At 5:00, Rachelle and I went to the Pastor's Conference at the Greensboro Coliseum. We registered as messengers and entered the arena. The first speaker went into a diatribe against people who believe God elected a certain number of people to go to heaven. He said if God's people simply were more faithful, the number of people who will get to heaven would increase and surprise even God himself. The theology in this type of teaching is aberrant, but what makes it so unpalatable is the way in which some in the SBC attack reformed thinking as incompatible with Baptist identity. In other words, if you don't agree with us and our understanding of free will, you can't be a true Baptist.

Of course, this kind of sharp attack happens on both sides of this issue, and it is one of the reasons cooperation is a must in our convention in order for missions ministry to continue to increase. We stayed for a few more messages and then returned to the hotel where several bloggers ended the day with a fellowship time in our suite. Art Rogers, Tad Thompson, Dorcas Hawker, Tim Sweatman, Kevin Bussey, Rick Thompson, Tim Sweetman (different from the Tim Sweatman I met in the elevator), Gene Bridges, Paul

Burleson, Ben Cole, and others. Several non-bloggers also enjoyed the fellowship. One was Sam Hodges, religion reporter for the *Dallas Morning News*. He was one of a handful present from the traditional media.

Sam's grandfather founded the Baptist Television Hour back in the days of M. E. Dodds (1879–1952), who pioneered preaching on the radio for the SBC. It was Sam's grandfather who moved the SBC from radio to television. His mother often sang as part of the Baptist Hour broadcast, and though Sam is not a Southern Baptist, he is familiar with our convention. Recently, Sam unintentionally distorted my views on the two new policies of tongues and baptism. He read to me a correction he was giving to his editor to run in the *Dallas Morning News*. The correction succinctly, precisely, and clearly represented my views. Sam increased my respect for the secular press, as did the female Greensboro reporter.[1]

The Southern Baptists who met during the fellowship time had played a key role in the direction of the convention that year. I believe the willingness these men and women displayed in opposing the IMB doctrinal policies led to people across the convention working to ensure diverse views were represented in convention offices. There were three announced candidates for Southern Baptist Convention president, six candidates for 1st vice president and at least four candidates for 2nd vice president. If someone had said six months ago that so many would run for convention offices, he or she would have been met with incredulous laughter. This simply shows how quickly things can change in our informational age.

One of the things I appreciate about this loosely knit group of bloggers is their unparalleled desire for transparency. Nothing is said behind closed doors. Everything is open for all Southern Baptists to see. All you have to do is read their respective blogs. One statement made at the fellowship was, "If you don't want all Southern Baptists to hear or read what you intend to say, then don't say it, because it shouldn't be said." How refreshing. All in all, the first day in Greensboro reminded me of why I am a Southern Baptist. There are thousands of sharp, dedicated, evangelical Christians who are committed to the Great Commission and identify themselves as Southern Baptists, and I enjoy being identified with them.

On Monday Rachelle and I attended the debate between Al Mohler and Paige Patterson on the subject of Calvinism. This particular event, designed by the leaders of the Pastor's Conference, was well attended. Dr. Mohler had just gone through a serious eye procedure and wore sunshades, but he was articulate and persuasive. Dr. Patterson used humor to make his case that

Calvinism is outside the bounds of the gospel, but the fondness both men had for each other was obvious. I left the debate wondering why Southern Baptists could disagree over Calvinism and still cooperate, but disagreement over the gifts or the administrator of baptism disqualified someone from cooperation. It made me wonder who set the standards of cooperation, since it was obviously no longer the *Baptist Faith & Message*. However, two people who spoke at the Pastor's Conference Monday night gave me incredible hope for the SBC. Joyce Rogers, wife of the late Dr. Adrian Rogers, spoke eloquently and passionately on precisely what I had been saying about our convention for the last six months. She then said that if her late husband were alive, he would be against "the narrowing of the parameters of cooperation within the Southern Baptist Convention." When she spoke, people listened. Ed Young also spoke that night, and though half the pastors left before his message, he gave a ringing endorsement of the IMB and Dr. Jerry Rankin. We went to bed Monday night knowing that the motion I would bring to the convention and the presidential election on Tuesday could possibly chart the course for the SBC for years to come.

The convention convened at 8:00 a.m. on Tuesday. The messenger registration eventually reached more than 11,000—fewer than I had expected but more than in the previous few years. The first motion presented on the floor of the convention at 8:45 a.m. was my motion requesting the appointment of an *ad hoc* committee from the executive committee to investigate my five concerns regarding the IMB. The rules for the convention mandated that I could only introduce the motion in the morning session, not speak to it, and the committee on order of business would set a time for debating the motion. When presenting my motion, I decided not to invoke convention bylaw 26 and force the convention to vote on my motion while in session. Rather, I accepted the decision of the committee on order of business regarding how my motion would be handled. Alan Blume, chairman of that committee, was a man I highly respected. His wife, Pam, had been a former IMB trustee, and the Blumes understood the need for SBC cooperation. At about 1:00 p.m. on Tuesday, I received a call from Alan Blume. He asked that I meet with him and a member of the committee at the platform. Alan was honest with me, but fair. He said the committee was going to refer the motion back to the IMB trustees, since he felt the trustees needed to be given an opportunity to deal with the recommendation themselves. He said, however, there would be two stipulations: (1) First, the convention would be asked to debate and vote on referring this motion back to the IMB at 7:40

that night, so that if it passed, it would be said to the IMB that this was the convention's action, not just Wade Burleson's. (2) Second, the IMB trustees' investigative committee would be required to report back to the convention in 2007, issuing findings and recommendations on all five points.

I thanked Alan for the committee's work and told him that though I felt it best that an independent panel be convened, I would not oppose the recommendation from the committee. As I left the platform, Dr. Rankin, who must have heard the decision of the committee to refer my motion back to the IMB, stopped me and pulled me into a hallway behind the platform. His expression was pained and his tone serious. He said I must not allow the convention to refer this motion back to the IMB. He said I must insist that an independent panel be convened. I told Dr. Rankin I had already informed Alan Blume that I would not oppose his committee's recommendation, and that if I did, it would not go over well with the convention. It's difficult to overturn a committee's recommendation before the entire convention. I know Dr. Rankin was frustrated that I would not force the issue of an independent panel, but the convention was not as aware of the bias of the trustees as were Dr. Rankin and myself. They would not overturn the recommendation from the committee on order of business. I was glad, however, that the IMB trustees would be forced to report back to the convention at the 2007 annual meeting.

The election for Southern Baptist president occurred Tuesday afternoon. There were three candidates, with Frank Page leading the way. Frank Page's large church gives 12 percent to the Cooperative Program, and he is the leading conservative in South Carolina. I had spoken with Dr. Page on a couple of occasions prior to the convention, encouraging him to run for president. I had publicly thrown my support behind Dr. Page, as had the majority of bloggers. Jerry Sutton, another candidate, had said publicly the day before the election that the debate over the new doctrinal policies at the IMB needed to be addressed. He suggested that the 2000 *BFM* be amended to include the new doctrinal policies.

I was shocked when I read Sutton's opinion. I posted on my blog the morning of the presidential election that a vote for Jerry Sutton was a vote for the continued narrowing of the parameters of the Southern Baptist Convention. If Jerry Sutton were to be elected president, the exclusionary, isolationist practices of the SBC would become more entrenched.

Dr. Ronnie Floyd was the third candidate. He is a good man and a good pastor. However, it was not the best year for Dr. Floyd to run for president.

His church's lack of support for the Cooperative Program (.27 percent) made it difficult for him to be elected. I predicted the night before the election that Dr. Frank Page would be elected president of the Southern Baptist Convention, and sure enough, he was—on the first ballot.

After we had cast our ballots for president, but before the results were announced, I saw Dr. Page in the hall. I greeted him, saying, "Hello, Mr. President." He smiled and reminded me that I was the first one to call him several weeks earlier when he and I talked on the phone about him running for president of the SBC. We had a good conversation, and I reminded Dr. Page of his pledge not to exclude from service godly, conservative Southern Baptists who affirm the Baptist Faith & Message, yet differ in areas of doctrinal interpretations not addressed by the 2000 *BFM*. Frank graciously reiterated his pledge to do so and said he was looking to open up the appointments to people throughout the SBC that had a sweet spirit, a commitment to inerrancy, and a willingness to serve. He also said he would not recycle appointments.

When Frank's election was announced, I was walking around the arena and happened to be stopped by a reporter in the underground hallway. He asked for my reaction. Soon others stopped, and eventually more than twenty-five reporters from around the nation stood four deep and asked questions for forty minutes. One of the repeated questions was whether or not I believed blogs played a role in the election. I said, "Absolutely." Baptist bloggers in 2006 may go down in history as the first bloggers who actually determined the outcome of a national religious/political election. When all three candidates were being nominated, my wife leaned over to me and said, "I feel like I know all three men because of the blogs." I attended the press conference for Frank Page, and he handled himself with class, dignity, and grace. Southern Baptists had a right to be proud of this man.

After the last business of the evening, which included the convention overwhelmingly passing my motion that an investigation take place within the board of trustees of the IMB, a large, informal group of bloggers, young leaders, and messengers from my church met in our suite at the Sheraton. Frank Page came by and we gathered around him and laid our hands on him and prayed. Morris Chapman also came by and spoke encouraging words. It felt like an old-fashioned revival meeting with all the Scripture, spiritual exhortations, and focus on Jesus Christ and the gospel. One of the messengers took pictures of the fellowship and prayer time. As our little prayer meeting was breaking up, I walked the new president of the SBC to the elevator. It was just Dr. Page and me in the hallway. Before he stepped on the elevator I asked him how he felt. He said he felt scared. I assured him that I would continue to pray for him. If I had known then what I know now, I would have asked him to pray for me.

Note

1. Sam Hodges, "Tongues Tied: The Lowdown on a Baptist Spat," *Dallas Morning News*, 9 December 2006, http://www.dallasnews.com/sharedcontent/dws/dn/religion/stories/DN-tongues_09rel.ART0.State.Edition1.3eb1173.html.

Chapter 20

REFLECTIONS ON THE
HISTORIC 2006 CONVENTION

Some have challenged the notion that events at the International Mission Board—and my blog—played any role in Frank Page winning the presidential election. Southern Baptists who are familiar with these issues likely recognize the influence of both, I think. Dr. Bart Barber, an adjunct professor of Southwestern Baptist Theological Seminary, and one who could not be considered a fan of my positions on the new doctrinal policies, wrote this comment on my blog:

> Bro. Burleson,
>
> I have been completely on the other side of all of this from you. I hope that won't prevent you from hearing me when I endeavor to step outside of this controversy and suggest something that I believe to be important.
>
> Your blog has played a significant role in this year's story of the Southern Baptist Convention. That makes its content, in my estimation, a valuable primary source for the people who (if the Lord tarries) will be trying to sort all of this out in 100 years.
>
> Yet blogs are nothing more than electrons—very ephemeral. Considering the way Blogger seems to run on occasion—very, very ephemeral. Have you considered taking any sort of action to preserve the content of your blog in a more permanent fashion? I should think that a suitable solution would contain both your posts and the comment log.
>
> The archivists at OBU's Mabee Learning Center would probably be as much help to you as anyone would. They also might constitute a suitable repository for the material. Another option to consider would be the Southern Baptist Historical Library and Archives in Nashville.
>
> For whatever it is worth . . . .
>
> In Christ,
> Bart Barber[1]

Though Dr. Barber seemed to be able to put aside personal animosity toward me, others in SBC leadership were not as gracious. There was a resolution presented at the 2006 Southern Baptist Convention that many said was aimed directly at me. I had publicly stated that a demand for abstinence from alcoholic beverages in order to cooperate in Southern Baptist missions was extra-biblical and unwise. In some countries, such as Chile, Germany, and others, the drinking of an alcoholic beverage is considered normal even by evangelical Christians. The difference between evangelicals and the lost in those countries is that Christians abstain from drunkenness.

My belief that abstinence was a Southern cultural phenomenon and unsupportable by Scripture itself caused some of the SBC leaders, including president of the Southern Baptist Conservatives of Texas Jim Richards, to take direct aim at me. Resolution 5, introduced at the 2006 Southern Baptist Convention, tied holiness to abstinence and demanded that all SBC leaders vow to abstain from the use of alcoholic beverages. Some shortsighted Baptists listened to the debate over Resolution 5 and thought that Southern Baptists who opposed it were advocating that everyone drink alcoholic beverages. Nothing could be further from the truth. This one issue illustrates clearly that Southern Baptists are in danger of demanding conformity to issues that reach beyond the Scriptures themselves. I took the opportunity to post an article I wrote, opposing Resolution 5, to illustrate the dangers of demanding conformity on tertiary issues in the Southern Baptist Convention. It is the most widely read post I have ever written.

> Some of my blogging friends believe the resolution on alcohol use in America, as amended by the Executive Director of the Southern Baptist Conservatives of Texas, is an attempt to embarrass me, or possibly remove me from the International Mission Board of Trustees.
>
> I would caution anyone about assigning motives to certain members of the resolutions committee or the leadership of the Southern Baptist Conservatives of Texas regarding me. In addition, I am never embarrassed about my interpretations of the Word of God, because I have such a high view of the inerrant, sacred text. If anything, I sometimes get embarrassed by the actions of my fellow Southern Baptists, but never what the Bible says.
>
> I teach my children and my church that abstinence is a wise choice for every Christian, and the best way to avoid drunkenness. I wholeheartedly support all believers who have an abstinence conviction. However, I believe the authoritative, inspired Word of God forbids drunkenness, not necessarily the drinking of an alcoholic beverage.

One person called me today and said this resolution is an attempt to "get me" off the IMB. I laughed. That won't work. If the trustees were to approve a policy of total abstinence for sitting trustees, I would, of course, abide by it. As I have said, I am policy driven. I would, however, without hesitation, argue against such a trustee policy prior to adoption because of my belief in the inerrant Word of God. The trustees of any agency have the right to set any policy they desire, even extra-biblical requirements for trustees, and though I will seek to prevent the adoption of any extra-biblical policy during my tenure on the IMB, were the abstinence policy to be adopted, I would abide by it.

In fact, I will go even further. Resolutions are not binding, but since I am elected by and represent the Southern Baptist Convention, and since the convention adopted a resolution urging abstinence by trustees, I will abstain from drinking an alcoholic beverage during my entire tenure as an IMB member.

However, let me use this "alcohol" issue as discussed by Southern Baptists at our convention as an example of the overall lack in our convention of sound, biblical exegesis. The idea that to drink a glass of wine, or any other alcoholic beverage, is a sin against God is so foreign to the teaching of the inspired, inerrant Word of God that for anyone to say to a Christian who has no abstinence conviction, "You are sinning against God when you drink a glass of wine" is a sin in itself. To do so would be to accuse Jesus of possessing personal sin, the epitome of liberalism.

Jesus drank wine. The disciples drank wine. Jesus turned the water into wine. Paul commanded Timothy "Drink a little wine for your stomach." The biblical prohibition is "drunkenness." The inerrant Bible says "Be not *drunk* with wine."

And make no mistake: Drunkenness *is* a sin. It is a scourge on our society. We must sharply rebuke anyone, including the alcohol industry, who minimizes or encourages drunkenness. Our church disciplines people for the sin of drunkenness, and we treat the sin very, very seriously.

However, the sin of drunkenness is similar to the sin of promiscious sex. We don't teach that a man should abstain from sex with his wife because other people are sex addicts. Similarly, we don't teach that individuals *must* abstain from alcohol because some commit the sin of drunkennes.

Likewise we don't *demand* that those who are single get married, or those who choose to abstain from alcohol drink. Some things are matters of *personal* conviction and conscience. The pastor's job is not to force those who use sex properly, or alcohol properly, to abstain from either because some others cannot control the lusts of their wicked hearts, but rather, the pastor's job is to teach the Bible and urge God's people to live by biblical principles.

I have never tasted beer. But I play golf every Friday with some wonderful men from my church who enjoy a glass of beer after the round. I don't condemn them for drinking beer and they don't condemn me for not drinking beer. And they don't get drunk. There have been three people in our church in the last fifteen years, only three, who have undergone loving church discipline for the sin of drunkenness. All three people must now be—by their personal choice and their corresponding accountability to our church—absolute teetotalers. They have shown their inability to control their appetite for alcohol. Their drunkenness is a dishonor to the Christ who has saved them and a shame to the body of believers with whom they have joined. Their conduct has been a breach of our church covenant which forbids drunkenness.

Fortunately, the grace of God is apparent in all three and they willingly accepted the counsel of their families and pastors and agreed wholeheartedly that abstinence is now a requirement in their lives. If they drink, we all identify it as sin for them and immediately confront them. Yet, they understand abstinence is not demanded from others in the church.

I believe one of the reasons Southern Baptists love to point to the act of drinking an alcoholic beverage as a sin in itself is because it is an action they can easily avoid and feel comfortable in their own self-righteousness. In fact, one messenger from Texas stated during the debate on the resolution that every Christian must *abstain* in order to be holy. Really?

The Bible teaches that claiming the righteousness of Christ is one's only hope of salvation. He is our holiness. We have his righteousness by faith. Imputed righteousness, of course, is not a license to sin, but the inspired Word of God **never** equates drinking an alcoholic beverage with sin. Drunkenness is the sin, according to God's word.

In fact, the Bible says wine was given by God for man's enjoyment. The Psalmist says that God gave wine to make men glad (Ps 104:15). Jesus did not preach against the use of wine; instead he did as most other Jews of his day. He drank wine in moderation. In ancient times it was normally diluted with water for drinking purposes, but it was one of the principal beverages in Palestine at that time—as it is today—and it was, and is, alcoholic.

Jesus' first miracle was to change water into wine (*oinos*). On this occasion Christ turned six jars of 20 or 30 gallons each into wine (*oinos*). This was no small miracle. This wine was of the finest quality—"You have kept the good wine until now "(John 2:10). At such wedding feasts, after people had drunk the better wine, the hosts brought out lesser-quality wines.

Jesus gave a parable involving the fermenting process of oinos in Matt 9:17. At that time, instead of having metal or glass bottles to enclose wine, the skins of animals were used. The fermentation of the wine would break an old inelastic skin, but it would not break a new stretchable skin.

Another proof that oinos is fermented wine is the fact that the apostle Paul said, "Be not drunk with wine [oinos]" (Eph 5:18). Paul did not mean to avoid getting drunk on grape juice! Paul instructed Timothy, 'Drink no longer water, but use a little wine [oinos] for your stomach's sake and your frequent infirmities" (1 Tim 5:23). He said to use only a little wine, not a whole lot. The purpose of this wine was to soothe Timothy's frequent stomach ailments; small amounts of wine can help some stomach problems.

Some of the Corinthian Christians were getting drunk at the Lord's Supper (1 Cor 11:21). They were using fermented wine, probably following the example that Paul had set for them. Paul did not tell them that they were using the wrong kind of wine. He simply told them to eat and drink at home, and to participate in the Lord's Supper in a respectful way. In Romans 14:21, Paul says that it is good not to drink wine or eat meat if it offends a weak brother. He is referring to fermented wine; grape juice wouldn't offend anyone. The implication is that there's nothing wrong with the wine in itself.

Both the Old and New Testaments contain many examples and commands against excessive use of alcohol and drunkenness. Drunkenness is listed as one of the works of the flesh (Gal 5:21). That means it is the result of the undisciplined, indiscriminate use of alcohol. Jesus warned his followers not to be drunk (Luke 21:34).

The apostle Paul told the Corinthian church to "put away from among yourselves"—to have no fellowship—with a person who cannot control his or her drinking (1 Cor 5:11-13). This refers to people who will not face up to or try to overcome drinking problems, not people who are working on and overcoming their problems. The Bible says that drunkards will not enter the kingdom of God (1 Cor 6:9-10, Gal 5:21). No one who abuses alcohol should be ordained an elder in the ministry of Jesus Christ (1 Tim 3:3, 8, Titus 1:7). If a minister drinks, it should be in moderation.

The following story is a beautiful narrative of reconciliation, conversion, and ultimate redemption—all initiated because of a glass of wine. Years ago a man came into our services and sat through the preaching time weeping. He was a wealthy, high-profile business man who had just gone through a heartwrenching divorce because of his own indiscretions.

After the service he introduced himself to me and set up an appointment to see me for some counseling. This began a six-month pastoral relationship with this man that eventually led him to an understanding of the gospel of Jesus Christ and the ultimate experience of Divine forgiveness.

All that was now needed was reconciliation with his ex-wife. He asked if I would counsel them. I said I would, but when he requested his wife to come with him to see me, she said, "No. He's a Baptist preacher. All he will do is condemn me."

The businessman was crushed. I asked him why his former wife was so hostile about Baptist preachers. He told me she grew up Roman Catholic and the only time she ever attended a Baptist Church the preacher yelled and screamed about the sins of the people in the pews including drinking, going to movies, wearing short skirts and long hair, etc. . . . and it turned her off from "the Baptist religion."

I suggested that rather than have her come to my office that the man might want to see if his ex-wife would have my wife and me over for dinner, just to get acquainted. To his surprise, she agreed. To our surprise, she was a gourmet chef. We entered the lovely home with the smell of French bread wafting in the air, and sat at the table meticulously crafted for a true dining experience.

Unfortunately, though the introductions were cordial, I could tell the evening might be a long one because of the chill toward this "Baptist preacher." As we sat down, I noticed the brilliant table settings, the scrumptiously prepared French gourmet meal, and the solemn expression on the woman's face. I also noticed there was tea and water on the table. So this Baptist pastor said, "You can't have a meal like this without wine. Where is the wine?"

I wish you could have seen her expression. She smiled and warmly said, "But I thought you were a Baptist preacher." "I am," was my response, "and this Baptist preacher knows a great chef when he sees one, and no chef worth her salt would prepare a meal like this without wine."

She asked my wife and I to follow her as she took us down to the cellar. She was a wine collector and she proudly showed us her collection, passed down to her by her grandfather. She meticulously chose a bottle of wine for the occasion and we made our way back to the table.

I led us in prayer and we thanked God for the food and the drink and his provision for us. We ate a wonderful meal and I enjoyed a glass of wine. Nobody around the table had more than two glasses. To make a long story short, the walls that had hindered the relationship came down. We enjoyed the evening with the couple and as a result five things happened:

(1) I was able to lead this woman to faith in Jesus Christ, showing her that Christ alone provided the righteousness she needed, and that she must forsake any trust in her own "self-righteousness." She trusted him and was baptized shortly thereafter.

(2) It was my privilege to perform the private ceremony where wedding vows were exchanged again and this man and woman were reunited in marriage.

(3) The couple became very active in our church and have led in our outreach of the lost in our community through Sunday school.

(4) They have personally given tens of thousands of dollars to the Lord's work through our church and Christian school, and have personally been able to lead several of their own family members to faith in Christ.

(5) They still have their wine collection, but have never been drunk since giving their lives to Christ as Lord.

Now, I ask this simple question to my Southern Baptist friends. What, if anything, is wrong with the events just described to you? I am convinced that we Southern Baptists have for too long avoided teaching our children the principles of God's Word, and instead, substituted a system of religious morality that is often contradictory to the Bible, and therefore, when kids leave Southern Baptists homes they go off the deep end into addictions, rather than live their lives in the enjoyment of the things of God *within the parameters established by God.*

I have heard the argument before that "Even if one person becomes a drunk then I will abstain from alcohol because of it." The power of the gospel is absolutely lost in that kind of thinking. The drunk is a drunk because of the sin in his soul. His soul is transformed by the gospel and the power of the Holy Spirit, not by observing cultural prohibitions of a Southern Baptist. Christians around the world drink beer and wine without getting drunk. It doesn't hurt their witness. It seems the only weaker brothers I keep running into are Southern Baptist pastors who "stumble" when they see a Christian drinking wine. We Southern Baptist pastors claim to believe the Bible, but I sometimes wonder what Bible it is we are reading.

Let's teach the Bible. Let's proclaim the gospel. Let's focus on the essentials. There is a lost world out there. It's time Southern Baptists were known for the transforming power of Christ rather than our cultural prohibitions.

In His Grace,
Wade[2]

I was about to find out that the Southern Baptist Convention, particularly Paige Patterson and those who hold to Baptist identity principles, were about to make life rough for people like Dwight McKissic, Sheri Klouda, and others.

Notes

1. "Pray for Frank Page," 20 June 2006, http://kerussocharis.blogspot.com/2006/06/pray-for-frank-page_20.html, comment 3.

2. "Conversion to Christ over a Glass of Wine," 14 June 2006, http://kerussocharis.blogspot.com/2006/06/conversion-to-christ-over-glass-of_14.html.

Chapter 21

WELCOME TO THE NEIGHBORHOOD, DWIGHT MCKISSIC

Southwestern Baptist Theological Seminary
Chapel Service
Tuesday, August 29, 2006

The motion I recommended and the convention passed at the 2006 Southern Baptist Convention, which called for an investigation into the actions of the trustees of the International Mission Board, was an embarrassment to Paige Patterson and his followers on the board and a challenge to their attempts to control the IMB. The backdoor attempts to demand belief in additional doctrines that exceed the 2000 *BFM* in order for missionary candidates to be appointed had been exposed. The Fundamentalists felt as if they were losing their grip on the SBC and the IMB, so they struck back.

When Paul Pressler wrote his book recounting the conservative resurgence, he was specific about the issue that needed correction in the SBC. In 1998 Pressler wrote,

> The issue in the convention was neither an interpretation of Scripture nor an effort to create unity of thinking on theological issues. . . . The liberals had said that after the conservatives finished with those who held different views of the nature of the Bible, they would begin attacking the charismatics (neo-Pentecostals). They also alleged that conservatives would later attack various other groups until they "purified" every aspect of Christian life. They said conservatives wanted to make everybody think just as they do.
>
> Such a charge was ludicrous, but it did worry some people such as my friends. . . . Charismatic worship and understanding of spiritual gifts is an

interpretation of Scripture. That was not our concern. Our concern was the nature of Scripture.

The liberals have tried to make much of the fact that some Calvinists exist within the conservative movement. Calvinism also is an interpretation of Scriptures. Although I am not a five-point Calvinist, I am perfectly content with persons who seek to convince others to have Calvinist convictions from the teaching of the Word of God.

An interpretation of Scripture is a derivative issue and not a primary one. Interpretation is not a hill on which to die. In fact, the presence of such persuasions as Calvinists and charismatics in the conservative ranks merely shows that conservatives never sought to have all Southern Baptists think exactly alike. All we wanted was for people to base what they believe on an intelligent study of what the Bible says.[1]

I'm sure Pressler meant what he wrote, but something had happened in the intervening ten years. On August 29, 2006, I listened to the Southwestern Seminary chapel message delivered by Pastor Dwight McKissic live on the Internet. After leaving during the message to attend to a previous engagement, I returned and went to the online archives of the Southwestern Baptist Theological Seminary (SWBTS) in order to listen to the remainder of Dwight's message. I discovered that the sermon had been removed from the SWBTS website. Dwight, a trustee of SWBTS at the time, had seemingly said something in chapel with which President Patterson disagreed. Interestingly, Dwight also happened to be a graduate of Southwestern.

I immediately called SWBTS and was told by the person responsible for the Internet broadcasts that all chapel messages are immediately archived and placed on the Web. But he had received a call from the administrative office of SWBTS saying that the message was not to be posted until it was "reviewed" by administration. Ultimately, the message by Pastor McKissic, which included a testimony of how he had discovered the meaning of the gifts and had prayed in tongues for years, did not pass the review, and Dwight's message was removed from the archives.

I later discovered the specifics of Dwight McKissic's sermon. It seems he recounted how, in 1981 as a Southwestern Seminary student, he experienced speaking in a "private prayer language" and that the experience has repeated itself in his Christian walk. Dwight went further and offered gentle criticism of the recently established doctrinal policies by trustees at the International Mission Board that banned any missionaries who practiced the private version of *glossolalia,* or speaking in tongues. McKissic later told the Associated Baptist Press,

I couldn't figure out how a policy that contradicts the teaching of many of our believing theologians could be enacted like that. That was amazing to me. I was so disappointed by the policy that I gave serious consideration to leading my church out of the Southern Baptist Convention. . . . [The policy] is an intrusion of privacy, an invasion of privacy, totally unnecessary, and would exclude a great number of Baptists who would make excellent missionaries. . . . [It is] extra-biblical.[2]

Jon Zellers, the seminary's associate vice president for news and information, issued a statement that was published on the seminary's website:

The statement said that while the seminary "is honored to have Rev. W. Dwight McKissic as a trustee" and "honored to have him in chapel," the seminary would not disseminate copies of the chapel sermon free of charge.

"[W]hile Southwestern does not instruct its chapel speakers about what they can or cannot say, neither do we feel that there is wisdom in posting materials online which could place us in a position of appearing to be critical of actions of the board of trustees of a sister agency. Any trustee or faculty member is free to communicate his concerns to the boards of sister agencies, but it is difficult to imagine a circumstance that would merit public criticism of the actions of a sister board. Furthermore, though most of Rev. McKissic's message represented a position with which most people at Southwestern would be comfortable, Rev. McKissic's interpretation of tongues as 'ecstatic utterance' is not a position that we suspect would be advocated by most faculty or trustees. In keeping with Baptist convictions regarding religious liberty, we affirm Rev. McKissic's right to believe and advocate his position. Equally in keeping with our emphasis of religious liberty we reserve the right not to disseminate openly views which we fear may be harmful to the churches."

The statement said Patterson had made the decision to limit distribution of the sermon "lest uninformed people believe that Pastor McKissic's view on the gift of tongues as 'ecstatic utterance' is the view of the majority of our people at Southwestern." Prior to the statement's posting, McKissic said he didn't believe Patterson had a problem with him or his view of tongues.[3]

He noted that he had lunch with Patterson and his wife, Dorothy, following the chapel service and neither one of them uttered one word of complaint about his message.

Though I had never personally met Pastor McKissic before his chapel message, I had spoken to him once. He was one of several Southern Baptists who called me to voice their support shortly after the recommendation for my removal. As soon as I could, I called Dwight to encourage him. I found him to be engaging in conversation, respectful of Dr. Patterson and Southwestern, and confused over the events that transpired as a result of his chapel message. I pointed out to Dwight that we had a couple of things in common in terms of our service on behalf of the SBC.

First, we both were completely shocked over public statements that contained charges never communicated to us privately and personally. As Dr. McKissic told the Associated Baptist Press, he had enjoyed lunch with Dr. Patterson and his wife following the chapel service. "I love Dr. Patterson, Dr. Patterson loves me, we had rich fellowship today," he said. "If they had a problem with it [the sermon], they didn't utter it to me at all."[4]

Dr. McKissic only became aware of the controversy over the seminary refusing to post his message—because it was "harmful" to churches and critical of a "sister agency"—when a reporter phoned him for an interview. He was stunned. In his mind, the entire chapel service was uplifting, biblically sound, and above all, Christ honoring. In addition, he was received with applause on at least three different occasions. Imagine what went through his mind when he learned his church members were being informed via the media that their pastor was teaching something harmful.

It is only appropriate that, when charges against a Southern Baptist leader are going to be made public, the person against whom the charges are directed be informed first. In fact, I would go further and say integrity demands that the person in question be informed privately before anyone else is told. For that not to happen in Dwight's public censure is unconscionable. Dr. McKissic should have been told in private that his views were harmful to Southern Baptist churches. He might have become angry with such a remark, but at least he would have been able to say, "They told me in private what they are now saying in public." I wish God would part the heavens and utter the following words so that every Southern Baptist would never forget them: "Do not make a public charge against a fellow brother without informing him specifically and privately what charge you are about to make."

Second, it is bewildering how conservative, evangelical Southern Baptist pastors who believe in the inerrancy of Scripture, and who base their messages on the sacred text, can be considered "harmful" or "heretical" by other Southern Baptists who disagree on interpretations regarding third-tier doctrines. The kind of attitude exhibited by Paige Patterson is pure Fundamentalism. In his sermon, McKissic quoted from several Baptist scholars who offer biblical support for private speaking in tongues, including a quotation from Patterson's April 6, 2006, chapel sermon at Southwestern: "What do we conclude? The apostle Paul clearly said, 'Do not forbid to speak in tongues,'" McKissic quoted Patterson as saying. "It would be a mistake for evangelicals to forbid others to speak in tongues."

Third, McKissic and I both have a love for the SBC and her autonomous agencies, including the presidents, trustees, and administrative staff of those agencies, but a growing concern that the SBC is narrowing the parameters of fellowship and cooperation. Dr. McKissic said to APB in a follow-up story,

> Because I said nothing during my message that contradicted the Bible or the 2000 *Baptist Faith & Message*, I fail to see how my comments are viewed as outside of the Baptist mainstream. I do believe that banning the free distribution of my message on the school website is a form of unnecessary censorship that is most unusual considering the fact, again, that many Baptist scholars and leaders . . . have expressed views similar to mine.[5]

I have never spoken in tongues. I don't even know that I agree with Dr. McKissic's interpretation of the texts regarding tongues, but I obviously agree with his assessment regarding the narrowing of the parameters of participation and cooperation in our convention.

We must resist the growing tendency of some to demand that third-tier doctrines, which in decades past have not been doctrines over which Baptists divided, be moved into the category of first-tier doctrines, and exclude fellow Southern Baptists who disagree or give principled dissent. As Al Mohler stated, "The misjudgment of true fundamentalism is the belief that all disagreements concern first-order doctrines. Thus, third-order issues are raised to a first-order importance, and Christians are wrongly and harmfully divided."[6]

Since I had sworn that I would never again sit silently by as another Southern Baptist was wrongfully treated by the Fundamentalist powers that be, I sought to encourage Dwight as much as possible. He later confided in me that the struggle with Patterson and the trustees at Southwestern had caused him health problems and a bout of depression. There were times when Dwight was so disillusioned with the verbal and personal attacks on him that I needed to encourage him to *remain* a Southern Baptist. My friendship with Dwight began in late summer 2006, and it will continue until we both go home to be with the Lord. One of the great privileges I have had since meeting Dwight is having him speak in my church. He, too, asked me to preach for his people in Arlington, Texas, at a conference on the Holy Spirit his church hosted in spring 2007.

The worship service at Cornerstone Baptist Church that Rachelle and I experienced with Dwight made a deep impression on both of us and has caused me to be astounded, again, that Paige Patterson or anyone else within the SBC would desire to exclude Dwight from denominational leadership or missionary cooperation because of his views or practices of the Spirit's gifts. I can assure you that at no time was anything done or practiced in the services Sunday that is prohibited in the Bible. More importantly, Cornerstone's worship services seem to follow what Scripture *prescribes* worship to be. There was both exuberance and reverance, emotion and doctrine, love and grace, Spirit and truth. Many of us could learn from Cornerstone, and I am happy they are part of our convention.

Second, it's time the Southern Baptist Convention reflected the diversity of our people within our leadership. I proposed at the September 2008 Oklahoma Baptist General Convention board of directors meeting that Oklahoma serve as a model for the Southern Baptist Convention on how to hold regional conventions throughout the United States, in conjunction with the annual SBC meeting. The technology exists today for messengers to vote via computer, and I think the worship, teaching, and testimonials at the different regional sites could reflect the diversity of our convention. This kind of networking would solve several problems:

(1) There would be greater participation in the direction of our convention by the members of the churches of our conventions instead of a select few who can travel across country to the site of the SBC host city.

(2) Since our convention was built on "cooperation" and not "conformity," various regional sites for the convention would allow true cooperation of a multitude of churches and church cultures.

(3) The policies and practices of our convention would truly reflect the diversity of our people.

My friendship with Dwight McKissic, including having witnessed his embarrassment of being censured by Paige Patterson and SWBTS trustees for simply living by his convictions, has convinced me even further that our Southern Baptist Convention is stronger through diversity of beliefs on tertiary matters. We must learn to cooperate in spite of our differences.

Notes

1. Paul Pressler, *A Hill on Which to Die* (Nashville: Broadman Press, 1999), 198.

2. Associated Baptist Press, "Trustee McKissic Endorses Prayer Tongue during Chapel Sermon," 29 August 2006, http://www.abpnews.com/index.php?option=com_content&task=view&id=1446&Itemid=119.

3. Ibid.

4. Ibid

5. Associated Baptist Press, "McKissic Responds to Patterson's Criticism of Sermon on Tongues," 30 August 2006, http://www.abpnews.com/index.php?option=com_content&task=view&id=1448&Itemid=119119.

6. "A Theological Triage Test," 25 August 2006, http://kerussocharis.blogspot.com/2006/08/theological-triage-test_25.html.

Chapter 22

"A MOMENTARY LAPSE OF PARAMETERS"

Sheri Klouda's Story
Posted to *Grace and Truth to You*
Wednesday, January 17, 2007

I grew more aware of conservative, evangelical Southern Baptists who were becoming victims of the horrible abuse caused by Fundamentalism's fury—Dwight McKissic, Wendy Norvelle, the Dobbses, and countless others who wrote to me to describe their experiences at the hands of Fundamentalists who desired to "purify" our convention. I received so many stories that I kept a file on my computer called "Horror Stories." My desire was not only to offer a word of encouragement to Southern Baptists who felt disenfranchised, but in some cases, to correct the problem of Fundamentalist abuse. One such horror story that dominated the media's attention in spring 2007 was that of Dr. Sheri Klouda.

Dr. Sheri Klouda joined the faculty of Southwestern in April 2002 as assistant professor of Old Testament languages. She received her Ph.D. from Southwestern in May 2002. She had previously been conferred her bachelor's and master's degrees from Criswell College in Dallas, and, as already stated, she served three and a half years as adjunct professor at Southwestern prior to joining the faculty as professor. In summer 2001, Sheri served as assistant professor of biblical Hebrew at Beeson Divinity School at Samford University in Alabama.

Her conservative credentials are unquestionable. During the same trustee meeting at which she was hired, the SWBTS trustees passed a resolution thanking fellow trustee Ralph Pulley for his twenty-two years of service as a SWBTS trustee. One can rest assured that all eight faculty members hired that day, including Dr. Klouda, were solid, evangelical conservatives who possessed a record of unashamedly defending the authority, sufficiency, and inerrancy of God's Word. Ralph Pulley and his fellow trustees would have guaranteed that to be the case.

Dr. Klouda was an exemplary employee of Southwestern and a tremendous representative of the Southern Baptist Convention to the evangelical world at large. She excelled in the classroom, building a strong reputation as both a scholar and teacher. Her classes were frequently full, and her students testified often of their admiration for Dr. Klouda. Donald Moore, a theological student at Southwestern who was diagnosed with Hodgkin's lymphoma during his tenure, expressed his appreciation for Dr. Klouda in an article published by the school's journal. "I was taking first-year Hebrew with Dr. Klouda at the same time I was going through my first round of chemo," Donald Moore said. "I thank God for [her] grace and good teaching and patience."[1]

Sheri Klouda gained the respect of the evangelical academic world. She served on the editorial committee and was a regular contributor to the *Southwestern Journal of Theology*. Sheri also contributed to *The Bulletin for Biblical Research*, a journal specializing in ancient Near East and biblical studies, and she was a guest lecturer at the 57th annual meeting of the Evangelical Theological Society at Valley Forge, Pennsylvania, in 2005, and the 58th annual meeting of the Evangelical Theological Society in Washington, D.C., in 2006. She also served as guest lecturer at SBL in 2006. In March 2006, Sheri received a grant from the prestigious Lilly Grant for Theological Scholars from the Association of Theological Schools in order to partially fund her work titled "Building a Biblical Theology for Today: The Theology of Intertextuality."

Paige Patterson was a hired as president of Southwestern Baptist Theological Seminary on June 24, 2003, a little more than a year after trustees had hired Klouda. The trustees voted unanimously to hire Dr. Patterson, just as they had Dr. Klouda a year earlier. Some of the faculty at Southwestern were concerned about the hiring of Paige Patterson. He was asked during a June 24, 2003, press conference following his appointment if he would hire women in the school of theology. He responded, "Dorothy [his wife] serves on the theology faculty at Southeastern," and that "provides somewhat of an answer." Then he added, "There are ample numbers of men who are well-qualified for those positions." Patterson said he planned to build the faculty with "God-called men."[2]

Patterson's philosophical perspective on the roles of women in theological education prevented him from feeling comfortable about women teaching biblical studies or theology to men. In September 2003, two months after his appointment as president of Southwestern and one month before his official inauguration, Paige met privately with all staff and faculty.[3] David Allen, the 2003 chairman of the board of trustees responsible for hiring Dr. Patterson, and who himself would be hired by Patterson in 2004 to serve as dean for the SWBTS School of Theology, said of that private meeting with faculty and staff, "While some speculate about Patterson's compatibility with our faculty, I have high hopes that our excellent faculty will work well with Dr. Patterson."

At that closed-door meeting in September 2003, Paige gave personal assurances to faculty that their jobs were safe, regardless of gender. Sheri acknowledged her concern at the time, but after the faculty meeting and the personal assurance by Dr. Patterson that her job was secure, she relaxed and continued in her commitment to invest her life and service in the school she loved. A few days after Patterson's inauguration, four professors resigned unexpectedly,[4] including Dr. Bruce Corley; however, Klouda placed her focus on serving her school and being loyal to President Patterson and the constituency that hired her.

Sheri was the primary provider for her family due to illnesses that have plagued her husband over the years. In July 2003, William and Sheri purchased a home in Arlington in order to be closer to the seminary so that she could spend more time at the school and with her family than on the highway commuting.

Just over a year after Sheri received the personal assurance that her job was secure, she was called to attend a meeting in June 2004, where she was informed that she would not be granted tenure because "she was a woman." Ironically, Dorothy Patterson was serving as professor of theology in women's studies, but unlike Sheri, Dorothy "only taught women." Though Paige and Dorothy Patterson often said that Dorothy worked "officially" under the auspices of the school of education at Southwestern, as of January 2007, her name continued to be listed on Southwestern's official website as teaching in the school of theology.

In June 2004, precisely a year after Patterson had been appointed president of the school, Sheri was told that "the president" would never recommend her for tenure. Why? It had nothing to do with her professional performance or collegiality, but simply her gender. The president would not give her tenure because she was the only female teaching biblical studies in the school of theology, and that was not the proper place for a woman. There were many qualified men who could fill that position, and it was the president's desire to replace her. Southwestern would give her two to three years to find another position at a reputable school, but she was to do her best to find another position as quickly as possible.

Sheri was stunned. In her mind she had the job of her dreams. While the issues surrounding tenure do not guarantee that a professor will retain his or her position at an institution, she saw herself as working toward tenure at Southwestern. She had invested her life, her family, and all her energy to be close to the school she loved. There was not one thing she had done to discredit her school. Rather, she was well liked by the students, loyal to administration and faculty, and had done her best to bring excellence to the school of theology in evangelical circles. She was being forced out because she was a woman.

If one wonders what goes on in the psyche of a man (or woman) who does not believe a woman should teach men Hebrew or teach men properly to exegete the Scripture through the study of the languages, one only has to read the words of Paige and Dorothy Patterson. On October 25, 2004, one year after he was inaugurated and four months after Sheri was told to look for another job, Paige Patterson gave an interview with Baptist Press.[5] He addressed the rumors that circulated a year earlier, just prior to his inauguration, that women would not be allowed to take classes with men at Southwestern Baptist Theological Seminary and "the rumor that women would be drummed out of the theology school altogether."

Patterson said he knew at the time that he would have to speak to the rumors one day, but he "sort of enjoyed watching the rumor mill work for a year. Every once in a while I've been known to feed one and watch how far it goes." Paige's confession here surprised me, and I wonder if the content of some of the rumors he 'fed' will one day be revealed.

According to the October 25, 2004, Baptist Press article titled "Women Are Treasured by God,"[6] Patterson said he purposefully scheduled a discussion of the issue of women in ministry because others often misrepresent his views on the subject; he called such misrepresentation a "diatribe and lie of the left." Of the many attempts to explain what the Apostle Paul meant when he wrote the passage about the submission and silence of women (1 Tim 2:12), Patterson said, "Oftentimes, the answer of the evangelical world is that a woman cannot serve as a senior pastor."

"Would somebody please find that in the text?" Paige asked. "It is not in the text. That is not said. There is no mention of occupation in this text at all. This is not a question of occupation. It is a question of an assignment from God, in this case that a woman not be involved in a teaching or ruling capacity over men." Patterson concluded by saying, "It is a prohibition of a woman teaching or ruling over a man . . . ."

There it is. Patterson's narrow interpretation of 1 Timothy 2:12 says it all and should cause our convention some serious concern. Paige is saying that this verse is not merely addressing "women pastors," but any woman in "authority" over a man. No woman shall teach a man—period. Dr. Klouda needed to be replaced as a professor because she was a woman.

Dr. Klouda was not a pastor of a church. Dr. Klouda was a professor at Southwestern. Dr. Klouda had been trained to teach Hebrew; in fact, Dr. Klouda had been trained to teach Hebrew at Southwestern Baptist Theological Seminary. The trustees of Southwestern unanimously voted to hire Dr. Klouda to be professor of Hebrew in 2002. It cannot be argued that the institution had religious convictions that a woman cannot teach men; the institution's ultimate authority (the trustees) hired Dr. Klouda. It cannot be argued that the institution had religious convictions against a woman being in a position of "authority" over a man; the institution's ultimate authority hired Dr. Klouda.

It is critical to understand that Dr. Patterson replaced Sheri Klouda with a male on the basis of an interpretative application of 1 Timothy 2:12 that, according to Patterson himself, goes far beyond a prohibition of women pastors. According to his rigid and narrow understanding of this Pauline text, Patterson believes it is God's will for a woman not to serve in any position of "authority" over a man. For our convention to treat in such a poor and humiliating manner a Christian who is as gifted and competent as Sheri Klouda—just because she is a woman—is a poor witness to the love of Christ in us, a shrouding of the sense of his justice over us, and a lack of appreciation of the equality he brings to us all.

If there is not a change in the way we as the Southern Baptist Convention view, treat, and appreciate women, there will be more lights that go out in our beloved convention than the shining luminary known as Sheri Klouda.

For those who say it is nobody's business what goes on among the faculty of Southwestern, I would gently disagree. This is a Southern Baptist institution, and it is our duty to ensure that things are done ethically, judicially, and biblically.

I called Sheri at her home in Upland, Indiana, one night in January 2007. She was hesitant to talk to me at first, but I eventually gained her trust as I shared with her that my only desire was to help rectify the ill treatment she and her family received. Sheri confirmed the facts of the story I was going to post. She told me she was hesitant for me to make anything public about her situation because she feared professional retribution. Future contracts to write books, opportunities to speak at academic conferences, and the possible hiring at another seminary could be in jeopardy if Paige Patterson sought to make trouble with her story going public. I appealed to her by asking her to consider the women who would follow in her footsteps in the Southern Baptist Convention. I also said that I was not necessarily asking permission to post her story, but rather, I wanted to ensure I had all the facts right.

In the end, it was my decision alone to post the article on my blog that introduced Sheri Klouda's troubles to the SBC world. I e-mailed Paige Patterson before I made public this story. I did not hear from Paige via e-mail, so I called him before I posted the article about Klouda in order to speak with him personally. He did not return my call. I went to lengths to deal with the matter privately, but I was rebuffed at every turn. Once I made the Klouda story public, SWBTS administration went through the proverbial roof.

Van McClain, chairman of the Southwestern Baptist Theological Seminary's board of trustees, told the *Dallas Morning News* that Dr. Klouda's hiring was a "momentary lapse of the parameters."[7] He also told the *Dallas Morning News* that my blog "is filled with inaccuracies."[8]

Upon reading Van's public statement, I immediately called him. It has not been my privilege to meet Van. Prior to its publication, I sent the Klouda post to several people to ask for corrections (if necessary), but Van was not one of them. Paige Patterson himself had not offered any corrections either, though he was on the list of people to whom I sent the post prior to publication. Since Van seemed concerned enough about "inaccuracies" to speak of them in general terms to a newspaper, I felt it appropriate to contact him by phone to learn more details. His secretary said Van was unable to receive my call, so I e-mailed him on Friday, January 19, 2007, and asked him the following four questions:

(1) Did you vote for Sheri Klouda to teach Hebrew at Southwestern Baptist Theological Seminary in 2002?

(2) Why do you now believe that she is not qualified to do so? Is it really the "statement of faith" (please show me where the *Baptist Faith & Message* 2000 says a woman can't teach a man Hebrew, or theology, or doctrine), or is it the narrow view of President Patterson that now guides you?

(3) Have you had any formal or informal discussions with Dr. Patterson about joining the School of Theology, teaching in the position vacated by Dr. Klouda?

(4) Would you please, in print, tell me where I am wrong in my post?

Van McClain e-mailed me back the following day, Friday, January 19, with the following two-sentence e-mail: "I have had neither any formal or informal discussions with Dr. Patterson about joining the School of Theology or teaching in the position vacated by Dr. Klouda. Nor am I seeking any faculty position at Southwestern."

I responded immediately, thanked him for his e-mail, and then closed by saying, "Van, thank you for your answer to one of my questions. I counted four questions, however, and must have missed your response to the other three."

Four days later he e-mailed me about the inaccuracies by sending a one-sentence explanation: "The vote for Klouda was not unanimous."

It was later revealed that the minutes of that meeting recorded a unanimous vote, so even SWBTS's claim that my blog was filled with inaccuracies was inaccurate itself. By now I was familiar with the tactic of those who don't like what is being said accusing the writer of "gossip" or "slander" or "inaccuracies." Yet, attempting to attack me did not stop me from continuing to ask the pertinent questions.

(1) Is it an ethical, moral, or just action to remove a woman from Southern Baptist service as a professor of Hebrew simply because she is a woman, particularly when the institution who hired her conferred upon her the very degrees necessary to fill the position she held, and in light of her outstanding service and accomplishments in that particular field?

(2) Some may argue that Southwestern Baptist Theological Seminary had "a momentary lapse of the parameters" when SWBTS hired a woman to teach Hebrew in 2002, but then the question becomes, Were the trustees who hired Dr. Klouda informed of the effort to remove Dr. Klouda, or did the

president take this action by himself, based upon his opinion that women should not teach in the theology department?

(3) How can we not challenge those who suggest that Southwestern Baptist Theological Seminary is a church and Dr. Sheri Klouda is a pastor? Is not SWBTS an institution of higher learning, and is not Sheri Klouda an educator? Are we seriously saying that a woman cannot teach a man Hebrew, cannot teach a man to exegete the Bible for himself, or instruct him in theology? Is this the direction in which we desire our convention to head? Is our ecclesiology so messed up in the Southern Baptist Convention that we call a seminary a church?

On a good note, our church raised several thousand dollars for Dr. Klouda and her family to help them during their financial hardships. God's people should watch out for their own, and Southern Baptists should take care of their own. I believe Sheri Klouda should have been given her job back. The judge eventually ruled that this was a "church" matter and the civil courts should not intervene.

I agree. It is a church matter, a convention matter. I have developed a friendship with Sheri and her family, and if my involvement in seeking to bring change to the Southern Baptist Convention accomplishes nothing more than to help the Kloudas and restore their faith in Southern Baptists, then it will have been worth it all. I am committed to seeing that we have no future horror stories like what happened to Sheri Klouda in the SBC.

Notes

1. This article has since been removed from the SWBTS website.

2. Baptist Press, "Patterson Tells Media He Wants "to Please Jesus" In His New Role," 25 June 2003, http://www.bpnews.org/bpnews.asp?ID=16181.

3. Baptist Press, "Patterson Responds 'Openly, Honestly' in Meeting with Southwestern Faculty," 25 June 2003, http://www.bpnews.org/bpnews.asp?ID=16180.

4. Baptist Press, "Four Seminary Faculty Submit Resignations," 4 November 2003, http://www.bpnews.org/bpnews.asp?ID=16998.

5. Baptist Press, "Patterson: Women Are Treasured by God, Have High Calling," 25 October 2004, http://www.bpnews.org/bpnews.asp?ID=19402.

6. Ibid.

7. Dallas Morning News, "Baptists at Odds Over Removal of Female Professor," 19 January 2007, http://www.dallasnews.com/sharedcontent/dws/dn/religion/stories/012007 dnmetnubaptists.176f48d.html.

8. Ibid.

Chapter 23

CONTINUED HOSTILITY
AT THE IMB

IMB Trustee Meeting
Richmond, Virginia
July 2006

Between the 2006 Southern Baptist Convention and the 2007 Southern Baptist Convention, the International Mission Board held six board meetings. Though I remained silent at every board meeting, never speaking publicly, the hostility shown me by trustee leadership only increased. They had been assigned the task by the SBC to "investigate" themselves, and Dr. Rankin's and my belief that trustee leadership would do nothing to correct the problems on the board was well founded.

The July 2006 IMB meeting in Richmond was the first one over which the new chairman of the board, John Floyd, presided. Over the next eighteen months, I had several conversations with John. He was always mild-mannered in conversation, but often patronizing. I think he was exasperated by my insistence that he answer my questions with specifics and not generalities. I made it a point to speak with John privately, and I didn't address him publicly until January 2008.

At the July 2006 trustee meeting, Chairman Floyd gave his report. He stated that blogs were lowering the morale of missionaries. Strangely, from the perspective of those missionaries who were visiting with me, my blog and other Southern Baptist blogs were energizing, motivating, and compelling missionaries and Southern Baptists to be informed and involved. I think Dr. Floyd was the one with lowered morale because he was being asked to answer for the policies he pushed through the board.

Dr. Floyd also indicated in his report that his major concern with the work of the International Mission Board was the sending of missionaries into the field without adequate training. His concern, I believe, is without basis or merit. If he is to convince me and others that inadequate preparation is a legitimate problem, he will need to provide evidence of such. I suspect this was Dr. Floyd's way of supporting ideological Fundamentalists who were alleging a lack of theological acumen at the IMB.

At my first trustee meeting a year earlier, I had asked Dr. Floyd for anecdotal evidence that the new doctrinal policies were needed in order to combat charismatic problems or inappropriate baptisms on the field. John ignored my question, and I never received evidence of problems on the field not handled properly by the IMB. I believe that had there been an attempt to answer my question with straightforward, clear communication when I initially asked it, and corresponding evidence of problems on the mission field, then my controversy with the board might have been avoided. As a duly elected trustee, I had a right to have my questions answered.

My request to see anecdotal evidence for the need of the "doctrinal" policies was finally answered in July 2006—one year after I initially asked. Dr. Floyd told me privately as we ate lunch together before the plenary session of the IMB trustee meeting that there was no anecdoctal evidence of IMB staff not dealing appropriately with charismatic problems on the field, and no unbiblical baptisms taking place on the field. Worse, he said, he and trustee leadership didn't need any evidence.

To him, the issue was doctrine. He was a Landmark Baptist who believed in the cessation of spiritual gifts. To John Floyd, every Southern Baptist needed to believe as he did. I appreciated his honesty in finally responding to my request for evidence that the policies were necessary. His response that there was no evidence, nor was it needed, only confirmed what I suspected from the beginning. The policies were pushed not because of problems on the mission field, but because there was a particular doctrinal mindset among IMB leadership. To those trustee leaders, every Southern Baptist had to believe their interpretation of Scripture; if not, he or she couldn't be part of the mission force.

Autumn 2006

Our trustee meeting in September 2006 was in Spartanburg and uneventful. I had not been assigned to serve on an IMB subcommittee for 2006/2007, and I experienced personal hostility from trustee leaders. However, several new trustees (voted in at the SBC in June) came up to me, introduced themselves, and said they had asked people to point out "Wade Burleson."

Invariably they remarked, "You are so quiet," as if they expected me to act otherwise because of what they had heard trustee leadership say through the media. I was making new friends, and I could see progress.

In October I traveled to India to meet with our missionary IMB personnel in Bangalore and spend a week with our church members who operate a 1,000-student English school and a 300-child orphanage. It was a great opportunity for me to see, again, firsthand the great work done on the field by Southern Baptists. Our problem with the IMB was not field personnel; our problem was a beaurocratic nightmare and disconnect from the field to the trustee board. The focus on keeping women from church leadership makes no sense in China and other places where house churches are mainly composed of women. The emphasis on proper "administrators" of baptism at the trustee level is ridiculous to a missionary trying to start a church among the Islamic tribes of West Africa.

Our Southern Baptist Convention needs to focus on the gospel and cooperation, so before I left for India I proposed a statement of cooperation for Southern Baptists. The statement is borrowed with permission, and with minor adaptations for our convention, from Dr. Michael Bird, a brilliant, conservative Greek and New Testament Baptist scholar who lives in Scotland.

Some trustees had tried to argue that I was good at pointing out problems with the SBC and the IMB but not as good at offering solutions. I felt that my five-fold recommendation to the convention, passed by the 2006 Greensboro SBC, was a start in the right direction, but I was hopeful this statement of cooperation could better define the future for the SBC.

A Southern Baptist Statement of Cooperation

The gospel is the story about Christ, God's and David's Son, who died and was raised and is established as Lord. We as Southern Baptists join together to proclaim the good news that God's Kingdom has come in the life, death, and resurrection of Jesus of Nazareth, the Lord and Messiah, in fulfillment of the Word of God.

The gospel we declare evokes faith, repentance, and discipleship—its accompanying effects include the forgiveness of sins, justification, reconciliation, adoption, wisdom, and the gift of the Holy Spirit. Southern Baptists accompany our proclamation of the gospel with cooperative works of compassion and mercy for those in need or distress.

We strive to advance Christ's kingdom on earth with the confession, proclamation, and application of the good news. The Bible is undoubtedly central to our cooperation, but Jesus Christ is the center of it. Therefore, we resolve to cooperate with one another, affirming the essentials of the gospel and our Baptist identity in these five doctrines:

(1). We affirm the authority, sufficiency, and reliability of God's infallible revelation to man in both his written Word and the Living Word Jesus Christ.
(2) We affirm both the full humanity and deity of Jesus Christ.
(3) We affirm Christ's substitutionary death for sinners, his resurrection from the dead, and his gift of eternal life to all who are in relationship with him by grace through faith.
(4) We affirm the Baptist distinctive of believer's baptism by immersion for those who have come to personal faith in Jesus Christ as Lord and Savior.
(5) We affirm that those apart from a relationship with Christ will face God's judgment.

The sole authority for faith and practice among Baptists is the Scriptures of the Old and New Testaments. Baptist confessions, including the 2000 *Baptist Faith & Message*, are only guides to interpreting the Bible, and have no authority over the conscience. We Baptists have historically differed in interpretation on finer points of doctrine not essential to Christian faith and Baptist identity. Yet, with all our differences on secondary issues, we as Southern Baptists desire to cooperate in ministry because of our love for the gospel.

Therefore, we intentionally put aside our differences on secondary issues for the sake of cooperative gospel ministry. We desire unity in the essentials, liberty in the nonessentials, but charity in all things. This statement of cooperation defines the necessary essentials that must be affirmed in order to participate in the cooperative ministries of the Southern Baptist Convention.

We desire to send to the world and our evangelical brethren through this statement of cooperation a sure and certain message: It is the gospel that unites Southern Baptists, and what unites us is greater than anything that might potentially divide us.[1]

I was considering offering this statement of cooperation for adoption at the 2007 SBC in San Antonio, but I felt that simply introducing the concepts of evangelical cooperation on my blog was a way to start a positive conversation about the SBC.

At the end of 2006, I had received close to 10,000 written letters, e-mails, or comments from fellow Southern Baptists, most of them positive.

My life had become richer through the relationships I had developed with Southern Baptists from all across our convention. I never could have dreamed that a recommendation for my removal from the IMB trustees in the first month of that year would ultimately lead to relationships with thousands of wonderful missionaries, pastors, and laymen across the world. Hundreds wrote to tell me that my blog had become a source of inspiration and a topic of conversation for them while in ministry. It also began to dawn on me that many people in the SBC knew far more about me than I knew about them.

All in all, 2006 had been a memorable, rich, and rewarding year for me. I would not wish my experience on anyone else, but I am glad God chose the path he did for me. I became a better man for it, and 2006 ended with the hope that the next year would be as rich and rewarding without as much conflict.

My message has been simple and consistent: to exclude otherwise qualified Southern Baptists from IMB leadership or cooperative missions ministry because of disagreement with interpretation of a tertiary doctrine is certain to stifle future growth in the Southern Baptist Convention. I didn't realize that trustee leadership would take such offense when I voiced my difference of opinion; trustee leadership didn't realize their actions to silence me would have the opposite reaction (maybe such tactics with others had been more effective?). The more aggressive they became, the more resolved I became. The more they failed on their promises to me, the more I pressed the issue to the convention regarding them. Throughout the debate, however, I had always been respectful of my fellow trustees.

I am of the opinion that if IMB trustee leadership had simply ignored my written posts in late 2005 and 2006, then no controversy would have erupted in our convention. I am a peaceful person by nature. I state my views, accept everyone who disagrees, and move on. I am not the guy who wears the rainbow wig in the stands waving the John 3:16 sign. I preach in the same pulpits where everyone else preaches. I attend the same conferences everyone else attends. I dress the same. I talk the same. I look the same. I am a Southern Baptist.

Why use a sledgehammer to squash a gnat? In the 161-year history of the Southern Baptist Convention no trustee has ever been recommended for removal from a trustee board. Yet, simply because I voiced dissent, this drastic action was taken. Why? It may be a little late, but if a similar thing happens again on an agency or board, I would suggest the following plan:

(1) Ignore dissent, or at least politely disagree, particularly if you are in the majority. When you seek to squelch it, you validate it. When you attempt to remove the dissenter, you make a hero of him.

(2) Make sure you know what you are doing before you do it. The day of proposing an action and then saying, "We must do this. Trust us, we'll explain later," have been buried forever. Thank God.

(3) Keep the main thing the main thing. Agencies should not delve into areas beyond their scope of responsibility. No agency that depends upon cooperative support of the entire Southern Baptist Convention has the right or the perogative to establish an arbitrary doctrinal standard that exceeds the *Baptist Faith & Message*.

There are those who say, "This fussing and fighting makes me wish I weren't a Baptist." Don't say that. The truth is, we may seem to "fuss and fight," but actually, we are establishing the fact that we are by nature Baptists; nobody dictates, demands, or dominates our beliefs. The word of God is our guide, and no human instrument will bind our conscience. The presence of free debate and dissent is a sign of a healthy Baptist denomination.

Congregations made up of Southern Baptists often fight, but in the friendly fight, friction sparks and shapes the steel that forms the future backbone of our Southern Baptist denomination.

Note

1. "A Southern Baptist Statement of Cooperation," 29 October 2006, http://kerussocharis.blogspot.com/2006/10/southern-baptist-statement-of_29.html.

Chapter 24

"WHAT IDIOT SAID THERE WAS NO INVESTIGATION?"

The Trustees Reveal Their Findings
January–February 2007

In nearly three years of service, I missed only one IMB trustee meeting—January 2007 in Ontario, California, January 30–31. I had made it known to trustee leadership and those who read my blog that I would not be present at the trustee meeting due to my son's state basketball playoffs and my wife's birthday. Perhaps I shouldn't have been surprised that trustee leadership decided to present their "official" response to the motion passed by the Southern Baptist Convention at the only meeting I couldn't attend. Not one time since the SBC passed the motion (i.e., that the IMB investigate itself in five specific areas and report back to the SBC) had a trustee leader called me to ask to see the e-mails, documentation, and other materials I had gathered over the previous year. Not one time was I asked to speak to the full board about my concerns, as I had been promised in the phone conversation with trustee leadership in February 2006. So when Rick Thompson called me from California and told me trustee leadership was "officially" responding to the SBC recommendation, I was shocked.

At this California meeting, the IMB trustees passed trustee leadership's official response to my motion, and immediately the press began to call requesting my response. I had asked that a fax of the report be sent to me, which it was, and I composed a point-by-point response to the report. I then posted my response on my blog on February 1.[1]

The entire motion appears in chapter 18. Below I have provided the five points of investigation, IMB leadership response to each point, and a summary of my reaction to that response.

The IMB was to investigate

(1) The manipulation of the nominating process of the Southern Baptist Convention during the appointment of trustees for the International Mission Board.

IMB Trustee Leadership's Official Response to Greensboro Motion (1)
"The International Mission Board has no authority to speak to the work of the nominating committee elected by the Southern Baptist Convention or to investigate the process by which it does its work."

My Response to Trustee Leadership Regarding (1)
I agree. This is why I asked for the executive committee of the Southern Baptist Convention to look into the matter, not IMB trustee leaders. However, these trustee leaders were the very ones manipulating the entire nominating process. To give the "investigation" over to the very IMB trustees who were contacting the nominating committee to seek to influence them regarding their appointments is like telling the fox to watch the hen house. The tampering of the nominating process by IMB trustees was exactly what the Convention said needed to be "investigated," and the one-sentence response by IMB trustee leaders showed they had no intention of letting anybody know what I knew about Fundamentalist trustees manipulating the process to get like-minded Southern Baptists to serve alongside them.

(2) Attempts to influence and/or coerce the IMB trustees, staff, and administration to take a particular course of action by one or more Southern Baptist agency heads other than the president of the International Mission Board.

IMB Trustee Leadership's Official Response to Greensboro Motion (2)
"It is assumed that any and all heads of SBC entities are concerned about the effectiveness of all entities in order for the SBC to fulfill its kingdom task in the world. While the IMB may exercise authority over its own president and elected staff, we are not in a position to question or investigate the actions and motives of heads of other entities."

My Response to Trustee Leadership Regarding (2)
Again, I agree. This is why I asked for the executive committee of the Southern Baptist Convention to look into the matter, not IMB trustee leadership. The IMB is not in a position to question or investigate the motives of heads of other entities, but *somebody* sure should be in a position to demand

that an agency head stop undermining the work, vision, and agenda of a fellow agency head—and that *somebody* is the executive committee of the Southern Baptist Convention (or the SBC herself). Of course, IMB trustee leaders were loyal to Paige Patterson at Southwestern Baptist Theological Seminary, and there was no way IMB chairman John Floyd would even begin to question the president of the Southwestern Baptist Theological Seminary where John's fellow administrator at Mid-America Seminary, Dr. Van McClain, served as chairman of the SWBTS board of trustees.

(3) The appropriate and/or inappropriate use of forums and executive sessions of the International Mission Board as compared to conducting business in full view of the Southern Baptist Convention and the corresponding propriety and/or impropriety of the chairman of the International Mission Board excluding any individual trustee, without Southern Baptist Convention approval, from participating in meetings where the full International Mission Board is convened.

IMB Trustee Leadership's Official Response to Greensboro Motion (3)
"The IMB does not allow formal business to be transacted in its closed trustee forums, but uses this time for prayer, personal testimonies, and preliminary questions and discussions regarding issues of mutual concern between senior staff and trustees. Official executive sessions are limited to matters dealing with sensitive personnel actions related to staff, missionaries, and/or trustees or those in which public exposure would result in detrimental consequences for personnel serving in sensitive and restricted locations around the world. Any actions that may be taken to exclude any trustee from participating in closed-board sessions by the chairman will have been made with support of the board as a last resort and in order to avoid disruption and distractions to the board fulfilling its assigned tasks with unity and appropriate decorum."

My Response to Trustee Leadership Regarding (3)
First, I am grateful that forums are now used to hear praise reports from the mission field, as well as testimonials and prayers from trustees themselves. This is the way it should be. However, in my personal experience, as well as that of others, this kind of forum has not always been the case at the IMB. I promise that as long as I serve as an IMB trustee that I will do everything in my power to ensure that closed doors will never again provide protection and

impunity for any trustee who unjustly attacks another IMB administrator, IMB missionary, or IMB trustee.

I have consistently and repeatedly advocated that the business of any agency of the Southern Baptist Convention be done in full view of the entire convention through plenary sessions. But for the safety of missionaries in security three zones or extraordinarily sensitive personnel matters, all the business of the IMB is appropriate for public viewing. I think every trustee now understands this point and is doing everything to insure that closed door meetings be spent in prayer and testimony and not politics.

Finally, a reporter for the *Southern Baptist Texan*, in an online article picked up by the Florida Baptist Witness, badly misinterpreted the last sentence of number three. The "official response" is dealing with when, how, and why a trustee may be barred from forum and closed sessions of the board. The article reported that I had been barred from IMB forums and closed-door executive sessions. That was not the case (nor would it ever be). Trustee leaders did not have any authority to bar me from a trustee forum or executive sessions of the International Mission Board. I had never missed attending a convocation of IMB trustees, and except for this meeting in Ontario, I did not miss another trustee meeting while I remained on the board. This type of reporting is evidence that Southern Baptists often misunderstand what is happening, even those who should be in the know. Later, *Southern Baptist Texan* editor Jerry Pierce informed me that the article had been revised to reflect the needed corrections.

(4) The legislation of new doctrinal requisites for eligibility to serve as employees or missionaries of the IMB beyond the 2000 Baptist Faith & Message.

IMB Trustee Leadership's Official Response to Greensboro Motion (4)
"While the *Baptist Faith & Message* represents a general confession of Southern Baptist beliefs related to Biblical teachings on primary doctrinal and social issues, the IMB retains the prerogative and responsibility of further defining the parameters of doctrinal beliefs and practices of its missionaries who serve Southern Baptists with accountability to this board."

My Response to Trustee Leadership Regarding (4)
Of all five statements in the "official response," this one causes me the most concern. In fact, for a board of trustees to "retain the prerogative and responsibility to further define the parameters of doctrinal beliefs . . . of its

missionaries" is *the* problem we face in the SBC. Fundamentalists in control of SBC boards are demanding conformity to their specific interpretations of Scripture, and then disqualifying from cooperative service those who disagree. To show the absurdity of this action, just ask yourself how the convention would feel if liberals were in control of the board and demanded that everyone deny the doctrine of substitutionary atonement before they be appointed to be an SBC missionary. There would be outrage. So, too, we ought to be outraged by Fundamentalists' desire to demand conformity on their interpretations of tertiary doctrines.

Dr. Bowden McElroy is a friend, a licensed professional counselor, and a Southern Baptist from Tulsa, Oklahoma. He is always calm and reasonable in his responses. Dr. McElroy's assessment, in the form of a comment on my February 1 blog, said this about statement (4) from trustee leadership:

> No matter what angle I approach this from, I keep hearing the underlying tone of superiority: "We know what's best for the SBC. We know what the Convention really meant when it adopted the BF&M." Or, as we say in Oklahoma, "I thought I told you to wait in the back of the truck." The mission statement of the IMB calls for the board to "Enlist, appoint, equip, and provide support for God-called Southern Baptist missionaries . . . who give evidence of piety, zeal for their Master's kingdom, [and] conviction of truth as held by Southern Baptists." Trustee leaders' official statement regarding (4) reveals the IMB trustee's belief that 'conviction of truth' can only be divined by them and the Convention is not to be trusted to articulate for itself what Southern Baptists believe.

Bowden was dead on. It was this arrogant response by IMB trustee leadership that led directly to us bringing to the Southern Baptist Convention for adoption what would later become known as the "Garner Motion" (see ch. 25). The Convention would pass the Garner Motion, an act that basically smacked IMB trustee leaders across the proverbial hand as if to say, "Don't you dare narrow the doctrinal parameters of missionary cooperation without asking the entire Southern Baptist Convention first!"

(5) The suppression of dissent by trustees in the minority through various means by those in the majority, and the propriety of any agency forbidding a trustee, by policy, from publicly criticizing a board-approved action;

IMB Trustee Leadership's Official Response to Greensboro Motion (5)

"All board approved actions result from a process of committee, and sometimes multiple committees, consideration before they are brought to a plenary session for adoption. All trustees have opportunity in the committee process and plenary session to express and advocate minority opinions. As in any democratic body, once the majority has determined the action to be taken, the board feels that the action should receive the unified public support of all trustees for the sake of effectively moving forward to fulfill our mission task."

My Response to Trustee Leadership Regarding (5)

I would agree with the statement above except in three circumstances—if the board's decision violates Scripture, or if the board's decision violates an individual trustee's conscience, or if a board's decision transgresses entity or Convention bylaws, then no matter how strong anyone's desire for unity is, the appearance of unity cannot become a stumbling block to seeking correction. Further, though it may have been the IMB trustees' prerogative to demand doctrinal conformity on these tertiary doctrines, the more appropriate question may be, "should they?"

The best way to handle dissent is to accept it as something healthy for our Convention, and if the dissenter has no biblical basis for his dissent then the Convention will ignore him, or . . . not.

Greensboro Motion (conclusion)

That to accomplish the committee's work all the trustees, officers, employees, and administrators of the International Mission Board, shall fully cooperate with the committee to accomplish the purposes outlined in this motion; and that the ad hoc committee make its final report and recommendation to the June 2007 Southern Baptist Convention and request that it be discharged.

IMB Trustee Leadership's Official Response to Greensboro Motion (conclusion)

"This official response shall be reported to the 2007 Southern Baptist Convention at San Antonio."

My Response to Trustee Leadership's Conclusions

I was so disturbed by the short, half-page responses by trustee leaders to an official recommendation of the Southern Baptist Convention that I called Dr. Rankin. He said there was no IMB trustee investigation, and trustee leaders simply wanted to put this motion behind them. He was clear that the "official" report was drafted quickly by a few trustee leaders; nobody had asked any questions or requested any documents, and trustee leaders just simply tried to make this recommendation from the SBC go away. After speaking with Dr. Rankin I wrote a post the next day titled "There Was No Trustee Investigative Committee."[2] Without naming Dr. Rankin, I wrote that an IMB administrator had revealed to me five things about the trustee response to the Greensboro recommendation:

(1) There was no trustee investigative committee.
(2) The response was designed to be generic and noncontroversial.
(3) Nobody investigated anything because it is not the business of the IMB to investigate any outside influence upon trustees by other agency heads. It is the business of the IMB to get on with the work of missions.
(4) The trustees felt they had the right to demand conformity to their interpretations of Scripture.
(5) The IMB, as well as every other SBC agency, is an autonomous agency, and can do anything the autonomous board desires regarding doctrinal standards, including going beyond the 2000 *BFM*.

I explained in my post that I now understood why nobody from the "investigative committee" had contacted me during the investigation. *There was no investigation.* I also now understand why I was confused about the *Southern Baptist Texan* headline concerning the "investigation" that read "Board Rejects Allegation of Impropriety." The reporter must have assumed that something was actually investigated.

My complaint has long been that the emphasis on a ban of a private prayer language and the pushing of a sacerdotal baptism policy, one that closely resembles tenants of Landmarkism, came from outside IMB administration and staff and worked its way into the board through trustees influenced by administrators and at least one head of another Southern Baptist agency. Further, I had contended that there was absolutely no anecdotal evidence that a problem existed on the mission field among our SBC missionaries that would call for correction by the implementation of those two policies. The Southern Baptist Convention Greensboro recommendation was a call to determine the real reason for the policies being forced upon the IMB, in opposition to the desires of her president.

I had hope in January 2007 that the trustees would vote to remove the two new doctrinal policies at the Memphis board meeting in March, but that did not happen. It was because of the trustees' whitewash response to the Greensboro motion that I and several others, including the executive committee of the SBC, began working on a motion to bring before the 2007 Southern Baptist Convention in San Antonio to put a firm and fast stop to any SBC board establishing a doctrinal parameter that exceeded the 2000 *BFM.*

A funny thing happened after I posted that an administrator of the IMB told me there was no "investigation" by the trustees. Jerry Corbaley posted an article on his blog, since removed, titled "What Idiot Said There Was No Trustee Investigation?" and went into another tirade against me. When I wrote a comment on his blog that said Jerry Rankin told me this, and I regretted that Jerry considered him an idiot, Corbaley called me a liar—then telephoned Rankin—only to have my account confirmed by the president of the IMB. Immediately Corbaley removed his foolish post and asked several Southern Baptist pastors to defend him on the blogs.

Notes

1. "The IMB Response to the Greensboro Motion," 1 February 2007, http://kerussocharis.blogspot.com/2007/02/imb-response-to-greensboro-motion.html.

2. "There Was No Trustee Investigative Committee," 2 February 2007, http://kerussocharis.blogspot.com/2007/02/there-was-no-trustee-investigative_02.html.

Chapter 25

THE GARNER MOTION
IN SAN ANTONIO

The 2000 BFM Is "Sufficient in its Current Form . . . "

After the January 2007 IMB trustee meeting in California, the IMB went about doing the work of missions and gathered in Kansas City in May. I attended all the IMB trustee meetings in spring 2007 and enjoyed visiting with missionaries, IMB staff, and Southern Baptists waiting to be appointed to the mission field. However, my focus had turned to even larger issues within the SBC, including addressing the wrongs of people injured by the application of Fundamentalist interpretations of Scripture (Sheri Klouda and Dwight McKissic), helping to stop sexual predators from hiding in the Southern Baptist Convention by creating a database of men in SBC ministry who had been convicted or credibly charged with such crimes, and doing whatever could be done to stop the narrowing of the parameters of cooperation among Southern Baptists. The Southern Baptist Convention in San Antonio was extremely important because messengers would finally have an opportunity to weigh in on the actions of the IMB in establishing as policy two "doctrines" that far exceeded anything in the 2000 *BFM*.

In February, the executive committee of the Southern Baptist Convention released a statement that said, "The *Baptist Faith & Message* is neither a creed, nor a complete statement of our faith, nor final and infallible; nevertheless, we further acknowledge that it is the only consensus statement of doctrinal beliefs approved by the Southern Baptist Convention and as such is sufficient in its current form to guide trustees in their establishment of policies and practices of entities of the Convention."[1]

The executive committee's statement is in direct contradiction to the "investigative" report of the IMB trustee leadership, released in the January 2007 IMB meeting, which said, "The IMB retains the prerogative and responsibility of further defining the parameters of doctrinal beliefs." Which

was it? Did the IMB trustees have that prerogative, or did the executive committee of the SBC get it right when they said no agency should be adding to
the 2000 *BFM* without Convention approval? Messengers at the 2007
Southern Baptist Convention in San Antonio would have the last word. I felt
confident IMB trustee leadership would be reprimanded for demanding
conformity on two doctrinal policies that exceeded the 2000 *BFM*.

Annual Meeting of the Southern Baptist Convention
San Antonio, Texas
June 12–13, 2007

On the evening of June 10, 2007, a group of Southern Baptists met at our
hotel to ensure that the Convention would speak to this matter and decide
once and for all whether the two policies passed by the IMB trustees were
appropriate.

Of the twenty-five people in our suite, one was a pastor named Rick
Garner. Rick is the pastor of the largest Southern Baptist Church in Ohio,
and he was chosen to bring a motion before the Convention that contained
the exact wording of the executive committee statement released in February.
We felt a Convention vote on this matter would correct the mistakes of the
IMB trustees in adopting two doctrinal policies that exceeded the 2000
BFM. We had a prayer time and discussed how to get the motion presented
to the Convention, and then dismissed around midnight.

The next morning, Rick Garner went to a microphone in the
Convention hall and made his motion, now famously called the "Garner
Motion."

> I move that this convention adopts the statement of the executive commit-
> tee issued in February of this year, and included in the executive 's report
> found in the 2007 Book of Reports, page 17, which reads "The *Baptist
> Faith & Message* is neither a creed, nor a complete statement of our faith,
> nor final and infallible; nevertheless, we further acknowledge that it is the
> only consensus statement of doctrinal beliefs approved by the Southern
> Baptist Convention and such is sufficient in its current form to guide
> trustees in their establishment of policies and practices of entities of the
> Convention."

I knew this vote over the Garner Motion would be more important than
any vote of the Southern Baptist Convention in the previous ten years. If the

2007 San Antonio Convention were to adopt the Garner Motion, it would send a strong and irrefutable message to the Fundamentalist trustees of Southern Baptist boards and agencies that the 2000 *Baptist Faith & Message* is the only consensus statement of doctrinal belief approved by the SBC, and to establish doctrinal guidelines or policies that exceed the 2000 *BFM* is an act contrary to the wishes of the Convention herself. If the Garner Motion were to pass,

(1) It would give to trustees a clear understanding that the Convention itself did not wish any SBC agency to demand absolute conformity on interpretations of tertiary doctrines not addressed by the 2000 *BFM* before one could participate in SBC missions and ministry.
(2) It would communicate to those who pray in tongues such as Dwight McKissic and Jerry Rankin, who believe in Calvinism such as Al Mohler and Tom Ascol, who believe in cessationism such as Paige Patterson and Russ Moore, who believe in Arminianism such as _____ (fill in the blank), and to pastors who hold to Landmarkism in their local churches and pastors who don't hold to Landmarkism in their local churches that there is plenty of room in the SBC for both interpretations of these tertiary doctrines. Neither side is free to demand that others take their position in order to cooperate in missions and ministry in the SBC.
(3) It would help Southern Baptists to focus on the main thing—sharing the gospel—and would insist we unite around the essentials and cease making tertiary doctrinal interpretations issues over which we divide.

Probably the more significant question we asked ourselves at the 2007 Southern Baptist Convention was, "What does it mean if messengers vote against the Garner Motion?" It would mean that a majority of SBC messengers believe the 2000 *BFM* is not sufficient, and that those Fundamentalist trustees who are narrowing the doctrinal standards of cooperation through the back door of board policy have been given Convention approval to do it.

A great deal was at stake. The vote, in my mind, was such an historic vote that I took the video of the debate and spent two days transcribing all that was said before the vote on the Garner Motion. Read carefully the debate printed below. When you finish, ask yourself this question: "Could there have been any possible confusion over the Garner Motion when messengers voted for its approval?" I think you will agree with me that there was no possibility of confusion.

Debate over Garner Motion, evening session, June 12, 2007

[The Garner Motion is read.]

President Frank Page: The committee of order on business has decided that this particular motion should be dealt with at this time, and so, we would like to know if Rick Garner is in this hall and, if so, would he like to speak to this motion. Bro. Rick (Garner), are you at microphone nine?

Pastor Rick Garner: Yes, sir.

President Frank Page: You moved. [Laughter] Would you like to speak to your motion sir?

Pastor Rick Garner: Yes, Mr. President.

President Frank Page: All right.

Pastor Rick Garner [speaking *for* the motion]: Mr. President, the *Baptist Faith & Message* 2000 stands as the doctrinal capstone of the conservative resurgence. It is the only consensus, and therefore, the only sufficient basis for doctrinal accountability among Southern Baptists. It is the privilege, it is indeed the sacred responsibility, of this convened body to inform our entities, agencies, and institutions of our continued and firm commitment to this instrument of doctrinal accountability.

The question before us this evening is this: Is the *Baptist Faith & Message* 2000 sufficient in its current form to guide the Southern Baptist Convention and all its agencies, entities and institutions? An affirmitive vote is for its sufficiency. A negative vote is a vote for its insufficiency and will effectively render the *Baptist Faith & Message* 2000 anemic to accomplish its purposes. I believe it is sufficient. My church believes it is sufficient. The executive committee report affirms it is sufficient, and this Convention believes it is sufficient.

If the *Baptist Faith & Message* 2000 is sufficient for the Southern Baptist Convention at large, then it should be considered sufficient for all Southern Baptist entities, agencies, and institutions.

Amos 3:3 says, "Can two walk together unless they are agreed?" We have all agreed that the *Baptist Faith & Message* 2000 is our convention's confession of faith. The only remaining questions is, "Will we walk together?"

Mr. President, thank you.

President Frank Page: Thank you. I would like at this point . . . what we are going to do, in case you are new, normally in these situations we allow persons to speak for, and in fairness to speak against, if there is someone—and we do believe because the button is pushed. And let me say this very quickly—we have a fancy box up here. It's nice, it's real nice. And it tells us who pushed what buttons, but it doesn't show us who it is. We don't know who it is, but it does tell us if you are pushing for or against, so I hope it is correct. Number 2 says they're against this. Would you like to speak against this?

Messenger: Yes I would.

President Frank Page: Name, church, and . . .

Messenger: Mr. President, it's . . . Robin Hadaway, missions professor, Midwestern Seminary, Kansas City, Missouri, messenger Pleasant Valley Baptist Church, Liberty, Missouri.

[Read carefully the following arguments professor Hadaway gives on why the motion should be voted down. Notice what he calls "doctrine" and why the 2000 *BFM* falls short of being "sufficient"—to me he articulates very clearly the problem we Southern Baptists would have faced had his view prevailed.]

Messenger Robin Hadaway [speaking *against* the motion]: I served as an IMB missionary for eighteen years and as an IMB regional for six of those years and I enforced the IMB policies. The IMB has long had a policy that divorced persons cannot be appointed as long-term missionaries. This is a doctrinal interpretation of 1 Timothy 3, and is also based upon the fact that divorced persons are not normally called to Southern Baptist pulpits in the USA and are especially problematic for our Baptist partners overseas. The executive statement on page 17 of the Book of Reports says, "The *BFM* is sufficient in its current form to guide trustees in their establishment of policies and practices of entities of the convention." Guide does not mean an exhaustive list. Let me list several doctrinal issues the 2000 *BFM* does not speak to.

Speaking in tongues or private prayer languages are not mentioned in the 2000 *BFM*, but do you want a seminary professor like myself, at your six seminaries, practicing glossalalia? This is not in the *Baptist Faith & Message*.

Last year's resolutions committee of which I was a member, and I am a member of this year's resolutions committee, passed a resolution on alcohol consumption. Our committee quoted Scripture, making it a doctrinal issue. The IMB does not appoint missionaries that drink alcohol, and neither do the seminaries. Alcohol is not in the *Baptist Faith & Message*.

The resolutions committee a number of years ago passed a resolution on gambling. Scripture was quoted, making this a doctrinal issue. Gambling is not mentioned in the 2000 *BFM* either.

Neither is the usage of tobacco.

Let's not make a creed of the *BFM*; let's keep it as a guide and allow the trustees of your boards, agencies, and entities to design policies and procedures to select godly men and women as missionaries, professors, and employees to serve in these agencies.

Otherwise, you may have missionaries and professors like me, with practices not in keeping with the vast majority of Southern Baptists. I urge the defeat of this motion.

[Other than the fact I am amazed that the good professor believes "quoting" Scripture makes something a doctrine, I would like to point out three problems with what Dr. Hadaway said: (1) To equate the Holy Spirit gift of glossalalia with divorce, tobacco, and alcohol would cause every mainline, conservative systematic theologian to raise his/her eyebrow. (2) Dr. Hadaway well illustrates the problem the Southern Baptist Convention is now facing—there are some who are attempting to force upon the entire convention their particular interpretations of holiness, and worse, they are attempting to make *everything* a "doctrinal" issue and dismiss from service anyone who disagrees. (3) A few of my fellow IMB trustees ought to be glad I am uninterested in enforcing the good professor's "doctrine" of tobacco. Of course, the passage of the motion rules null and void Dr. Hadaway's attempt to make everyone look like him.]

President Frank Page: Thank you, Robin. Now do we have at microphone number nine again someone to speak for this particular motion?

Messenger Dwight McKissic [speaking *for* the motion]: Yes, Mr. President, my name is Dwight McKissic, I pastor the Cornerstone Baptist Church in Arlington, Texas.

It's really a simple matter. Are we going to let the parents make rules for the house, or our we going to let the children rule the house? The agencies and entities should be subordinate to the Southern Baptist Convention.

When I gave my church a doctrinal statement, all of our leaders were asked to read it and believe it, the 2000 *Baptist Faith & Message*. We buy into the convention based on that document. Then, when agencies circumvent that document, it leaves a church like the one I pastor in a quandary. "Pastor, you sold us on the Southern Baptist Convention based on the contents of this document. Now decisions are being made that are not consistent or compatabile with this document that affects the identity and image of our church."

I don't let my four children decide what the McKissic household believe. Dwight and Vera McKissic decide what we believe and what we stand for. Joshua said, "As for me and my house, we will serve the Lord." We need the convention itself to speak to this issue and not the children.

[Loud Applause]

President Frank Page: Thank you Bro. Dwight. One more. Microphone number five, do you speak against this motion?

Messenger: No sir, I'm here to speak for this motion.

[It was here that the messengers could see Art Rogers at the microphone, ready to speak for the motion. Behind him one can see on the video screens Dr. Hershael York and Dr. Richard Land prepared to speak *against* the motion. Dr. York adamantly attempts to get the microphone monitor to allow him to speak, but Art came to the microphone first, and by rule, Art did not have to give up his spot until he had the opportunity to speak.]

President Frank Page: To be fair, we've got to go with someone against. All right, we'll try number eight. Microphone number eight over yonder.

Messenger: Yes, sir. My name is Barbara Turner and I am a messenger from the Mountain View Baptist Church in California. And, uh, I did not grow up in a Christian home; however, I had people who took me to church and so forth, and I accepted Christ after a Baptist camp, not a Southern Baptist. However, when I moved I had a neighbor who took me to the closest church, which was a Southern Baptist church. And as I started learning about that church I picked up a little paper, really a little card, that was called the *Baptist Faith & Message*. And as a young teenager, really preteen, I read that and thought about it quite a bit. And, you know I believed the things that were in that document. I felt like, yes, this is what I believe, this is what I want to subscribe to, and this is a body of believers that I want to join with. And I put a lot of thought in that, even as a young person, just as I did my salvation, knowing that God would want to call me to things. That document was written in 1963. It was put together thoughtfully with many great leaders, including Herschel Hobbs, who many people still read his commentaries. I have nothing against the 2000 as far as submission or whatever. However, I have a problem with saying you must subscribe to this particular *Baptist Faith & Message* or you can't serve. I guess I cannot serve because I believe in both of them. And I think there's a problem, and so I believe it should be *Baptist Faith & Message*—period, and not *Baptist Faith & Message* of a certain year. And I also believe, as it is stated, that it is a statement of faith, this is what we believe, but we are autonomous. I believe when we are saying we must set this as a guide, we are not using this as a guide; we are using it as a creed, and that goes up against who we are as Baptists. Thank you.

[Barbara knew exactly what she was saying. However, what she may not have been aware of was that those who were *against* this recommendation desire to tighten the 2000 *BFM* even further, "de facto," by tightening the doctrinal parameters and narrowing the definition of what it means to be a Southern Baptist by using trustees of Southern Baptist agencies to change the doctrinal parameters "out of the view of the entire Southern Baptist Convention."]

President Frank Page: Thank you, Barbara. Let me ask at this time, microphone number one, you have pushed a button saying you have a motion. Would you please give me your name and your church and clarify what you are asking, please?

Messenger: Leroy Cole, West Tyler Baptist Church, Alabama. I call for the question.

[I do not know Leroy Cole, but his motion to cease debate and vote on the recommendation passed by a two-thirds majority raising their ballots in favor to end debate, at least according to the ruling of the chair. It was at this moment that one of the lower points of the convention occurred. Several who were *against* the motion (and possibly a few who were for it) booed and hissed and shouted at the chair because they didn't feel the motion to end debate had actually passed. Dr. Page graciously ruled that the debate would continue for five minutes because it was a close vote, but then he said, "Do not holler at me [applause]. Do not holler at me. I have a litte bit of redneck in me. Don't holler at me." (Good for the president).]

President Frank Page: Five more minutes. Microphone number three speaking for.

Messenger Bob Cleveland [speaking *for* the motion]: I'm Bob Cleveland, lay messenger from First Baptist Church, Pellham, Alabama. I came to the Southern Baptist Convention, to a Southern Baptist church, from the

United Methodist and the Presbyterian churches. In each case I was given, in those denominations, a book and they said, "Here's what we believe." And I actually read it. And when I came to our church, I asked Bro. Mike before I ever joined, if we had such a book and he said, "Well, no. We have no creed but Christ." But here's the *Baptist Faith & Message* which is a consensus statement of our faith. And I read it. And I went back to him and said, "You know, there's a lot of things this doesn't cover."

And he gave me Hershel Hobbs's book on the *Baptist Faith & Message*, and I read that, and I read about what Hershel Hobbs said the fundamental Baptist distinctive is and that's soul competency in religious matters. And I said, "Whoa," this is the most responsible doctrine I've ever seen because it says it's me and God and I'm responsible for what I believe. I cannot blame it on somebody else.

Now if I wanted to change what Southern Baptists believe confessionally I would never attack the *Baptist Faith & Message*, I would go to missionary sending organizations, both US and foreign, and change what they can be to be missionaries. And then I would just wait until the Southern Baptist Convention changed what they believed.

And if I wanted to accelerate the process I would go to some of the seminaries and change what you had to believe so that they would believe just like me to be a professor. And that would send out pastors into churches here that would believe just what I wanted them to believe. I would never have to touch the *Baptist Faith & Message*.

We are like the frog in a pot of hot water. You can put him in cool water and turn the heat up and the frog will literally boil to death before he knows he is in trouble. We will change the *BFM* because we will change what Baptists believe if we don't vote for this recommendation. Now I know we can't tell the entities what they have to do, but we can tell the entities of the SBC what we believe being a Southern Baptist means, and this is it, and I urge you to vote for it. [Applause]

[Bob, who is a layman, understands better than anyone I've ever heard that Southern Baptists had better be careful in handing over the ability to define what a Southern Baptist *is* to either a seminary or an agency.]

President Frank Page: Thank you, Bob. Now, we will call on microphone number twelve and ask if you are speaking *against* this particular issue.

Messenger Jeremy Green [speaking *against* the motion]: I'm Jeremy Green, pastor of First Baptist Church of Joshua, Texas. According to the preamble of the *Baptist Faith & Message*, our confessional statement includes only those doctrines that we hold precious and as essential to the faith. If Southern Baptists believe that these doctrines are essentials, then why are certain trustees and employees now not even affirming the bare minimum doctrinal standards of our convention as adopted by each entity. Baptist polity and our trustee system both necessitate that each individual trustee boards maintain the right and responsibility to employ other doctrinal parameters as needed.

The *Baptist Faith & Message* is a sufficient guide, but it is not the *only* guide. I believe that voting *for* this motion is the first step in the wrong direction. I encourage the messengers to vote against this motion. Thank you, Mr. President.

[I thank Jeremy for making clear, right before the vote, what a vote *for* the motion meant, and what a vote *against* the motion meant. The convention heard him, and they voted. Contrary to his desire, and others', to move our convention beyond the 2000 *BFM* to reflect their narrow doctrinal views on matters that are *not* essential to the Christian faith and Southern Baptist identity, the convention said let's keep our parameters of cooperation as broad as possible.]

President Frank Page: Thank you, Jeremy. Now, here is where we are. Our time is up. If you would like to extend the time, it will require a motion and two-thirds majority to extend the time for discussion. [End of debate]

The vote to extend time to debate the motion to adopt the executive committee statement on the 2000 *BFM* failed. Then the vote occurred on the original motion. The Garner Motion passed by an overwhelming margin. I was vindicated. The trustees of the International Mission Board had acted contrary to the wishes of the Southern Baptist Convention. Fundamentalists were livid at the outcome of the vote. Many of them tried to argue that the Convention didn't know what it was doing. The IMB trustee leadership was furious. The Convention had just told them they were wrong.

The trustee leadership, including John Floyd, not only paid no attention to what the Convention had said, but they said they didn't care what the

Convention wanted; they would do whatever *they* wanted. Now there was the absurd action of trustee leadership, the same people who said I "resisted authority," resisting the greatest authority in the Southern Baptist Convention—messengers from local churches.

This blatant disregard for the Convention's desires, evidenced by the IMB trustee leadership refusing to rescind the policies, led me eventually to understand that victory would only be won when individual trustees were removed by either attrition or the appointment of trustees who understood cooperation. After the 2007 Southern Baptist Convention, certain trustee leaders of the IMB doubled their efforts to marginalize me.

Note

1. Baptist Press, "Executive Committee—BF&M a 'Sufficient' Guide for Entity Trustees to Form Policy," 21 February 2007, http://www.bpnews.net/bpnews.asp?ID=25015.

Chapter 26

CENSURED

IMB Trustee Meeting
Richmond, Virginia
July 2007

At the July 2007 IMB trustee meeting in Richmond, Virginia, I was beginning my third year as a trustee with the International Mission Board. I flew to Richmond International Airport Monday afternoon, July 16, and drove to the International Learning Center outside of Richmond to attend the trustee forum at 3:30. At dinner I ate in the ILC cafeteria with a wonderful missionary couple and their children (unnamed due to security). The dad is a physician and the mom is a nurse serving with the IMB in a security 3 country in Central Asia. I enjoyed our July trustee meeting, which is always held at the ILC, because of the opportunities I have to meet missionary families. The ILC is where IMB missionaries are trained and oriented for their missionary service. It is located in the beautiful rolling hills of central Virginia.

I was interested to see IMB trustee leadership's response to the Convention's adoption of the Garner Motion. There was none. John Floyd, chairman of the board of trustees, chose (again) not to appoint me to a regional or standing committee of the IMB for 2007/2008. That was his perogative as chairman, and I did not make an issue of it. Dr. Floyd and trustee leadership continued to be perturbed by the Convention's reaction against them, and I was the logical person on whom to take out their frustrations.

Trustee leadership did nothing at this meeting to reverse the two doctrinal policies that the Convention said were wrong. Further, Fundamentalist trustees continued the attack against Dr. Rankin and myself. Winston Curtis, a fellow pastor and trustee from Oklahoma, made a motion that the IMB send a copy of *The Camel: How Muslims Are Coming to Faith in Christ* to all sitting trustees. My ears perked up when I heard this motion because I had read a few days earlier a blog post by Dr. Bart Barber of Southwestern Seminary on "the camel book." The book was written by a couple of missionaries, one of whom is directly affiliated with the IMB. Winston proceeded to explain his concern that a conversation was taking place "across the convention" about the appropriateness of using this book or, more accurately, the method of witnessing to Muslims as taught by this book, and the trustees needed to know what was being discussed.

For those unfamiliar with *The Camel*, it teaches a unique method of sharing the gospel to Muslims by using portions of the Koran and teaching them of the "true" Allah, One who can only be known through his Son Jesus Christ. I have read the book, and while I don't agree with everything in it, I found it a particularly helpful book in contextualizing the gospel of Jesus Christ, both linguistically and culturally, to the Muslim people without compromising the heart of the gospel. After a few procedural matters, it was felt that Winston's motion was not needed since IMB staff stated they would be happy to send the book to all trustees and would do so within the week. Winston withdrew his motion and we trustees were informed that we would be receiving *The Camel* soon.

What happened next gave more indication regarding Winston's concerns. Dr. Gordon Fort, vice president of Overseas Operations for the International Mission Board, gave an excellent report and then paused at the end to discuss why it was essential that the name "Allah" be used for "God" when conversing with Arabic-speaking people in their native tongue. "Allah" is the Arabic word for God and precedes the Islam religion as a word. Dr. Fort explained that Wycliffe Bible translators use Allah when translating the Hebrew names Yawheh and Elohim, similar to the way the English word "God" is used to translate those same Hebrew names. Gordon further explained there is no Arabic equivalent to convey the idea of a Supreme Being other than "Allah," and when missionaries use the word "Allah" for God, they tell their listeners that the only way to know the one true "Allah" is to come to faith in Jesus Christ. Clyde Meador, another vice president for the International Mission Board, affirmed Gordon's remarks by speaking beautifully in Arabic John 3:16, demonstrating that the word "Allah" is understood by Arabic-speaking people the same way that "God" is understood by English-speaking people.

Winston Curtis followed the remarks of Gordon and Clyde by saying he is a conservative, Bible-believing Christian, and it was not his desire to open our boards or Convention to liberalism. He felt that when we speak of God to people in other nations, we ought to use the "Bible" names for God such as Yahweh, Elohim, and El-Shaddai. Of course, as Winston spoke to us in English, he used the English word "God" thirty-five times (I counted), and Yawheh only once, Elohim once, and El-Shaddai once. I couldn't help but chuckle that Winston seemed to contradict the very point he was attempting to make. Winston used the English word "God" the way Arabs would use the Arabic word "Allah"; both words convey concepts of the Supreme Being of the Universe, identified for us in Scripture as God (or "Allah" in Arabic), the Father of our Lord and Savior Jesus Christ.

Gordon pointed out that some may have "other" problems with *The Camel* other than the use of the word "Allah" for God, and I believe that may be true. However, I am hopeful that no missions professor from Southwestern, or anyone else in the SBC who disagrees with IMB missionary David Garrison's premise (the co-author of the book) will lose sight of the fact that our missionary personnel are only doing what the Apostle Paul did on Mars Hill—starting at the place where the people who need Christ are and taking them to where they need to go, to repentance from their sin and then to faith in Jesus Christ as their Lord and Savior.

At this same July 2007 trustee meeting, Hershael York, professor at Southern Seminary, a brand-new trustee, questioned Rankin about his theology. When I had first come on the board, sitting Fundamentalist trustees tried to make an issue of the "poor" theology of Dr. Rankin and IMB staff. My experience as a trustee proved that there was excellent theology and highly trained staff. Regardless, York's questioning of Rankin revealed an undercurrent, particularly at SBC seminaries, that the SBC is "doctrinally deficient" and the Convention needs help from people who know doctrine. Hershael York asked the only question of Dr. Rankin after the president's report. "Dr. Rankin, I only ask because I'm curious and have heard this said before. Is your focus on the unreached people groups driven by an eschatological motive?" Dr. Rankin answered by quoting Matthew 24:16: "The gospel of the kingdom shall be preached to the whole world, and then the end shall come," and said that eschatology does not compel the IMB's mission (or his), but obedience does. Dr. Rankin said the timing of the coming of the Son is up to the Father, and nothing we do will define when he comes. It is up to God. We are simply to obey his commission. As I listened to the exchange between Hershael York and Jerry Rankin, I couldn't help wondering why the chairman of the board didn't interrupt York and tell the "rookie" trustee to sit down and be quiet—as this "rookie" trustee was told when I questioned trustee leadership (not IMB staff) in my first year. I would assume that rookie trustees who agree with trustee leadership are free to say whatever they desire.

An event occurred in the cafeteria of the ILC that was a precurser of things to come for me. The cafeteria is beautiful at the ILC, and the cook staff does a great job. I was one of the first in line, and by the time I got my tray and drink I entered the cafeteria to find Jerry Corbaley sitting by himself. I went to him and said, "Jerry, do you mind if I sit next to you?" Jerry said, "Truthfully, I do." I said, "Jerry, I would just like to sit here and visit with you over dinner as a brother in Christ and enjoy your company." Jerry said a few choice things about me and then said that if I sat down he would get up and leave, and if I followed him he would make it a "public issue." Well, I sat down anyway because I feel it is important that we as trustees get along even if we don't see eye to eye on certain things. Jerry promptly stood up, took his tray, and moved to another table.

Trustee Mike Gonzales from Texas was at the table behind me, and I asked if I could join him. He graciously said yes, and I moved and had a wonderful dinner with him and his family. That evening, we would all witness Mike's daughter, her husband, and their three children being appointed as a new missionary family. Soon, the Gonzaleses left and several trustees came to sit with me, including Mike Smith of Texas, Simon Tsoi of Arizona, Ken Kuwahari of Hawaii, Gene Williams of Florida, Rochelle Davis of Michigan, and my good friend John Click of Kansas. What began as a sad supper ended up being one of the most enjoyable times I have had with the IMB. I laughed as these men told stories—enough to fill a notebook of illustrations for me—and I genuinely enjoyed their company.

But those men around the table were not trustee leaders. Jerry Corbaley was. Jerry and the other trustee leaders, particularly Chuck McAlister, John Floyd, Joe Hugley, and others who remained from the 2005 leadership were particularly hostile. The influence my blog had obtained over the years—by July 2007, more than 2 million hits—had caused trustee leadership to consider using everything in their arsenal to marginalize me. The next weapon was censure.

IMB Trustee Meeting
Ridgecrest, North Carolina
September 2007

At the September trustee meeting in Ridgecrest, North Carolina, Dr. Floyd, chairman of the board, reminded all trustees that they needed their passports. Regional committees would fly to the regions they served in spring 2008. The IMB would pay for the trip for all trustees (except a small portion of the fee). During the break, I asked Dr. Floyd to which region I should go in the spring. He said that since I was not on a regional committee, I would not be participating in the spring trips. I then asked Dr. Floyd for his rationale for not appointing me to a regional committee again this year. He said I had never apologized to the board and I continued to blog.

I reminded Dr. Floyd that *before* the March 2006 vote to rescind the recommendation for my removal, a recommendation that had to come before the entire 2006 Greensboro Southern Baptist Convention, I was publicly asked if I would apologize before the board. I said at the time before the entire board, "I have no problem apologizing for something that I know is wrong, but I will not apologize for what I know is *not* wrong. Not only do I not wish to apologize, but I stand by every word, sentence, and paragraph I have ever written on my blog." The vote to rescind the recommendation for my removal was still *unanimous*, even after every trustee heard me say this publicly before the entire board.

I told John that I would not apologize now and I would not stop blogging. I also told him that I accepted his decision not to appoint me to a regional committee. In the past year I had been to the South Asia regional office and the Pac Rim regional office. I would be going in January 2008 to the East Asia regional office, and I had plans to go to the Central Asia regional office as well. The regional leader for Middle America and the Carribbean was a member of our church, and we were considering partnering with him for mission opportunities. Our youth were considering a partnership with the Western Europe region. I told John Floyd that trustee leadership might be seeking to remove me from involvement in Southern Baptist mission work, but they would not succeed. I ended my conversation with Dr. Floyd with these words, spoken in as soft and gracious a voice as possible: "Dr. Floyd, I will not apologize to the board for my blogging. I will continue to blog for the good of the Southern Baptist Convention and the International Mission Board."

What happened next was particularly interesting. Jerry Corbaley, after visiting with Dr. Floyd, sent a 153-page letter to every trustee calling for me to be censured and removed from the board. I published the entire letter on my blog,[1] knowing that my best defense against the hardball religionists who dominated trustee leadership was for everything being done in secret to be revealed. Corbaley, Floyd, McAlister, and other trustee leaders were angry that I continued to influence not only trustees, but also the Southern Baptist Convention. This lengthy letter was an attempt, once again, to marginalize my influence by attacking my character. I am not sure who the "Fathers and Mothers" are to whom Jerry addressed the letter, but he sent it to IMB trustees only and begged they keep it secret. I published it four days later after calling Jerry Corbaley four times to visit with him, only to have him hang up on me each time. I share here a small portion of the letter.

October 18, 2007
Dear Fathers and Mothers, Sisters and Brothers,
I apologize for adding this task to your workload, but this letter addresses gross and habitual sin on the part of Trustee Wade Burleson. The proof is undeniable. The sin is highly offensive to God. The sin is affecting tens of thousands of Southern Baptists, and some of our own missionaries are being swept up in this sin. You, the Board of Trustees, are responsible before God, the Southern Baptist Convention, and yourselves, to address this trial of faith in a serious and strait-forward [sic] manner. It is absolutely necessary that the Board speak publicly and decisively to Mr. Burleson's sin in a way that is not subject to Mr. Burleson's reinterpretation of your action . . . .

Trustee Burleson is an unrepentant slanderer and an unrepentant gossip. He continues to initiate slander and gossip against the trustees of the International Mission Board. Since January of 2006 I have made it very clear to Mr. Burleson personally that I believe he has slandered the Board of Trustees and that I consider him a divisive man. Having concluded such, both 1 Corinthians 5:11 and Titus 3:10 clearly dictate my relationship to him. According to God, I am not to associate with him, not to eat with him, and am to have nothing to do with him. Have I sinned in this conclusion?

By far the best option is for Wade Burleson to publicly confess that he has sinned through slander and gossip; and to repent of such in the international venue in which this sin occurred. It would be wonderful if Mr. Burleson demonstrated the fruits of repentance in the months ahead. This is God's preference, our preference, and my preference.

Another option is to seek his removal from the Board of Trustees immediately. And then release a very public and very clear statement regarding his slander and gossip. It would be Christian faithfulness to use the terms "slander" and "gossip," and the phrase "unrepentant sin." It would be faithful stewardship on the part of the trustees to publicly and clearly state that Mr. Burleson's interpretations of Board actions, procedures, and motivations are unworthy of trust. From my reading of Mr. Burleson's writings about Board actions, procedures, and motivations, his opinions are deceptive. If I am wrong, I think you should tell me so. Whether he intends them to be deceptive or not does not change the end result.

If Mr. Burleson does not seriously repent and seek to resign quietly, the Board should still release a very direct statement about his slander and gossip. May I point out to you all, that it is the public slander and gossip that is the sin, and not Mr. Burleson's presence on the Board? To be sure, his actions on the Board since June of 2006 have not been "combative," as his previous months on the Board most certainly were. I thank him. But since he is still a member of the Board, his slander is our business, and the responsibility to confront him is our responsibility. Allowing an unrepentant slanderer to just "go away" is irresponsible to the point of sin. "Do not entertain an accusation against an elder unless it is brought by two or three witnesses. Those who sin are to be rebuked publicly, so that the others may take warning. I charge you in the sight of God and Christ Jesus and the elect angels, to keep these instructions without partiality, and to do nothing out of favoritism." 1 Timothy 5:19-21. Furthermore, a habitual slanderer and gossip will continue to slander others and gossip, whether he is on the Board or not.

Another option is to refer the whole complex matter to the IMB Executive Committee or some other committee. The problem with this action is that slander has a life of its own after it hits a gossip venue. Slander hurts people. Slander destroys people. "If you keep on biting and devouring each other, watch out or you will be destroyed by each other." Galatians 5:15. Any referral to a committee will consume two months at a minimum. Probably longer. During this extended time a lot more damage will be done to the reputation of the Board, and a lot more Southern Baptists will be deceived, and our missionaries who are entering the slander and gossip venue will get themselves into more trouble with God. Mr. Burleson's blog gets 1,600 hits per day, that's over 53,000 per month. A faithless or timid response by the Board of Trustees will only empower his momentum.

It is an option, though a very poor one, to do nothing in the hope that the Convention will not reappoint him to a second term. However, this will allow the behavior to continue for another 18 months. During this time another slate of new Trustees will rotate on to the Board who have never even seen the IMB Executive Committee Report of May of 2006. About 25% of those serving on the Board now have no memory of Mr. Burleson's combative first six months on the Board.

Perhaps there are other options that the Board of Trustees might consider. Wouldn't it be better to decide sooner, rather than later, so that the net effect of the sin is less? Is this scandal getting better? God doesn't think so.

For my part, I see the possible unpleasant circumstances of this letter more clearly than I see God's resolution to our apparent dilemma. Unpleasant circumstances are a present reality. They will remain a reality, whatever we do. Therefore, since we do not see a nice and tidy administrative solution; we ought to do what God says and leave the future circumstances to Him. Has it come to that? Is obedience to God a problem?

But now I am writing you that you must not associate with anyone who calls himself a brother but is sexually immoral or greedy, an idolater or a SLANDERER, a drunkard or a swindler. With such a man do not even eat. 1 Corinthians 5:11

Warn a divisive person once, and then warn him a second time. After that, have nothing to do with him. Titus 3:10

Those who sin are to be rebuked publicly, so that the others may take warning. I charge you, in the sight of God and Christ Jesus and the elect angels, to keep these instructions without partiality, and to do nothing out of favoritism. 1 Timothy 5:20,21

That means it is not a matter of siding with a friend, or with a political ally. It is not about siding with a victim, not about being personally offended, and not about taking political advantage of the scandal. It is about slander, not partiality nor favoritism. God is watching. Our King and Savior is watching.

I charge you, in the sight of God and Christ Jesus and the elect angels, to KEEP these instructions . . . .

My initiative in sending this letter is the response of a Christian man who has been subjected to public, habitual, international slander and gossip since January of 2006. What should a Christian response be to public, habitual, international sexual abuse; or public, habitual, international abuse by a drunkard; or public, habitual, international abuse by a swindler? God is the one who places all of these sins in the same category. Please consider my response in His context. You may know for certain that I am praying, and curious, as to what your response will be.

If you decide that I am slandering Mr. Burleson, then please obey God and do to me as I intend that you should do something about him (Deuteronomy 19:15-20).

For my part, if the Board of Trustees thinks I should resign because of my behavior; you have only to ask. There is absolutely no need for such a decision on your part to be referred to the Executive Committee of the Southern Baptist Convention; there is no need to wait for the Convention to vote.

Final Point: The Southern Baptist Convention is going through a period of political turmoil. Fine. The Convention will decide what the Convention decides; and Jesus will continue to build His church through many different churches and groups of churches. Meanwhile, the IMB will continue to send missionaries into all the world to share the gospel and make disciples of all the nations. In view of the importance of the Great Commission, the stark contrast between heaven and hell, and the opportunity to glorify the name of our great God and Savior Jesus Christ; can we as Trustees abstain from making the work of the International Mission Board a political football?

Your brother in Christ,
Jerry Corbaley

By fall 2007 I had become familiar with the tactics of Fundamentalist trustee leaders at the IMB, and though I knew they intended to make life unpleasant for me and to influence other people's opinion of me, each and every time they sought to accomplish their goal, it would always backfire. On the day IMB trustees received Corbaley's 153-page e-mail, I wrote my own letter to every trustee of the IMB.

Friday, October 18, 2007
1:48 p.m. Central Standard Time

Dear Fellow Trustees,

I am thankful for God's mercy in relation to the answered prayers of our trustee body in terms of health and family. I continue to pray for each need that arises and I am grateful for the prayer ministry of the IMB board and the e-mail updates sent to all trustees. Our church spent time in prayer last night for the family of the 29-year-old Christian in Gaza who operated the Palestinian Bible Bookstore and was murdered for his faith in Christ. The IMB's administrative decision to send us a timely update with information on this Christian martyr made our prayer time for all our missionaries very real, very fervent, and very personal.

I visited with my wife Rachelle, and we felt it wise to send to you just this one e-mail in response to the 153 page letter from Trustee Jerry Corbaley. I have made it a practice these past eighteen months not to respond to personal attacks on me or my character and I am choosing not to respond to this letter. I would encourage us all to keep our focus on missions and the support of our missionaries in the field. I will continue to pray for our work and for each of you who serve as a trustee of the IMB.

In His Grace,
Wade

What IMB chairman John Floyd, trustee Jerry Corbaley, and the rest of the trustees did not know at the time was that my last meeting as an IMB trustee was going to be the November 2007 trustee meeting in Springfield, Illinois. For more than a year, a pulpit committee from out of state had sought to convince me to become pastor of their church. The men and women who were on that committee would not take "no" for an answer from us. Emmanuel Baptist Church, Enid, Oklahoma, shares similar philosophies of Christian cooperation, Christian grace, and Christian ministry as her pastor. It had been a garden of Eden for my family for the previous sixteen years. The pulpit committee had been to Emmanuel, and they knew that the spirit and teaching of our church was what their church needed. After a grueling process of determining direction for my life, we had accepted the invitation of the pulpit committee to become their pastor on the condition that they wait for the holiday season to pass and allow me to bring an end to my participation on the International Mission Board and activism in the Southern Baptist Convention and allow our sixteen-year ministry at Emmanuel Baptist Church to end in a manner appropriate to the loving people who had supported us for so long. In addition, my son and I had primary roles in the annual Christmas pageant seen by more than 10,000 people in our little community of Enid, so we couldn't relocate until after we fulfilled our commitment to our church and city.

Emmanuel Baptist Church in Enid, Oklahoma, runs like a well-oiled machine in terms of her ministry, both locally and internationally. The large, competent professional staff allowed me to be involved on a national level in terms of the Southern Baptist Convention, but I knew that the new church would need my entire focus and attention to get her on track in terms of ministry and reaching people in a manner similar to the way Emmanuel does. I was going to give up my blogging, my involvement in SBC politics, and everything associated with my desire to turn the Convention back toward a more cooperative ministry so that I could focus on restoring an effective local ministry where I was being called to pastor. Though the pulpit committee of this new church knew that the national publicity I had received in the previous eighteen months would cast a negative light in the minds of some in the church who did not know me but would be voting on me as pastor, they were confident that anyone who read what I wrote on my blog—as they had—would see that my writings reflected my views of Christian ministry and were filled with grace and truth.

However, I thought that if trustee leadership understood that I would be resigning from my post at the IMB, that my last meeting with the IMB would be the November 2007 trustee meeting in Springfield, Illinois, and that I would cease blogging in January 2008, they would not go through with an attempt to embarrass me with a public censure.

I was wrong.

Note

1. "Disagreement Is Not a Sign of Corrupt Character," 23 October 2007, http:// kerussocharis.blogspot.com/2007/10/disagreement-is-not-sign-of-corrupt_23.html.

Chapter 27

RESIGNATION

IMB Trustee Meeting
Springfield, Illinois
November 2007

The next International Mission Board trustee meeting was held in Springfield, Illinois, November 6–8. When I arrived in Springfield on Monday afternoon, November 5, I knew that trustee leadership wanted to censure me and was orchestrating events for that to happen. Chairman John Floyd asked that I meet with trustee leadership behind closed doors. I couldn't be sure what the meeting was about, but I assumed Dr. Floyd wanted to discuss the possibility of censuring me. I went into the meeting desiring simply to convince them that for the good of the International Mission Board and the good of the Southern Baptist Convention, it would be best not to make "Wade Burleson" an issue again. Rather, they should allow me to fade into the sunset.

John Floyd called me into the room, and I sat at a table surrounded by IMB trustee leadership. Across from me was Chuck McAlister. Moderating the meeting was John Floyd. He explained that they were going to bring a motion to the board that I be censured unless I apologized for my blog. I told the trustees that, once again, I would not apologize for simply disagreeing with the board of directors or expressing dissent. I asked Dr. Floyd about the Convention's adoption of the Garner Motion and wondered when trustee leaders would be recommending a reversal of the doctrinal policies. When I mentioned the Garner Motion, John Floyd became flustered. He said the Convention didn't know what they were doing, and the Garner Motion had no bearing on actions of the IMB. Not surprisingly, nobody around the table disagreed with him. John Floyd said I was going to be censured because I had *continued* to be critical of the actions of the IMB trustees, violating the new policies the board had established in March 2006. These policies, what some were calling the "Burleson Guidelines," forbade any trustee from expressing public disagreement with board actions. He said unless I issued a public apology for expressing public dissent, trustee leadership was likely to bring a motion that I be censured. John then gave me an opportunity to respond.

I told John that I did not wish to be censured. I explained that it would be detrimental to Lottie Moon giving, it would be a distraction from our work as a board, and it would not be best for the Southern Baptist Convention. However, I would never apologize for voicing my dissent—ever. So we were at another impasse.

I reminded trustee leaders that for 162 years, the International Mission Board did fine without a guideline that forbade public dissent. However, on the day the motion for my removal was rescinded in March 2006, the IMB board of trustees passed a policy that said (I looked down at my notebook), "Individual IMB trustees must refrain from public criticism of board-approved actions . . . . [T]rustees are to speak in positive and supportive terms as they interpret and report on actions by the board, regardless of whether they personally support the action." I also reminded them that I had voted against this new policy and was on record as calling it the worst policy ever passed in the history of the Southern Baptist Convention. To stifle free and courteous dissent is to deny our Baptist heritage and identity. I knew that the last paragraph of the new "Trustee Standards of Conduct" made it clear that if a trustee chose to "publicly dissent" and voice his opposition to a board action, he would either be censured or suspended from active involvement with the board. Only the Convention could remove a trustee, and they had once had that opportunity, but obviously felt uncomfortable in going forward.

I knew that the only way Southern Baptists would have known about the new doctrinal policies that were excluding otherwise qualified SBC missionaries from the mission field was through my blog. The only way Southern Baptists knew SBC agencies were narrowing the doctrinal parameters of missionary cooperation and participation was through people like me keeping others informed.

I told my wife that I was going to continue to publish my courteous dissent of the policies that excluded otherwise qualified Southern Baptists from missionary appointment. Everyone who reads my blog knows that I have been only affirming of the vision of President Jerry Rankin, am absolutely supportive of the Cooperative Program and the Lottie Moon Offering, and desire more—not fewer—missionaries on the mission fields. I initially chose to express my public dissent against the two new doctrinal policies to help get those missionaries on the fields, the very place where they belong. When the Southern Baptist Convention approved the Garner Motion, I not only felt affirmed in my gracious and courteous dissent, but I had also looked forward to trustee leadership rescinding the two doctrinal policies that went beyond the 2000 *BFM*. That, sadly, did not happen.

When I saw that the two unbiblical and narrow policies were not going to be reversed by IMB trustee leadership after the 2007 Convention, I wrote a post[1] about the unwillingness of our agencies to follow the desires of the SBC. This was one of the posts Jerry Corbaley used as the basis for his recommendation that I be censured. I told John Floyd and the others around the table that after hearing their animosity toward the Garner Motion, I would assume that my particular post challenging them for not reversing the doctrinal policies upset them as well. I closed by reminding trustee leadership that to dissent publicly is *not* a question of loyalty, is *not* evidence of a lack of unity in the Spirit, but is the *only* way to ensure that the boards and agencies of our Southern Baptist Convention maintain our Baptist identity, live by Christian principles of openness and transparency, and refuse to change the *Baptist Faith & Message*—the doctrinal basis of our cooperation—through hidden agency policies.

I then suggested a solution to the impasse. I informed trustee leadership that I would shut down my blog on December 6, 2007, the two-year anniversary of the start of the blog; that I would resign from the IMB before the end of the year (December 31, 2007); and that I would apologize to any trustee who felt "disparaged" by my blog. I also requested to speak to the entire trustee board for thirty minutes, without interruption, before I resigned. I requested that I speak to the trustees in the public session, but since I knew trustee leadership would not allow that, I said I would acquiesce to the opportunity to speak to the full trustee board behind closed doors before I resigned.

The trustee chairman asked me to put my proposal in writing and dismissed me from the meeting. I went to the seating area outside the conference room to write the proposal, but I was interrupted by another bizarre event. Jerry Corbaley walked to where I was seated and sat down. I stopped writing and greeted him. I later discovered he was asked to help trustee leaders make their case for a censure of me, but they wanted him out of the room while I spoke with the leadership. Since I knew I would be resigning from the board, I tried to make amends with Jerry. I said, "Jerry, listen, I want you to know that even in the midst of our disagreements, I love you as a brother in Christ, and I really do desire to work with you for the common good of our Convention." Jerry interrupted and said, "I will not talk to you; we do not have a witness." I said, "Jerry, the Holy Spirit is enough for us both. He is able to bring reconciliation in the hearts of Christian bro—" Jerry didn't let me finish my sentence. He stood, walked over to the doors where trustee leaders were meeting with IMB staff, opened the door, and shouted, "Are you ready for Mr. Burleson? If you aren't, you need to ask him to leave. He is harassing me."

Jerry then left the waiting area. Distracted, I tried to finish writing the proposal I had made in the allotted time of five minutes. When John Floyd stepped out to check on me, I had not finished it, so he asked that I meet with a subcommittee later that night in order to hammer out the proposal. I told John Floyd I would be happy to do so.

Later that night, I gave more information to this three-man subcommittee, chaired by future IMB chairman Paul Chitwood from Kentucky. I gave them the reason for my decision to resign as accepting the pastorate of a church outside of my home state. I reiterated to this small committee of three that I did not want myself to be the issue at this IMB meeting during the important Lottie Moon season, and if they would leave well enough alone, I would be gone by the first of the year. However, if the executive committee proceeded with a censure, then I would not be resigning. I told the subcommittee that if I was censured at this meeting, my church back home knew me and understood my heart. I could not put my family at risk by leaving Emmanuel at a time when trustee leadership sought to make me a major issue again. I would refuse to go to the church who was asking me to become their pastor if I was "censured." In other words, if they censured me, they guaranteed my continued participation in the Southern Baptist Convention. I told the subcommittee that I did not want the information about my going to another church to be spoken of to the board since I had not had the opportunity to tell my church yet. If they simply led the rest of trustee leadership to let the matter of my censure go and do nothing about it, the focus of IMB could be on missions, and the Wade Burleson "issue" would disappear for good.

I was led to believe after that meeting with the subcommittee that my proposal had been accepted. No trustee leader informed me that they would be recommending a censure motion. I did not meet again with trustee leadership and attended all the plenary sessions of the board at that November 2007 meeting. However, at the conclusion of the last public business session, trustee leadership called trustees into executive session (closed-door session) and made a motion to censure me. Trustee leadership did not afford me the opportunity to speak to the board, and none, including John Floyd, revealed to the board my four-part proposal to overcome this impasse. They allowed the question to be called after only one person spoke, a trustee who urged trustee leadership not to go down this path. One of my trustee friends said after the meeting, "Those railroad tracks went right across your chest." I just smiled, knowing that my chest had become Grand Central Station.

I was not upset over the 2007 censure. My courteous dissent on my blog violated the March 22, 2006, new guideline that forbids trustee dissent. I knew that a censure from trustee leadership would more than likely occur. What did surprise me, however, was the dogged determination to marginalize me even though I offered a proposal that would allow trustee leadership to end the impasse for the good of the IMB and the SBC. When the censure became public the next day and the press started reporting on it, a former trustee sent me an e-mail asking this great question: "Is public dissent only forbidden when trustees express disapproval of trustee decisions, or is public dissent also forbidden by trustees for decisions made by the IMB president and his administrators?"

I believe Southern Baptist trustees should be free to express courteous public criticism and dissent for decisions made by *both* IMB trustees and administrators. The great Czeck dissident Vaclav Havel once wrote, "You do not become a 'dissident' just because you decide one day to take up this most unusual career. You are thrown into it by your personal sense of responsibility, combined with a complex set of external circumstances. You are cast out of the existing structures and placed in a position of conflict with them. It begins as an attempt to do your work well, and ends with being branded an enemy of society."[2]

After the motion to censure passed a verbal vote, with several shouted "no's" from trustees who voted against it, we were dismissed. I immediately called the chairman of the pulpit committee asking us to come in view of a call and informed him that I would be pulling out of the process. I explained that I could not put his church, or his committee, in the position of having to defend a storm of criticism that would come for calling a pastor who had been the only person in the history of the Southern Baptist Convention to be recommended for removal from an agency and then be officially "censured" by a group of sitting trustees. He tried to talk me out of it, but after a few minutes of thoughtful discussion, he came to the understanding that I could not help his church get started on refocusing ministry if I were constantly defending myself to people who did not know me. The members of that committee had become good friends of both my wife and me, and it was difficult to refuse their invitation. However, within a few short days, we knew we had made the right decision.

The deacons at Emmanuel Baptist Church, Enid, met on the following Sunday night and voted unanimously to express their unqualified support for their pastor. They were also gracious to my family and me in other ways I learned about later. In addition, our deacon leadership personally invited John Floyd to Emmanuel, all expenses paid, to sit down and get to know their pastor and our church. John Floyd declined. I did not know that the deacons' meeting had been called, and I was not present for it, having a previous commitment in Oklahoma City for Oklahoma's Centennial. The support and love shown to me and my family during the censure confirmed it was not God's desire for us to leave Emmanuel. Our people know their pastor. They know I believe courteous dissent is essential for any healthy organization, including our church. Sunday school teachers are free to teach opposite of what their pastor teaches on tertiary issues of Scripture. Deacons and members are free to express publicly their disapproval of church actions. All members of Emmanuel are asked, when they express dissent, to maintain a gracious, loving, and courteous spirit. The official "censure" of me at the IMB sealed my decision not to cease my efforts to reform the Southern Baptist Convention until leaders who could not display this same spirit were removed.

Upon my return to Enid, and after communicating with IMB legal counsel, I sent a letter to all IMB trustees.

November 28, 2007
Dear Fellow IMB Trustees,
    The November meeting of the International Mission Board resulted in a censure brought upon me by a majority vote during Executive Session. I realize not all of the trustees were present, and not all trustees present voted for the censure, but this letter is being sent to you, as well as all other IMB trustees, to request a personal response to me of four questions you will find later in this letter.

In order for the focus at this crucial time of the year to be on Lottie Moon and not Wade Burleson, I made it known to the Executive Committee on the Monday afternoon prior to our last Board meeting that I would resign by the end of the year, I would shut down my blog on December 6, 2007, and I would personally and publicly apologize to any trustee who personally felt disparaged by my blog. Ironically, I had never been approached privately by any IMB trustee about any personal embarrassment felt because of my blog. But, having received an overwhelming amount of negative publicity myself over the 2006 recommendation for my removal, I understand what it means for people to *feel* disparaged. All that ever had to happen for an apology to occur was for those feelings to be made known to me. The Executive Committee did so Monday afternoon on behalf of the three trustees (John Floyd, Winston Curtis, and Jerry Corbaley). I made my apology known to the Board in the Executive Session on Tuesday night.

However, I also let the Executive Committee know on Monday afternoon that I *would not* apologize for expressing my public dissent over Board approved actions. When a subcommittee of three people, sent by the Executive Committee, met with me on Monday evening to work out the details of my proposal, I gave to these three men the specifics of my offer above. I told them I could not apologize for publicly dissenting because the new policy that states trustees must publicly support what they cannot privately support was adopted the day the motion for my removal was rescinded by IMB trustees on March 22, 2007. In effect, the recommendation for my removal would have allowed the SBC to decide the matter if my public dissent was appropriate. That recommendation was taken out of the Southern Baptist Convention's hands and brought back internally to the IMB.

I believe the new policy that officially stifles minority dissent is very unwise. I agree with much in the March 22, 2006, *Guidelines of Trustee Conduct*. For instance, I wholeheartedly agree that Executive Session confidentiality rules should be upheld, and I have never broken those rules. I also agree that everything said must be voiced with grace and civility, and I earnestly seek to exhibit such Christian grace in everything I write and say. But I cannot agree with the portion of the policy that stifles the public expression of a minority opinion, and I cannot agree with the practice of conducting IMB business behind closed doors. The Baptist way to handle dissent is simply to ignore it, but to respect the place that it has in our history and among our people. Soon it goes away. That is, if the majority have sound reasons for their actions.

It is apparent to me that the Garner Motion at the 2007 Southern Baptist Convention specifically advises SBC trustee boards to consider the 2000 *Baptist Faith & Message* as the *sufficient* doctrinal standard for cooperation. Doctrinal policies that go beyond the 2000 *BFM*—and exclude otherwise qualified Southern Baptists from missionary cooperation—are in direct violation of the will of the SBC. It is my belief that the IMB is in violation of the wishes of the SBC, and I am simply fulfilling my role as a trustee elected by the SBC at large. My dissent over the November 2005 policies is firm, but civil. That will not change.

I was censured because I have been consistent, intentional, and unyielding in my desire to see the International Mission Board correct the two wrongs which occurred over the adoption of two policies that exceed the 2000 *BFM*. As all of you should know, the two new policies, which passed Board approval on November 15, 2005, forbid any Southern Baptist from being appointed for missions service who (a) honestly admitted when asked that he/she had a private prayer language, and/or (b) was baptized by an administrator of the ordinance, deemed qualified by the candidate's local church, but "unqualified" by the trustees of the IMB.

Because my proposal was rejected and I have now been censured, I will not cease voicing my disagreement—both publicly and graciously—with these policies until they are either reversed or the Southern Baptist Convention instructs me to cease expressing my minority dissent. You have seen me serve with quiet faithfulness, always speaking respectfully the couple of times I have spoken, and you know me to be cordial. However, when it comes to public dissent, I answer to a higher authority than an internal IMB trustee policy that forbids it.

What concerns me, however, is that the censure, the negative publicity, and the distraction from Lottie Moon could all have been avoided. My proposal, which was intractable due to the facts I presented to the three-man subcommittee, was *conditioned* upon the Executive Committee not issuing a censure and thus distracting our Board and my future ministry. I would have resigned my trusteeship from the IMB by January 2008. I respectfully request that you e-mail me with your personal answers to the following four questions:

1. Did you know of my offer to the Executive Committee before you voted for the censure?

2. Were you surprised that I was not allowed to speak prior to the vote for censure?

3. Did it concern you that "Question" was called after only one person spoke in opposition to the motion; and did you think a motion of such magnitude was fully and freely debated?

4. Would the information gleaned in this letter have changed your vote?

I look forward to your responses.

In His Grace,
Wade Burleson

Nobody from the trustee board contacted me over the 2007 holiday season in response to the above letter except for those who informed me that they voted against the censure. It was becoming increasingly frustrating to deal with Fundamentalist trustees, or at the very least sycophant trustees, who seemingly had an aversion to focusing on the mission work of the IMB for the sole purpose of getting everyone to conform to their demands and punishing those who did not.

IMB Trustee Meeting
Gainesville, Florida
January 2008

I had told my wife that I would remain a trustee of the International Mission Board only as long as I could have a good attitude during trustee leadership attempts to punish me and as long as mission work was not harmed by my presence on the board. After the November 2007 meeting, I knew I was going to be a distraction to the mission work on the board as Fundamentalist trustee leadership would do everything in their power to prevent my being reassigned to a four-year term as an IMB trustee at the 2009 Southern Baptist Convention. Derek Gaubatz, legal counsel for the IMB, contacted me in December 2007. Derek had been in all the trustee leader meetings, and he said what trustee leadership wanted was an apology from me for my public dissent.

I told Derek I knew that was what trustee leadership wanted, but they were not going to get it. Derek then said I was going to be a continuing issue at every trustee meeting, and mission work would be harmed unless some kind of resolution came about. I did not wish to be a continued distraction to the SBC missions ministry, so I asked Derek to draft a letter that he felt would be an acceptable "apology" to trustee leadership, without violating my convictions that dissent was healthy. If we could come up with a letter acceptable to the two of us, I would sign off on it, and then maybe we could get this IMB fiasco behind us. Derek worked hard to draft a letter that I would read at the January 2008 IMB trustee meeting in Gainesville, Florida. At the last board meeting, I requested to read the following letter in the final public session.

My Fellow Trustees,

I want to briefly share with you what a great privilege it is to serve with you as a trustee. It is my belief that God has uniquely gifted and called each one of us to this role so that we can work together to advance the IMB's mission. My earnest desire is to be a working member of our team so that we can accomplish that mission together. While I understand that some of you may harbor doubts about my ability to actually be a "team player," I want you to know that I am committed to being a team player and that perhaps you have not yet seen or understood a full picture of me. Accordingly, as we move forward into a new year of serving the IMB together, I would like to say a few words to clear the air of past events, express my commitment to working with you within our internal standards, and then once I've spoken, let the proof of my verbal commitment be seen in my future actions.

To begin with, I do admit that I have in the past intentionally violated our newly revised (Spring 2006) internal standards of conduct. In particular, I publicly disagreed with certain actions taken by this board, rather than speaking in supportive terms or staying silent on matters about which I disagreed. The new standards of trustee conduct, adopted in the Spring of 2006, state that a trustee must publicly affirm a board approved action even if he cannot privately support it. I want you to know that I never expressed my dissent out of a desire to harm the work of the IMB or any of you, my fellow trustees and brothers and sisters in Christ. Instead, I did so out of an exercise of my conscience. Simply put, I believed in my conscience that it was the right thing to do to further our mutual goal of supporting the IMB's purpose of cooperatively taking the gospel to all peoples of the world. I recognize that many of you may have been upset by my decision to express my disagreement and feel that it has hurt the work of the IMB. Scripture teaches us that sometimes we can exercise our conscience in a way that offends others. I am sorry that this seems to be the case here.

Therefore, it is my goal going forward, to the extent it rests in my power to do so, to live at peace with all of you and not cause you offense. It is also my goal to have a greater focus on the work of the IMB than on me. Accordingly, I commit to you this day that I will no longer violate, intentionally or otherwise, our new trustee standards of conduct. If I find myself in disagreement with a policy or proposed policy of the Board, I will express my disagreement using the channels that are available—for example, plenary forum sessions, trustee forum sessions, and private communication with fellow trustees—but will not take my disagreement outside of those confines to the blogosphere or world at large. In fact, if this statement is accepted, I intend to shut my blog down immediately after this board meeting. I should add that it is possible, however unlikely, that an occasion might arise where I believed that we had enacted a policy that violates Scripture or conscience. If that were to happen, I would resign and express my disagreement outside the structure of the IMB or understand I will be censured. I do, however, consider such a future occasion to be unlikely. It is my belief that God has blessed the work of the IMB because it is carrying out a mission close to his heart and that so long as we collectively continue to seek him in prayer, he will guard us from error and bless our work.

I do look forward to working with you as a fellow servant this year and in the years to come.

In His Grace,
Wade Burleson

After I read the letter, John Floyd requested that everyone who was not a trustee leave the room, that the doors be closed, and trustees would do business. John informed the board of trustees that the letter was not an "acceptable apology." He said that I would remain under censure, and would not be appointed to an IMB committee. Derek later told me he was surprised by trustee leadership's reaction. I was not. After that closed-door meeting, I called my wife, my father, and the rest of my accountability group and told them I was resigning from the board. I knew I would always be the issue to Fundamentalist trustees, and I was becoming a distraction to the work that needed to be done.

I also felt that I could be a better influence for the future direction of the SBC without serving as a trustee of the IMB. It had been a rocky ride as Fundamentalists sought to "deal" with me, but I left on my terms, precisely when I wanted to leave, and knew that my two-year effort to turn the Southern Baptist Convention toward a more gracious and cooperative stance was only beginning. So, on Tuesday, January 29, 2008, just a little more than two years since the initial trustee recommendation that I be removed from the International Mission Board, I resigned. On my blog, I posted the reasons I resigned. I wrote,

> It became crystal clear to me tonight that it would be impossible for me to continue as a trustee of the International Mission Board. The appropriate forum for my continued service to the Southern Baptist Convention is now outside the IMB Board of Trustees. I deem it better to be censured by man than to be condemned by conscience. It is my decision to resign, effective immediately, from service as a trustee of the International Mission Board. I will continue to work to effect change within the Southern Baptist Convention and will post later this week my plans for the immediate future.[3]

I was flooded with hundreds of letters and e-mails of support from across the Convention after my resignation. Many remarked how proud they were that I had fought the good fight for as long as I did. Others were asking me not to quit blogging for the overall good of the Southern Baptist Convention. I appreciated all the e-mails and letters of encouragement. I also can honestly say I never one time questioned or regretted my decision to resign from the moment I made it.

I had enough of hardball religion at the IMB. A new game was about to begin.

Notes

1. "Patience Is the Operative Word for the SBC," 10 July 2007, http://kerussocharis.blogspot.com/2007/07/patience-is-operative-word-for-sbc.html.

2. Vaclav Havel, *The Power of the Powerless* (New York: Sharpe, 1985), 63.

3. "A Decision I Believe Is Best for the Future of All," 29 January 2008, http://kerussocharis.blogspot.com/2008/01/decision-i-believe-is-best-for-future.html.

Chapter 28

FUTURE

The *Christian Century* magazine posted an article in fall 2008 in which the writer introduced me as "a pastor in Enid, Oklahoma, who often needles SBC officials, asked September 24 on his blog . . . ."[1]

When I read the article, I paused for a moment to ponder the word "needles." I looked up a definition for the word and it said, "to goad, provoke, or tease." Someone once opined that perception is personal truth, reality is objective truth, and rare is the occasion when the two actually meet. I do not perceive myself as a needler of Southern Baptist Convention leadership, but I accept that the *Christian Century*, Fundamentalist SBC leaders, and a handful of others do see me that way. I perceive myself as a supporter of the SBC (I led my church to increase Cooperative Program giving last year), a defender of SBC missionaries, agency employees, and administrators (we hired them to do a job, and we should trust them to do it well). I've been a Southern Baptist for the long haul (for my entire life, and I willingly continue my affiliation with the Southern Baptist Convention).

But frankly, if SBC Fundamentalist leaders make stupid decisions, they need someone to "needle" them from within the Southern Baptist Convention. My wife and I were rocking along the earlier part of this decade, raising a family, pastoring a church, loving Oklahoma and our Southern Baptist Convention, when we both were awakened to a radical change occurring within the SBC—a change that caught us by surprise.

We discovered missionaries were being fired. At the time we said nothing because, as most Southern Baptists, we believed the issue was related to a denial of the Bible as the inspired, inerrant word of God, and, by golly, we want Bible believers on our mission field.

Then, when I became a trustee of the International Mission Board, I realized to my horror that the issue in the Southern Baptist Convention was not a battle for a belief in the inspired, inerrant word of God. I trust my moderate friends will be patient as I restate what I just wrote in the preceding sentence. Had it been proven to me at the grassroots level of the SBC that the problem with our Convention was a denial by some of the sufficiency, inspiration, or inerrancy of God's word, I would never have second thoughts about my involvement in "the battle for the Bible." Some may wish to debate with me the propriety of using the word "inerrant" to describe the Bible, but I have no problem using the word in reference to God's Word. I discovered as a trustee of the IMB, however, that inerrancy is no longer the issue in the Southern Baptist Convention; we are battling a more serious problem. Frankly, because of the way I have seen some of my fellow Southern Baptists who hold to inerrancy treated in this new millennium by other Southern Baptists who also profess to hold to inerrancy, I now have doubts about the veracity of the claim that the issue in the Southern Baptist Convention was ever a battle for a belief in the inerrant Bible in the first place.

The problem in the SBC is a rejection of conservative evangelicals who disagree with Fundamentalist interpretations of the sacred Scriptures. I have seen an excellent Hebrew professor fired from teaching Hebrew at Southwestern Baptist Theological Seminary (Sheri Klouda), forced into financial straits, all because of a Fundamentalist interpretation that a woman should not teach men. I have seen an outstanding female supervisor (Wendy Norvelle) at the International Mission Board promoted by Dr. Rankin to be the vice president, only to see Rankin's recommendation overturned by Fundamentalist trustee leaders who forced their interpretation of the Bible that "no woman shall lead a man" upon IMB administration. I have seen IMB trustees force their Fundamentalist interpretation that certain spiritual gifts have ceased, a belief that exceeds the 2000 *BFM* and in some minds contradicts the inerrant word of God, and keep otherwise qualified Southern Baptist missionaries from serving on the mission field. I have seen IMB trustee leaders force their Fundamentalist Landmark beliefs on an entire board, and thus remove from the possibility of missionary service any Southern Baptist church member whose baptism did not take place in a Southern Baptist church. I have seen Fundamentalist trustees fire a missionary couple in Africa because they refused to "cease and desist" from cooperating with another conservative, evangelical missionary couple—who happened to be non-Southern Baptist—in planting a church among the bush tribes of Africa. I have personally been witness to Southern Baptist Fundamentalist leaders spreading vicious rumors against people (other than me) who dared speak out to oppose their views. I have seen Southern

Baptists threatened, excoriated, fired, mistreated, lied about, and dismissed, all because they dared to express an opinion different than the Fundamentalist interpretation of sacred Scripture on tertiary matters that have nothing to do with being Christian or even Southern Baptist. The best way to identify these Baptist Fundamentalists is with the label "Baptist identity," for truly, the Fundamentalists would rather demand people conform to their interpretation of what it means to be Southern Baptist than to cooperate with people who hold a differing view. In other words, their "Baptist identity," as they interpret it, precedes any identification with Christ and his commandment to love one another.

That, my friend, is why I speak out. The people in leadership who are hurting Southern Baptists by their demands for conformity must be removed from Convention leadership. Why? The Convention is built on cooperation (i.e., the "Cooperative Program"), and demands for conformity disqualify anyone who is to lead in cooperation. I will continue to speak out until the sleeping giant we call the Southern Baptist Convention wakes up and realizes that what began as a "conservative resurgence" somehow became a "Fundamentalist fury." It's time the fires of Fundamentalism's fury are quenched. If my writing plays any part in quenching those fires, and if in so doing, the *Christian Century* writes that I "needle" the SBC leaders who exalt Fundamentalism (Baptist identity), then so be it.

I plead guilty.

My future is laid out for me. I will continue to write about our beloved Southern Baptist Convention. I will continue to oppose Fundamentalism's fury. I will continue to step to the plate in the game of hardball religion until we can decide as a Convention to call the game and begin cooperating for the purpose of spreading the gospel of Christ.

Note

1. "'Female Pastors' Story Rattles SBC Nerves," *Christian Century*, 21 October 2008, http://www.christiancentury.org/article.lasso?id=5427.

AFTERWORD

Adrian Rogers preached a message titled "Truth or Consequences" at the 1990 Southern Baptist Pastors' Conference. The outline of Dr. Rogers's sermon went thus:

(1) It is better to speak the truth that hurts and heals, than falsehood that comforts and kills.

(2) It is better to speak the truth alone, than to be wrong with the multitude.

(3) It is better to die for the truth, than to live for a lie.

Dr. Rogers's words ring as loudly for me today as they did when I first heard them nearly twenty years ago. The truth that I have spoken these past three years has not been a comfortable word to Fundamentalists who desire to exclude from Southern Baptist cooperative ministry all who do not interpret Scripture the way they do. I also realize that there have not been many in the SBC opposing the narrowing of the doctrinal parameters of cooperation, though the number is increasing daily. I can say, in good conscience, that I would not change one thing I did while serving as a trustee of the IMB. Each of my actions was based on truth and done with the ultimate good of the Southern Baptist Convention in mind. Their effectiveness will be measured as time passes and others evaluate them.

I close with an answer to a question asked me by my son. He said, "Dad, what is the greatest hurt and the greatest blessing in being a Southern Baptist?" I answered without hesitation—"People." It's because of people we call Southern Baptists that I remain a Southern Baptist. They have been a blessing to me. And the others? Well, let's just say they introduced me to hardball religion, and, ultimately, I think they'll lose the game.

APPENDIX

Excerpt from *Old Landmarkism and the Baptists* by Bob Ross

The term LANDMARKISM is a nickname which refers to ecclesiastical views arranged as a logical system or ecclesiastical order and popularized by the late James Robinson Graves (1820–1893). According to Landmarkers, there is no authority in either the Word or from the Spirit for doing the work of the Great Commission; this authority comes solely from the local Baptist church.

The system of Landmarkism, sometimes called "church truth," involves the authenticity of a church as an organization, the administration and administrator of baptism, and the ordination of ministers. It is asserted that a church is unscriptural, baptism is invalid, and ministers are not duly ordained unless there is proper Church Authority for them. This is Landmarkism's "chief cornerstone."

Some writers of the past referred to this position as "high churchism." Consequently, the Landmark view is that Baptist Churches ALONE have the authority of Christ to evangelize, baptize and carry out all aspects of the commission. The system further involves the perpetuity, succession, or continuity of Baptist churches through which authority has descended through the ages and will continue. This position, though not uniformly defined among Landmarkers, is believed to have been taught by Christ in such verses as Matthew 16:18, 28:19-20.

While Landmarkers in general profess either an inability to demonstrate the succession or no necessity of doing so, their efforts to advocate their system of "church truth" are almost invariably characterized by several quotations from secondary sources and their own respected authors, supposedly establishing the historical claim. Generally therefore, they believe that (1) the true and scriptural organization of a church, (2) the valid administration of baptism, and (3) the proper ordination of a gospel minister, MUST all be enacted upon the authority of a sound and true, scriptural church, namely, a church that was born through the authority of a "mother" church continuing in like manner back to the original apostolic church of Matthew 28 where "church authority" first "began."

In refuting these errors, Baptists and other Christians today can believe in the continuity of Christianity since Christ and may devote themselves to regulating their faith and practice by the Scriptures (in an orderly manner) without adhering to the Landmark teachings of church authority and succession. The authority which validates baptism, or any other scriptural action of our time, does not reside in the church institution any more than does the authority which validates salvation itself; authority resides in Jesus Christ and is expressed in His Word. The church itself is dependent upon this authority, but this authority is not dependent upon the church.

This book advocates no new or novel views in opposition to Landmarkism. The first Confession of Faith set forth by English Particular Baptists is the well-known Confession of 1644, and in Article 41 it states, "The persons designed by Christ, to dispense this ordinance (baptism), the Scriptures hold forth to be a preaching disciple, it being no where tied to a particular church, officer, or person extraordinarily sent, the commission enjoining the administration, being given to them under no other consideration, but as considered disciples."

Landmarkism, as a system, is of relatively recent origin among the Baptists, although various items in the system have been obvious at certain times in our history. But at least not until J. R. Graves popularized all of the related concepts in systematic form did a significant segment of Baptists finally become a fragmentation from other Baptists (in the Preface of his book, *Old Landmarkism; What Is It?*, Graves takes credit for "inaugurating the reform" which became known as Landmarkism).

May this book assist all who read it to see Landmarkism in its proper perspective among the Baptists.

—Bob L. Ross

David Rogers's Letter to IMB Trustees (January 2006)

Dear IMB Trustee,

After much prayer and thought, I have decided to write and express my concerns to each of you regarding the developments at the IMB which have been in the news recently. I am writing, first of all, as a missionary of the IMB, who, having dedicated 16 years of his life to ministry in Spain, has a lot of investment at stake in the future direction of the IMB. I am also writing as the son of Adrian Rogers, with a sense of stewardship of the heritage I have received, as well as concern for a God-honoring and accurate representation and application of my father's spiritual legacy. I can only wish my Dad were here today to share his wisdom and leadership skills in relation to the situations we are presently facing. It is impossible for me to know exactly how he would have responded regarding each detail concerned. I do, however, believe I knew my Dad well enough to give a general approximation of what he may have thought regarding these issues. At the same time, I acknowledge that each of us is ultimately accountable to God, and our understanding of His will in the light of His inspired Word, and not to the opinions or memory of any fallible human being.

Having said that, I must say now that I am concerned with what seems to me to be a general direction on the part of the Board of Trustees, much of which I have only recently been made aware. It would seem to me that much of the ground gained for the glory of God and the advance of His kingdom through the "conservative resurgence" in the SBC, in which my father played such an integral role, is in danger of being commandeered in a new, more extreme direction.

Specifically in regards to the direction of the IMB, I believe some very helpful adjustments in focus and parameters have been made in the wake of the "conservative resurgence." We, as Southern Baptists, have been able to clarify that a steadfast commitment to the authority of God's Word, and a proper understanding of "all things whatsoever I have commanded you" preclude any *a la carte* self-styled commitment to "missions" as our bottom line. We, at the same time, have made what I understand to be a great push towards the evangelization and discipling of all the *ethne* of the world than ever before. Though we as Southern Baptists are definitely not perfect, and have undoubtedly committed many errors, it is my opinion that God's blessing has been upon the Southern Baptist mission enterprise in a mighty way during this time.

I also believe that God has used the spiritual and strategic leadership of Jerry Rankin to help us make bold steps of faith, and to open our eyes to what God is doing around us, and to how we, as Henry Blackaby would put it, can "join Him in what He is already doing." After having recently read the book, *To the Ends of the Earth*, I am not hesitant to say, in the light of 16 years of international missionary service, as well as whatever spiritual insight God may have given me, that I believe that God has given us as Southern Baptists a great gift in Jerry Rankin, and that His blessing and anointing is upon Dr. Rankin's leadership.

I am especially encouraged by Dr. Rankin's emphasis that the kingdom of God is broader than the Southern Baptist Convention, and that God's way of working entails using the entire Body of Christ around the world, with each group and member making their own unique contribution working together in a beautiful kaleidoscope of service to Christ towards the fulfillment of the Great Commission. I am in agreement that we need to be careful to discern who are our true partners in the glorious task that Jesus has given us, and to not compromise biblical convictions, especially regarding essential doctrine, on the altar of "false unity." I am concerned, however, that there appears to be a drive on the part of some to "rein in" the progress we have made in these areas, giving an undue emphasis on certain points of doctrine, which, in my opinion, are not clearly spelled out in Scripture, and seeking to narrow the parameters of biblical cooperation a few steps beyond the healthy adjustments we had already made.

Specifically, I do not think the recent policy change approved in the November Trustee meeting disqualifying missionary candidates who acknowledge having a "private prayer language" or those who were baptized by immersion as believers outside of a church deemed to be doctrinally compatible with Southern Baptists is a move in the right direction.

I myself do not practice a "private prayer language." However, in the course of my Christian ministry, I have known many fellow servants of Christ who have professed to have had this experience and for whom I have the utmost respect, due to their evident love for Christ, His Word, and His work, as well as sterling Christian character. Of course, there are a few exceptions to this, as there are as well with otherwise perfectly orthodox believers, who do not practice a "private prayer language." At the same time, while I recognize that sincere, godly interpreters of the Word of God take the view that certain supernatural gifts ceased at some time in the past, it seems to me that other equally sincere, godly, and objective interpreters of the Word of God have come to different conclusions.

I personally do not see how putting this new limitation upon Southern Baptist missionary service is going to make a positive difference in our faithfulness to Christ or in our effectiveness in carrying out His Great Commission. It does concern me, though, that some otherwise perfectly qualified candidates for missionary service might be disqualified because of this, especially in light of the previously existing policies limiting public expression of *glossolalia* and the "persistent emphasis of any specific gift of the Spirit as normative for all or to the extent such emphasis becomes disruptive to the Baptist fellowship."

I also feel that the new policy stating that "baptism must take place in a church that practices believer's baptism by immersion alone, does not view baptism as sacramental or regenerative, and a church that embraces the doctrine of the security of the believer" and that "a candidate who has not been baptized in a Southern Baptist church or in a church which meets the standards listed above is expected to request baptism in his/her Southern Baptist church as a testimony of identification with the system of belief held by Southern Baptist churches" does not have scriptural justification and goes beyond what Southern Baptists have traditionally accepted. Others have already written eloquently, exposing the flaws in Landmarkist ecclesiology. I imagine most, if not all of you, are well familiar with the arguments on both sides of this issue.

I would like, however, to point out the biblical example of the baptism of the Ethiopian eunuch, which leaves the question of any local church "sponsorship" or "supervision" of the baptism very much up in the air. We also have the testimony of the roots of the Anabaptist movement, in which the initial "baptizers" had not yet been scripturally baptized themselves.

I am not saying that those who approved the new policy change on baptism are necessarily sympathetic on the whole towards Landmarkism. However, I do recognize the policy as reflective of at least one "plank" of Landmarkist argumentation, and a "plank" for which I believe there is no biblical basis. And, it concerns me that we, as a denomination, may be making steps in that direction.

Another related issue that is on the minds of all involved has to do with the proposed dismissal of Wade Burleson from the Board of Trustees. Since I was not present during Trustee meetings in order to personally observe Mr. Burleson's behavior in that setting, I must reserve judgment regarding that. At the same time, I have carefully read through Mr. Burleson's "blog," and reflected deeply both upon the ideas expressed therein, as well as the tone in which they are expressed. My opinion is that, while Mr. Burleson, just like any of the rest of us is not perfect, and may here or there say things which might be able to be expressed in a more circumspect manner, what I have read there written by Mr. Burleson is a long way from amounting to, in and of itself, "slander," "gossip," "broken trust" or "resistance to accountability."

It would seem to me that if the Trustees are indeed accountable to the Southern Baptist Convention as a whole, and to the churches which comprise it, then Mr. Burleson acted in good faith making known to those who have the bottom line responsibility for decisions made something of the issues involved behind those decisions. Before the "conservative resurgence," it was frequently argued that many of the various boards and committees of the SBC were out of step with what the majority of Southern Baptists believed, and thus, it was necessary to make Southern Baptists aware of what was going on. In my concise but humble opinion: "what's good for the goose is good for the gander."

At this point, I would like to reiterate it is impossible for me to know exactly how my father would have addressed each of these points. Each of us is our own person. However, having grown up under the wings of this great man of God who has been so influential in Southern Baptist life, I can honestly say I think that he would be in general agreement with the gist of what I am saying here.

How each of you respond to this is between you and God, taking into consideration your accountability to the SBC as well. I pray God will give you the grace and wisdom to act in a way glorifying to His name and advantageous to the advance of His kingdom.

Your co-laborer in the Harvest, David Rogers

Transcript of Phone Conversation with IMB Trustee Leaders (February 2006, after the St. Louis meeting)

Tom: The more we've thought about it [the motion for removal], the more that we're inclined to go to our next board meeting and just suggest to our trustees that we withdraw the request of the Southern Baptist Convention. We are going to just take that off the table altogether; not contingent on anything from your end at all. This is just something that we ought to do.
Wade: Well, I'm appreciative.
Tom: Uh . . . anything that you would want to do you're still free to do. We didn't want you to feel like this was a deal being brokered. We wanted you to feel free to do whatever you wanted to do without feeling like you had to leverage it out with us.

Wade: I appreciate it, Tom. It's a difficult time. I want to work within the board to do whatever I can to correct what I believe to be some issues that we need to look at, but I'm not sure of the timetable. I will follow your leadership as to when those things I need to address can be spoken before the entire board. I'll be prepared to do it at the next meeting; but as I said, I'll do it within the confines of the board at the time that you suggest.

Tom: I think that's very nice and very helpful. I still intend . . . to follow through on those things that are under my control. I would still like to suggest that the appropriate committee revisit the doctrinal policies just to make sure that we're able to put a proper context and a sharpening of the reasoning for them. We never before have had to put a rationale for a policy or a guideline because there usually was never enough interest to warrant putting out a rationale to the press. I will refer the policies back to personnel committee for some clarification. I will also ask that we issue a statement of support for President Rankin. I still intend to do that. I'm going to tell people he's only cussin' when he's drunk; so that ought to help him some. But I just wanted you to know, we're still on track for those things.

Wade: Tom, let me ask a question. I understand that you have said there is nothing that needs to be leveraged or brokered in order to rescind the motion to remove me. I need to know how many IMB trustee leaders are sitting around the table listening to our conversation.

Tom: Okay, we've got the nine that are on the executive committee, which is the standing committee chairman and the officers. Then we have Dr. Rankin and Clyde Meador here.

Wade: All right, I need some wisdom from you. In Oklahoma your efforts to remove me have been pretty big news; the Associated Press, my church, and my hometown newspaper have all made it pretty big news. I guess what I need is wisdom on what will be said when you take your recommendation for my removal off the table. Will there be an explanation as to why you made it in the first place and then remove it so quickly?

Tom: Well, we, that's what this conversation is about. Even after we get off the phone with you we're gonna work on that. We do need some kind of a news release about this and we want it worded well. I've worked on a statement that I might could just put out as chairman that would be constructive. It would probably [be] something such as, "It is my intention to request of our board that we rescind our action in January to recommend to the SBC in June that Wade Burleson be replaced as an IMB trustee. We have found workable options to resolve conflict that were not known during our January meeting. I've consulted with my board officers and with our standing committee chairman and they agree with me that we should move forward with a motion to withdraw our request for SBC action." It's a statement of fact, in other words.

Wade: All right. I'm not sure what you mean by you "found" workable options to resolve the conflict since the January meeting, but I guess it is allowing me to express my concerns to the full board instead of removing me, right?

Tom: Do you have anything working in your heart or head right now that you want to do as far as addressing the board in the March meeting?

Wade: Well, you know, Tom, like I've written to you in e-mails in months past, e-mails I sent to all the trustees, at some point, and again I leave the time to your discretion, I would like to share with the entire board what you heard me share in St. Louis. Our board needs to work to end the undermining of our administration. We cannot function properly as a board if we allow trustees, even some of you men seated around that table, to continually undermine our president. I'll express my concerns to the full board at your discretion; but from the beginning I really feel like folks need to know the story that you now know. We need as a board to deal with the issues I laid out to everyone at St. Louis. I realize that there's disagreement over some things and I understand that. But you have seen the documentation that I have. I think some things must be dealt with if we're going to function as a board that supports our president and staff. If we don't feel like we can, I think we need to remove him, but we can't continue this secret, outside-the-board-meeting attempt to undermine the work of the IMB.

Tom: Yeah, well, I agree with that. I think everybody here now agrees with that as well. I just think that your commitment to doing it within the board instead of making it public is the proper approach.

Wade: Absolutely.

Tom: I think that there are avenues for that to happen. In fact, I believe new avenues are being created for some of your concerns. For example, after the November meeting we challenged the orientation committee to sharpen the definitions in the Blue Book and to bring back a recommended procedure for accountability whenever trustees are out of line with some of the things that we say must be a part of trustee decorum. There will probably be a report from this committee in the May trustee meeting. So assuming that the amendments to the Blue Book are in place in the May meeting, then any issues that anybody has, starting in July, will have a way to be addressed; in matters of deportment or integrity, hidden agendas, all of that would have a means for proper procedure within the board. I think that's probably the best way to address this.

Wade: I agree. I mean, that's all I could ask for.

Tom: Yeah, well, that's what we're gonna give ya (laughter). Tell me, there's gonna come an awkward moment or two in our next meeting as we work through this. I want you to be prepared for that.

Wade: Once the motion for my removal is rescinded, I will be at all executive session meetings and trustee forum meetings. As you know, I was baffled and confused for the recommendation for removal in the first place. So if the intention of trustee leaders is to take it back, I don't know that I have anything to say. I'll be more than happy to be at all the executive sessions and forums and continue my service as a trustee, putting the past behind us.

Tom: Yeah. Jerry's got something . . . .

Jerry: Wade, I haven't been in the whole meeting. I was late getting here, but the spirit and sense of the group here is kind of a willingness to go the direction Tom has mentioned. I think it's because it is so much out there in the news and everything, and there is negative publicity about it. I think a statement to come out of this meeting, even before our board meeting in March, to let people know that a rescission may of the recommendation to remove you is coming. I don't know if the trustee leaders want to do that or not. But after the board meeting, or after this meeting, whenever that happens, I mean, it's going to be meaningless apart from a statement from you. Regardless of how you feel about the accusations against you and what others have said about you, I think the spirit of dealing with the issues that concern you on this board and resolving them within board process will go a long way. I wonder if a statement to the press, at the time this recommendation to rescind the motion comes out, just a statement of apology, you know, for doing anything that's confrontational that helped to create this conflict. That would go a long way toward the board, I think, being conciliatory and working through this.

Wade: I appreciate that, Dr. Rankin. I appreciate what you've said. I will say categorically that I will not apologize for anything. I cannot. Now I will issue a statement, and it will be this: In the spirit which I have sensed from our chairman and from trustee committee chairmen, I look forward to working with my fellow trustees in the cooperative mission work of the Southern Baptist Convention and fulfill my fiduciary duties as a trustee of the International Mission Board on behalf of the SBC.

Dr. Rankin: Mm-hmm.

Wade: Now if my blog continues to be an issue with trustee leaders, all that has to be done is a guideline or policy that states "trustees shall not blog" and I will not blog. But what I'm saying, Doc, is this: I stand by everything that I have said. So to apologize for my blog, I will not do.

Tom: Brother Wade, a rule that prohibits blogging probably will not happen until March or May, you know, because of the time involved.

Wade: I understand, and I guess here's what I'm saying. If you've read my blog, you've noticed that I've taken the high road in this sense. I've only discussed the issues that are pertinent to the health of the Southern Baptist Convention. I know in my heart that what I have done is right.

Tom: Wade, we're not going to challenge you on that, okay? Like I told you earlier, we're not brokering a deal here. What we're gonna do is get this thing off the convention's table. We're creating ways to deal with the impasses within the board so that we should be able to work through the issues like this in the future. So if you don't feel led to make any kind of a statement, conciliatory statement or apology or anything like that . . . ."

Wade: Okay, let me ask a question, Tom. I do feel led to issue a statement, and I always desire reconciliation. But in terms of any "apology," I guess my question is this: When I'm accused of gossip and slander and set outside the board without ever being shown what the gossip and slander is, and then just a few weeks later that motion is rescinded without me ever acknowledging I've done anything wrong, where's the apology supposed to come from?

Tom: Well, brother, I imagine the appropriate place for that would probably come from whoever made that motion. I think you and he have been in contact with each other about that. But I also want you to know that though that might be true as far as behind closed doors—the board has internally heard that language "gossip and slander"—but the only time that anyone in the Southern Baptist Convention has heard that outside of the board has been published by those other than the trustees who voted on that motion. We were behind closed doors. We never put those words in public, and so the only way for you to be accused of that publicly would be for somebody other than us to have put it out there.

Wade: Okay. I know you changed the words of the motion when you made them public. Let me just ask a question for information. I was only in the public session where people and press—I believe Mary Nickel's daughter was present—where the statement of trustee leadership regarding the recommendation for my removal was read into the record by you. You stated, for the record and in public, that I was being removed "for gossip and slander." So when you say it's not public, press is always in public sessions unless they choose not to be present. So I'm confused.

Tom: Well, we, I'll put it this way: We did not publicize it.

Wade: Okay, I'm sorry. I understand that. I thought I heard you say, "we did not make it public."

Tom: It's not officially a matter of record until the minutes are approved at the following meeting, and it's only released to the press at that point. And then we don't even release the minutes in whole. We will only release excerpts from the minutes upon request after they've been reviewed by staff and not contain any damaging information to people on the field.

Wade: I understand. So if I understand you correctly, and you shared this with me a few days ago as well, your intention is to remove "gossip and slander" from the official record of the IMB?

Tom: The motion to rescind will supersede the motion to remove you. We will withdraw this whole issue from the convention. The original motion is being taken off by this new motion. And basically this new motion rescinds the motion by replacing it.

Wade: Hmm. Tom . . . and forgive me for pressing here, but I just need to be clear for my wife's sake, for my sake.

Tom: Sure.

Wade: The "gossip and the slander" language will not be in the minutes so that one hundred years from now people who read the minutes will not read "Wade Burleson is being recommended for dismissal for gossip and slander."

Tom: I'm not sure; I will have to double check that, but we, you know, I will work on seeing how that can be accomplished.

Wade: I appreciate that, Tom, because that's the issue for me. That's why I can't apologize; because "gossip and slander" is the basis for the motion. For me to apologize acts as if I am agreeing that I gossiped and I slandered; and I totally deny that. So I guess my spirit is this: I do want reconciliation and I do want to work within the board and I do want to do whatever is possible to make the IMB better, but I cannot issue an apology."

Tom: That's all right. Listen, would you do me a favor and consider this: As I'm thinkin' through this parliamentarily I think all we can do is that we could, in the minutes, we could amend them to have in those minutes in parentheses: "this motion was left moot by a new motion that was adopted at the next meeting." You know what I'm saying?

Wade: Yes, sir, and that's a very good possibility. I would say this. If when the action is taken to remove the "gossip and slander" and whatever it is that's done, I think you might find that I would be very willing to say that I regret and even could apologize for anything that looked as if it was confrontational, because that was not my heart. But what I'm saying is this: For me to issue a statement of apology prior to that being removed, I'm afraid there'll be confusion that I'm agreeing that I "slandered and I gossiped."

Tom: I understand and I'm not pressing you for that, you understand?

Wade: Yes, sir. No, I do understand and I . . . but I want you to hear my heart that I don't want those nine folks around the table to think . . . .

Tom: I hear your heart. I understand exactly the logic of this. But I just want you to know that in my opinion—now I'm speaking to you as a friend or a counselor—in my opinion, if your statements come a meeting or two after the news release of what the board is doing, you will have lost the advantage of having you be seen as side by side with the board. You will not get as much understanding or appreciation because of the distance factor between our removing the motion and your statement.

Wade: Well, Tom, I appreciate your expression of concern for me, but I am quite capable of enduring the risk of trustees not seeing me "side by side" with them on this issue. I will be able to express my desire to work with my fellow trustees in the process that is established by the IMB. And I give you my commitment to do everything I can to work within those parameters.

Tom: Yes.

Wade: So I guess if there's a statement that needs to be forthcoming from me to make things go smoother in the public eye regarding the IMB, I'm more than happy to work on a statement and I'm more than happy for you to see it before it's released, but there will be no apology.

Tom: Mm-hmm.

Wade: Let me reiterate: There will be no apology from me in the statement. There will be an expression of gratefulness for the rescission of the motion and there will from an expressed desire to continue to work with my fellow IMB trustees and perform all my duties as a trustee as I have done from the beginning, within the parameters the Blue Book that guides trustee conduct and behavior.

Tom: Well, that's between you and Jesus, brother. Good point; we're just leavin' that between you and him.

Wade: Okay, my wife wishes to ask a question.

Tom: Yeah.

Wade: She said what about you apologizing to me? What about an apology from trustee leadership for allowing the recommendation for my removal to come before the board in the first place?

Tom: I don't know . . . you want us to apologize to you for making the motion?

Wade: I guess I'm just wondering why I'm being asked to apologize when, if you are the ones retracting the motion . . . ."

Tom: . . . I'm not asking you to apologize, brother.

Lonnie: Wade, the officers and the chairmen, we put no conditions on what—this is Lonnie, by the way—what we see is the right thing to do. I appreciate Dr. Rankin's part in expressing his desires, but please, we never have asked for an apology. When Tom first began the conversation today, he said that what we have been discussing is doing this within the trustee family where it needs to be handled to begin with. So what we're going to recommend to our board is not contingent on what you do.

Wade: Lonnie, thank you. I guess we were getting a little confused just because we felt like we were getting off track and I'm sorry. I understand Dr. Rankin's heart in this. He wants a public perception of peace. But Lonnie, I think you know of why I am concerned. I think you and Tom both can understand that if there's a charge that is floated, say for instance like embezzlement or misappropriation of funds, or slander or gossip, or whatever it may be, and then an apology is issued from the person being falsely charged, and that apology has nothing to do with the charges, then people get really confused as to whether or not somebody is guilty of what he is being charged with doing. All I'm saying is this: I can be guilty of a number of things. I know that with all my heart. I can be bullheaded; I can be recalcitrant, I understand. I have no problem with admitting my sins, when I know I am guilty. I ask the Lord continually, and my wife who is sitting beside me, and everyone who knows me and loves me to help me see those sins to which I may be blind. The issue before us is a recommendation for removal for gossip and slander, and I know I am not guilty. Nobody even had the Christian decency to point out what they thought was "gossip and slander" behind closed doors, and then you guys removed the language when you went public. I have a hard time apologizing for anything until the recommendation for gossip and slander is off the table.

Tom: It's gonna be off the table.

Wade: Okay, I hear you. I really appreciate that. You have my commitment to work within the process to do what I can to correct the problem. God bless you guys.

Tom: Yeah, thank you and I appreciate your precious wife as well. I know I'm always better with my wife at my side. Would you do me a favor? Do you have the little blue book "Ordered of God" handy?

Wade: Yes, sir.

Tom: Okay, would you look at page 33? And I'm not gonna read that to you, but just . . . number 18 under 33. If you would just review that and look at it. It's just a statement in there about, you know, what we expect of trustees as far as being positive in public. It is a part of our . . . you could almost make that fit the blog, it requests, that you were talkin' about. If you wanted something to cite to say to your readers, you know, I really need to quit blogging because it's outside of an adopted board policy. You could cite that number 18 if you needed to. If you're looking for a way out, to quit blogging and cite it as a board policy, then that would be a spot where you could pick that.

Wade: Okay, well, in my view I've always been positive about the SBC and our mission work . . . . Of course, I'm not positive about the doctrinal changes. As you know, I believe they violate our convention's understanding that only the convention can establish the doctrinal parameters of our cooperation through the *Baptist Faith & Message.*

Tom: Well, just aware of it. You don't have to read it or anything like that. I just wanted you to be aware of it and let you just . . . .

Wade: Okay. I appreciate that, Tom.

Tom: Yes, sir. Well, I love ya. I appreciate you talkin' with us and you know, just uh, we'll, we're gonna come out with some kind of a good, positive press release on this in the near future. So you be praying for us in that, if you would.

Wade: I will and I appreciate you guys taking the time today to talk with me.

Tom: Okay, God bless, brother.

Wade: God bless you.

Tom: Bye-bye.

Wade: Bye.